HURDLE: THE BOOK
ON
BUSINESS PLANNING

How to develop *and implement*
a successful business plan.

By: Tim Berry

Palo Alto Software, Inc., Fifth Edition, July, 2004

Publisher:

Palo Alto Software, Inc.

144 E. 14th Ave.

Eugene, OR 97401

USA

Fax: 1 (541) 683-6250

Email: info@paloalto.com

Library of Congress Catalog Number: 00-109560

ISBN 0-9712185-0-1

Book layout by Teri Epperly, Steve Lange. Editor, Steve Lange, Sara Prentice Manela.

About the Author

Tim Berry has also written *On Target: The Book on Marketing Plans* (in 1999, co-authored with Doug Wilson), *CPA's Guide to Business Planning* (published first in 1998 by Harcourt Brace, republished by Aspen Publishers, and now in its fifth edition, published by Palo Alto Software), as well as several other books on business planning with spreadsheets that were published in the 1980s by Dow-Jones-Irwin, Microtext/McGraw-Hill, and Hayden Books. His business software has been published by Palo Alto Software and M & T Publishing. He has been a professional business planner since 1974, as an employee of Business International and vice president of Creative Strategies, as a consultant to Apple Computer, as a member of the founding board of directors of Borland International, and as president and founder of Palo Alto Software. He has given seminars on business planning in 13 countries on four continents, in two languages.

Berry holds a Stanford MBA degree, an MA *with honors* from the University of Oregon, and a BA *magna cum laude* from the University of Notre Dame.

Acknowledgements

I want to thank Paul Berry for not just cover design, but for inspiration as well. I was recently introduced to the phrase "Entrepreneur in Heat." If you have to ask what that means, then you've never been involved with somebody starting a business. The shortcut is simply "EIH." Paul has been EIH a lot lately.

Teri Epperly and Steve Lange have done a wonderful job with this book, designing the layout, managing the graphics, and patiently waiting on me through the ups and downs of my developing software, writing this and one other book, and managing a company all at the same time.

To Vie Radek, Cristin, Megan, and most of all Vange, thanks for putting up with me while this was coming together.

Sample Business Plans

This book includes two complete sample business plans. One sample is a computer store that is actually a composite of several computer reseller businesses the author consulted with during the early 1990s. The other was a consulting company that was accepted for financing by a major venture capital firm, although it was never actually formed. Both were originally published as part of *Business Plan Pro®* published by Palo Alto Software, Inc.

Workbook

Also included is the Hurdle Workbook. The workbook pages provide a place to write ideas on your business while you read and gather information. The text outline was taken directly from *Business Plan Pro®*. As you read through this book, we recommend you go to the topic reference in the workbook.

Hurdle book online!

The electronic version of this manual (portable document format .pdf) can be viewed and downloaded from our business resources website at:

http://www.bplans.com/ho

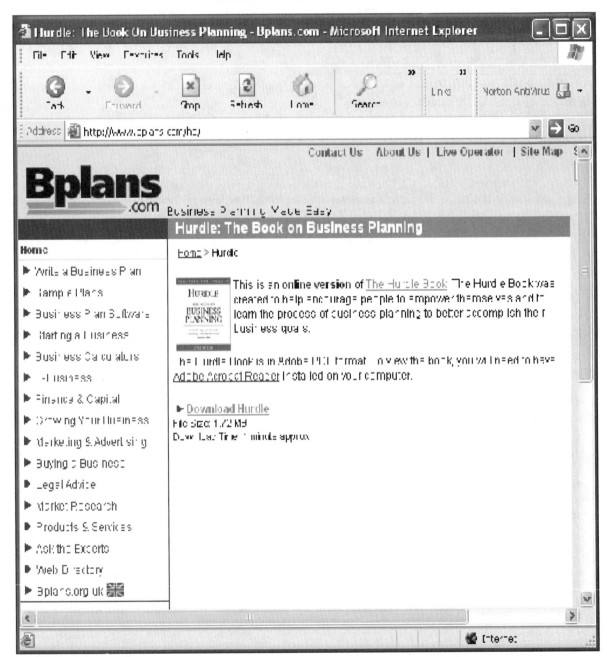

Table of Contents

Part 1: Fundamentals

As you start the planning process, begin with a general view of the whole project. Review your goals and consider your options.

Part 2: Tell Your Story

A standard business plan includes company backgorund information, history, and basic descriptions.

Part 3: Gathering Information

A good plan will include useful information about your market, your customers, and the busines you are in.

Part 4: Forecasting

Forecasting is more art than science, a combination of good research, logic, simple math, and educated guessing. It's hard to forecast but it's harder to run a business without forecasting.

Part 5: Financial Analysis

The financials aren't as hard as you think, particularly if you have the patience to follow the steps. A good plan includes sales, cash flow, profits, and related financials.

Part 6: Strategy and Tactics

Strategy is focus. You also need tactics to implement the strategy, and tactics require concrete milestones and well-defined management responsibilities.

Chapter 1:

IT'S ABOUT RESULTS

Some years ago, I was having lunch with Professor James March, a business school professor whose class I'd enjoyed years earlier, as a grad student. I was then in my late 30s, making my living mostly through business plan consulting. I'd had some successes. One of my plans was for a company that went from zero to more than $100 million of sales in four years. Apple Computer's Latin American group increased sales from $2 million to $27 million during the four years I'd done its annual plan. I'd had some failures too, but we won't mention those.

"So what is the value of a business plan?" Professor March asked at one point.

"Thousands of dollars," I answered. "Tens of thousands, in some cases."

"Wrong," he answered, to my shock. "Very wrong."

The value of a plan is the decisions it influences, he explained, and ultimately, how much money is in the bank as a result.

He was very right, although I was fairly smug about my successes and didn't like his response. And the underlying lesson is vital to this book.

I've absorbed the idea into my work on business planning. Plans should be measured by results. No matter how well researched, beautifully written, or excellently presented, what really makes a difference is how it impacts the results of the business.

What Makes a Good Plan?

Figure 1-1 shows a business plan as part of a process. You can think about the good or bad of a plan as the plan itself, measuring its value by its contents. There are some qualities in a plan that make it more likely to create results, and these are important. However, it is even better to see the plan as part of the whole process of results, because even a great plan is wasted if nobody follows it.

The plan depends on the human elements around it, particularly the process of commitment and involvement, and the tracking and follow up that comes afterward. I'm going to deal with those elements in coming chapters of this book. They are vital. But for now, let's look at the qualities that make the plan itself better or worse.

Successful implementation starts with a good plan. There are elements that will make a plan more likely to be successfully implemented. Some of the clues to implementation include:

1. Is the plan simple? Is it easy to understand and to act on? Does it communicate its contents easily and practically?

2. Is the plan specific? Are its objectives concrete and measurable? Does it include specific actions and activities, each with specific dates of completion, specific persons responsible and specific budgets?

3. Is the plan realistic? Are the sales goals, expense budgets, and milestone dates realistic? Nothing stifles implementation like unrealistic goals.

4. Is the plan complete? Does it include all the necessary elements? Requirements of a business plan vary, depending on the context. There is no guarantee, however, that the plan will work if it doesn't cover the main bases.

FIGURE 1-1: PLANNING IS A PROCESS, NOT JUST A PLAN

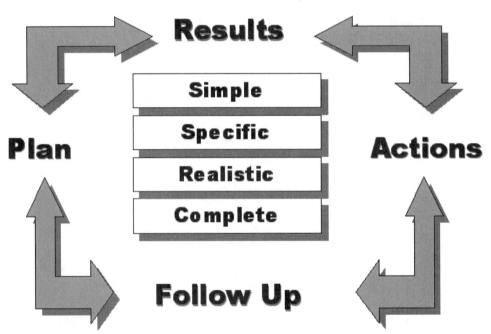

A business plan will be hard to implement unless it is simple, specific, realistic and complete. Even if it is all these things, a good plan will need someone to follow up and check on it.

Use of Business Plans

Preparing a business plan is an organized, logical way to look at all of the important aspects of a business. First, decide what you will use the plan for, such as to:

- Define and fix objectives, and programs to achieve those objectives.

- Create regular business review and course correction.

- Define a new business.

- Support a loan application.

- Define agreements between partners.

- Set a value on a business for sale or legal purposes.

- Evaluate a new product line, promotion, or expansion.

No Time to Plan? A Common Misconception

"Not enough time for a plan," business people say. "I can't plan. I'm too busy getting things done."

Too many businesses make business plans only when they have to. Unless a bank or investors want to look at a business plan, there isn't likely to be a plan written. The busier you are, the more you need to plan. If you are always putting out fires, you should build fire breaks or a sprinkler system. You can lose the whole forest for too much attention to the individual trees.

Keys to Better Business Plans

Business Plan "Do's"

- Use a business plan to set concrete goals, responsibilities, and deadlines to guide your business.

- A good business plan assigns tasks to people or departments and sets milestones and deadlines for tracking implementation.

- A practical business plan includes 10 parts implementation for every one part strategy.

- As part of the implementation of a business plan, it should provide a forum for regular review and course corrections.

- Good business plans are practical.

Business Plan "Don'ts"

- Don't use a business plan to show how much you know about your business.

- Nobody reads a long-winded business plan: not bankers, bosses, nor venture capitalists. Years ago, people were favorably impressed by long plans. Today, nobody is interested in a business plan more than 50 pages long.

A Business Plan Fable

Once upon a time there were three entrepreneurs who set out to seek their fortunes. Each of them developed a business plan.

The first business plan was built of straw. It was easy to complete, but it was mostly just puffery. For example, it had objectives like "being the best" and "excellence in customer satisfaction" without any way to measure results. It had a lot of talk, but few specifics. I'd almost say it was written like a sales or public relations piece, except that not even those can really afford to skip the hard facts.

The second business plan was built of sticks. It was built on what a venture capitalist I know calls "hockey stick" forecasts. You can probably guess what that means. I've seen a lot of them. Sales grow slowly in the past but the forecast shoots up boldly with huge growth rates, just as soon as something happens. Usually the something that is supposed to happen is investment, usually with other people's money, and as soon as this plan gets the money, then wonderful things will happen. As one of my favorite teenagers would say, rolling her eyes with eloquent sarcasm, "yeah, right," and "oh, brother."

The third business plan was built of bricks. You can see them in Figure 1-1. Bricks are specifics, especially "ownership", such as in specific job responsibilities, or specific people in charge of well-defined activities. Bricks are milestone dates, deadlines, budgets, and concrete, measurable objectives.

Then came the real world, as awesome as the big bad wolf in a similar fable. The real world was phone calls and daily routine. It was business problems and changes in economic environment, customers paying slower than expected, costs going up on one product, down on another. In business school they called it the RW, pronounced "are-dub." I won't say anything about huffing and puffing.

The real world blew the plan of straw apart in an instant. It was worthless, forgotten, lost somewhere in a drawer, never to be referred to again. Nobody remembered what it said. It was useless.

The real world blew the plan of sticks apart too, in an instant. Nobody had paid much attention anyhow, because the forecasts were so wildly optimistic. Nobody had been given responsibility, and nobody would have taken it. The plan was simply ignored. It was useless.

The plan of bricks, however, stood up to the real world. As each month closed, the plan of bricks absorbed plan-vs.-actual results. Managers looked at the variance. They made adjustments. Each manager kept track of milestones and budgets, and at the end of each month the actual results were compared to the plan results. Managers saw the performance of their peers. Changes were made in the plan—organized, rational changes—to accommodate changes in actual conditions. Managers were proud of their performance, and good performances were shared with all. And the company lived happily ever after.

Summary

Business plans are realistic. They provide a roadmap and a timeline for a business' actions. They are tools for effective decision making.

Business plans don't sell new business ideas to venture capitalists. Venture capitalists invest in people and ideas, not plans. A business plan, though necessary, is only a way to present information.

Chapter 2:

PICK YOUR PLAN

As we noted in Chapter 1: It's About Results *business planning is about results. Make the contents of your plan match your purpose. Don't accept a standard outline just because it's there.*

In the United States business market, there is a certain standardization about business plans. You can find dozens of books on the subject, about as many websites, two or three serious software products, and courses in hundreds of business schools, night schools, and community colleges. Although there are many variations on the theme, a lot of it is standard.

What is a Business Plan?

A business plan is any plan that works for a business to look ahead, allocate resources, focus on key points, and prepare for problems and opportunities. Business existed long before computers, spreadsheets, and detailed projections. So did business plans.

Unfortunately, people think of business plans first for starting a new business or applying for business loans. They are also vital for running a business, whether or not the business needs new loans or new investments. Businesses need plans to optimize growth and development according to plans and priorities.

What is a Start-up Plan?

A very simple start-up plan is a bare-bones plan that includes a summary, mission statement, keys to success, market analysis, start-up costs and funding, and break-even analysis. This kind of plan is good for deciding whether or not to proceed with an idea or venture, to tell if there is a business worth pursuing; but it is not enough to run a business with.

Is There a Standard Business Plan?

A normal business plan, that follows the advice of business experts, includes a standard set of elements. Plan formats and outlines vary, but generally, a plan will include standard components such as descriptions of company, product or service, market, forecasts, management team, and financial analysis.

Your plan depends on your specific situation. If you're developing a plan for internal use only, not for sending out to banks or investors, you may not need to include all the background details that you already know. Description of the management team is very important for investors, while financial history is most important for banks. Make your plan match its business purpose.

What is Most Important in a Plan?

What's most important in a plan? It depends on the case, but usually it's the cash flow analysis and specific implementation details.

- Cash flow because it is both vital to a company and hard to follow. Cash is usually misunderstood as profits, and they are different. Profits don't guarantee cash in the bank. Lots of profitable companies go under because of lack of cash. It just isn't intuitive.

- Implementation details because that's what makes things happen. Your brilliant strategies and beautifully formatted planning documents are just theory unless you assign responsibilities, with dates and budgets, and then regularly and consistently follow up and track results. Business plans are really about getting results, improving your company.

Can you Suggest a Standard Outline?

There are predictable contents of a standard business plan. For example, a business plan normally starts with an Executive Summary, which should be short and interesting. People almost always expect to see sections covering the Company, the Market, the Product, the Management Team, Strategy, Implementation and Financial Analysis.

If you have the main components, the order doesn't matter that much, but here's the order I suggest.

1. Executive Summary: Write this last. It's just a page or two of highlights.

2. Company Description: Legal establishment, history, start-up plans, etc.

3. Product or Service: Describe what you're selling. Focus on customer benefits.

4. Market Analysis: You need to know your market, customer needs, where they are, how to reach them, etc.

5. Strategy and Implementation: Be specific. Include management responsibilities with dates and budgets. Make sure you can track results.

6. Management Team: Describe the organization and the key management team members.

7. Financial Analysis: Make sure to include at the very least your projected Profit and Loss and Cash Flow tables.

I don't recommend developing the plan in the same order you present it as a finished document. For example, although the Executive Summary obviously comes as the first section of a business plan, I recommend writing it after everything else is done. It will appear first, but you write it last.

This book, therefore, discusses the business plan in the order you develop a plan, rather than the order of the document outline.

Standard Tables and Charts

There are also some business tables and charts that are normally expected in a standard business plan.

Cash flow is the single most important numerical analysis in a plan, and should never be missing. Most plans will also have Sales Forecast and Profit and Loss statements. I believe they should also have a separate Personnel listing, projected Balance sheet, projected Business Ratios, and Market Analysis tables.

I also believe that every plan should include bar charts and pie charts to illustrate the numbers.

Pages 2.4 and 2.5 include a complete standard business plan outline. It explains in detail where the tables, charts, and topics fall in a standard outline and where you can find the related discussions in this book.

Form Follows Function

However, as we noted in *Chapter 1: It's About Results*, business planning is about results. Make the contents of your plan match your purpose and adjust the outline to match your type of plan.

For example, if you are developing an internal plan for company use, you don't need to include a section about the company. If your plan focuses on well-known existing products or services and is intended for internal use only, you may not even need to include the details about the products.

Another example that comes up frequently is the level of detail required in your market analysis. Business plans looking for investors need to have some convincing market data, but a plan for a small local business, to be used mainly by a small group of people close to the company, may not need as much research. Is there an opportunity to improve the company and the plan by learning more about the market? Then do it. If not, it may be overkill.

Investor Summaries and Loan Applications

When a plan is used to back up a loan application or explain an opportunity to potential investors, it may require a special summary document as well as a complete plan. Many investors like to see a brief summary, and a loan application doesn't always require a complete plan. If you develop your plan in the right way, you can use the summary paragraphs of the main sections—company, market, product, etc.—to create these specialized summary documents.

Timeframes: Is Three Years Enough?

Opinions vary regarding the span or length of focus of a business plan—its timeframe. I believe a business plan should normally project sales by month for the next 12 months, and annual sales for the following two years. This doesn't mean businesses shouldn't plan for a longer term than just three years, not by any means. It does mean, however, that the detail of monthly forecasts doesn't pay off beyond a year, except in special cases. It also means that the detail in the yearly forecasts probably doesn't make sense beyond three years. Plan your business for 5, 10, and even 15-year timeframes; just don't do it within the detailed context of business plan financials.

Summary

Beyond my outline recommendations above, or the specifics in the menus of a program such as *Business Plan Pro®*, please remember that your plan is yours. You make the choices that best suit your needs.

Outline order and sequence in a standard business plan.	Where the process is covered in this book.
1.0 Executive Summary	*Chapter 17: Strategy is Focus,* helps you write the main summary.
1.1 Objectives	*Chapter 3: Initial Assessment,* talks about Objectives, Mission, and Keys to Success.
1.2 Mission	
1.3 Keys to Success	
2.0 Company Summary	*Chapter 5: Describe Your Company,* covers the company text section in your business plan as well as the related tables, either the Start-up or the Past Performance table.
2.1 Company Ownership	
2.2 Company History (for ongoing companies) or Start-up Plan (for new companies.	
2.3 Company Locations and Facilities	
3.0 Products (or services, or both)	This is in *Chapter 6: What You Sell.*
3.1 Product (or service, or both) Description	
3.2 Competitive Comparison	
3.3 Sales Literature	
3.4 Sourcing	
3.5 Technology	
3.6 Future Products	
4.0 Market Analysis Summary	We cover this in *Chapter 9: Know Your Market.*
4.1 Market Segmentation	*Chapter 11: Market,* also includes the market analysis table and chart.
4.2 Target Market Segment Strategy	
4.2.1 Market Needs	
4.2.2 Market Trends	
4.2.3 Market Growth	
4.3 Industry Analysis	This is all in *Chapter 8: The Business You're In.*
4.3.1 Industry Participants	
4.3.2 Distribution Patterns	
4.3.3 Factors of Competition	
4.3.4 Main Competitors	

Outline order and sequence in a standard business plan.	**Where the process is covered in this book.**

5.0 Strategy and Implementation Summary

5.1 Strategy Pyramids

5.2 Value Proposition

5.3 Competitive Edge

5.4 Marketing Strategy

    5.4.1 Positioning Statement

    5.4.2 Pricing Strategy

    5.4.3 Promotion Strategy

    5.4.4 Marketing Programs

5.5 Sales Strategy

    5.5.1 Sales Forecast

    5.5.2 Sales Programs

5.6 Milestones

6.0 Management Summary

6.1 Organizational Structure

6.2 Management Team

6.3 Management Team Gaps

6.4 Personnel Plan

7.0 Financial Plan

7.1 Important Assumptions

7.2 Key Financial Indicators

7.3 Break-even Analysis

7.4 Projected Profit and Loss

7.5 Projected Cash Flow

7.6 Projected Balance Sheet

7.7 Business Ratios

7.8 Long-term Plan

Much of this is covered in *Chapter 17: Strategy is Focus.*

Chapter 18: Make it Real, also covers the recommended Milestones table.

Implementation and plan-vs.-actual analysis comes up again in *Chapter 19: Plan for Implementation.*

The sales forecast discussions and the forecast itself are all the subject of this book's *Chapter 10: Forecast Your Sales.*

Chapter 7: Management Team, covers this text and the Personnel Plan table.

Chapter 14: The Bottom Line, covers the Profit and Loss and General Assumptions tables.

Chapter 3: Initial Assessment, includes the Break-even table as part of the Initial Assessment.

You deal with Cash Flow and the Cash Flow table in *Chapter 15: Cash is King.*

The Balance Sheet table is covered in *Chapter 13: About Business Numbers.*

The Business Ratios table appears in *Chapter 16: Finish the Financials.*

Long-term plans are discussed in *Chapter 18: Make it Real.*

This page intentionally blank.

Chapter 3:

INITIAL ASSESSMENT

*Start your business plan with a quick assessment. "Feasibility" is the formal term for it, although I prefer to think of it as finding out "is there a **there** there?" Even for an ongoing business, take the time to step away from the business and look at the basics. Do your business numbers make sense?*

Before anything else, take a step away from the idea, try to separate your feelings and identity for a while, and ask yourself about this business.

Quick Count of Customers

What you need most to start a business is customers. Nothing else is more important. Whether they are individual consumers, families, businesses, government organizations, or whatever, a business needs customers. So ask yourself:

- Does anybody want what I intend to offer?
- Will they pay money for it?

Don't worry too much about the difference between wants and needs. We don't want to narrow businesses down to those based on needs, when in the real world wants is just as important. Nobody needs perfume, stuffed mushrooms, or music, for example. Businesses do very well supplying non-essential goods and services—as long as somebody is willing to pay for them.

And it doesn't always matter who pays for them, as long as somebody (or some organization) does. Nonprofit organizations normally don't charge money for all services; the free medical clinic, for example, can survive if segments of society—donors, government agencies, etc.—are willing to pay.

Develop a Mission Statement

Use the mission statement to define your business concept. A company mission statement should define underlying goals (such as making a profit) and objectives in broad strategic terms, including what market is served and what benefits are offered.

What Business You Are In

Ask yourself what business you are in, and don't narrow yourself down. One of the classic business examples is the railroads, which lost a chance to expand in the twentieth century because they incorrectly defined themselves. They thought they were in the business of running trains on tracks. They didn't understand they were in the business of transporting goods and people. When trucks and buses and highways grew, the railroads were left behind.

My company, Palo Alto Software, is not in the business of software development. It is in the business of helping people do their own business plans, by providing business know-how through software and documentation. The broader definition helps us understand what we're up to.

Customer Satisfaction

Leading experts in developing customer satisfaction look to a mission statement to define customer satisfaction goals. Developing customer care programs depends on spreading the idea and importance within a company. That should normally start with a statement included in your mission statement.

Workplace Philosophy

Some mission statements also define internal goals such as maintaining a creative work environment and building respect for diversity. Experts in employee relations look immediately to a mission statement for a definition of a company's stand on some of these fundamental issues.

Value-Based Marketing

Experts developed the value-based marketing framework to help companies understand their business better. This framework starts with a business value proposition, which states what benefits a business offers, to whom, and at what relative price level. For example:

- This automobile manufacturer offers reliable, safe automobiles for families at a relative price premium.
- This fast food restaurant offers quick and consistent lunches at a low price.

Understand Keys to Success

Focusing on what I call "keys to success" is a good idea for getting a better view of the priorities in your business. Just about any business imaginable is going to depend a lot on three or four most important factors. For example, in a retail business, the classic joke is that "location, location, and location" are the keys to success. In truth, that might translate into location, convenient parking, and low prices. A computer store's keys to success might be knowledgeable salespeople, major brands, and newspaper advertising.

Focus is very important, and the keys to success framework helps you develop focus. There is what I call a law of inverse focus. I can't prove it with detailed research but I've seen many times that, beyond three or four key items, the more items on a priority list, the less chance of implementation. Thinking about keys to success is a great way to focus on the main elements that make your business work.

Explore Sales and Costs

Basic Questions

You also need to think about prices and costs. Ask yourself:

- How much will the customers pay?
- How many customers are there? How many will actually do business with me?
- How much will it cost me to make or deliver what each customer wants?

You don't need to answer these questions thoroughly or provide back-up research and documentation—not yet, at least. That comes later as you develop the full business plan. What you do want is to have a good general idea of the answers before you proceed. You don't want to rush into a bad business.

Do worry about cost compared to price. You don't need a detailed study, not yet, but you do need to have a good idea. If the frozen dessert costs you $10 to make and you plan to sell it cheap in the summer at the beach, then maybe the business has a problem. You also have to cover wages and salaries, rent, and other fixed costs. Make sure there is an underlying business proposition.

You don't have to be the first of a kind, or the first in your market, to have a good business. Your community probably has lots of some kinds of businesses—restaurants, food stores, clothing, so many different kinds of businesses are so common—and they don't all have to be first or unique. What you do need is customers.

Simple Break-even Analysis

Some people find a simple break-even analysis is a good way to get a quick view of the underlying running expenses, pricing, and costs in a business. This doesn't have to be a carefully researched and detailed break-even at this point. That will come later as you develop a full plan. For initial assessment, a simple estimated break-even might still be useful. The simple Break-even Analysis table is shown in Figure 3-1.

FIGURE 3-1: BREAK-EVEN ANALYSIS

Break Even Analysis	
Monthly Units Break-even	1,222
Monthly Sales Break-even	$397,262
Assumptions	
Average Per-unit Revenue	$325.00
Average Per-unit Variable Cost	$248.07
Estimated Monthly Fixed Costs	$94,035.00

The Break-even Analysis table calculates a break-even point based on fixed costs, variable costs per unit of sales, and revenue per unit of sales.

Make the following three simple assumptions:

- Average per-unit sales price (per-unit revenue):

  The price that you charge per unit. Take into account sales discounts and special offers. For value-based businesses, make the per-unit revenue $1 and enter your costs as a percent of a dollar.

- Average per-unit cost:

  The incremental cost of each unit of sale. If you are using a units-based Sales Forecast table (for manufacturing and mixed business types), you can project unit costs from the Sales Forecast table. If you are using the basic value-based Sales Forecast table for retail, service and distribution businesses, use a percentage estimate. For example, a retail store running a 50% margin would have a per-unit cost of .5, and a per-unit revenue of 1.

- Monthly fixed costs:

  Technically, a break-even analysis defines fixed costs as costs that would continue even if you went broke. Instead, you may want to use your regular running fixed costs, including payroll and normal expenses. This will give you a better insight on financial realities.

Figure 3-2 shows a Break-even chart. As sales increase, the profit line passes through the zero or break-even line at the break-even point.

FIGURE 3-2: BREAK-EVEN CHART

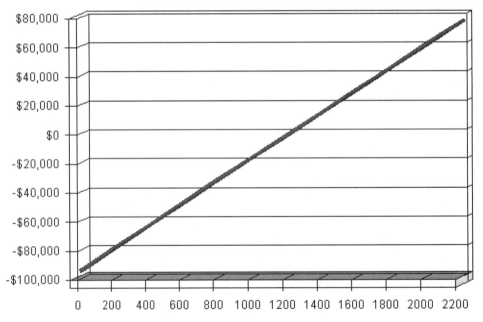

The Break-even chart shows that the company needs to sell approximately 1,200 units per month to break even.

The chart shows that the company needs to sell approximately 1,200 units in order to cross the break-even line. This is a classic business chart that helps you consider your bottom-line financial realities. Can you sell enough to make your break-even volume?

Of course the break-even analysis depends on assumptions made for average per-unit revenue, average per-unit cost, and fixed costs. These are rarely exact assumptions.

Consider Your Objectives

Objectives are business goals. Set your market share objectives, sales objectives, and profit objectives. Companies need to set objectives and plan to achieve them.

Make sure your objectives are concrete and measurable. Be specific, such as achieving a given level of sales or profits, a percentage of gross margin, a growth rate, or a market share. Don't use generalities like "being the best" or "growing rapidly" as your objectives.

For example, "being the best" or "maximize customer satisfaction" cannot really be measured. Much better objectives would set measurable goals, such as holding gross margin to 25 percent as a minimum, or selling more than $3 million, or achieving six percent profit on sales and 10 percent return on equity.

If less tangible goals are critical to a plan, find a way to measure them. For example, if image and awareness are vital, then plan for statistically valid surveys to measure the improvements in image and awareness. You can also set goals for market share, and purchase research to measure the actual share. Or, if you want to focus on customer satisfaction, plan for a survey to quantify satisfaction or specify numerical objectives regarding returns or complaints.

Pause for Reflection

At this point, you've defined your business, your financial break-even point, and your total potential market. How does your business look from this viewpoint? Does it make sense? Can you make the sales you need to break even? Is the market big enough? Are your projections realistic? Can you bring together the keys to success?

Especially for potential start-up companies, a moment of reflection is critical. Many people dream of starting a business, but that dream turns into a nightmare if the new business isn't successful.

If you think you can make your break-even numbers work, and you believe you have enough customers to make it, then go on to develop the plan. If not, either do more research and revise the idea, or give up and try something else.

This page intentionally blank.

As you start the planning process, begin with a general view of the entire project. Review your goals and consider your options.

Chapter 4:

STARTING A BUSINESS

It is dangerous to fall in love with the idea of starting your own business without understanding the realities.

Customers First

A business plan is not the most important single requirement for starting a business. Many other things are more important. For example:

- **Customers**: The first thing you need to start a business, maybe even the only thing you really need, is customers. It all starts with at least one customer.

- **Customer needs**: Your business must fulfill some type of customer need in order to be successful. Sometimes customer needs can be intangible, like security or prestige. Some customer needs seem frivolous, but they still matter. Make sure there is a market for your service or product. Your business will fail if it doesn't address a customer need.

Myths on Starting a Business

There are several myths about owning and operating a business that should be avoided at all costs. These common myths cause a lot of problems:

- The myth of "being your own boss": You are not your own boss when you own a business. Your customers are your boss. Your bank is your boss. Your fixed costs are your boss.

- The myth of "independence": Owning a business doesn't make you independent—not needing money makes you independent. As long as you need money, you can't be independent.

The folklore of business start-ups generally underestimates the risks. Imagine yourself missing mortgage payments when you can't cover your business costs and facing employees when you can't make payroll. Those negative images are also part of business ownership.

A Simpler Plan for Start-ups

Business advisors, experienced entrepreneurs, bankers, and investors generally agree that you should develop a business plan before you start a business. However, not all business plans are the same. You might develop a fairly simple plan first as you start a small business, and that might be enough for you. You can also start simple and then elaborate as you prepare to approach bankers or investors.

Don't let me, this book, business plan software, or any other source force you into doing more of a business plan than what you need. A plan can help you move forward, make decisions, and make your business successful. Not every plan is the same, not every business needs the same level of detail.

For a simple example, imagine a woman making jewelry at home and selling it at a local flea market on the weekend. A business plan could give her a chance to step back from the normal flow and look at ways to develop and improve the business. The planning process should help her understand her business. It should help her define what she wants from the business, understand what her customers want, and decide how to optimize her business on her own terms. She might benefit from developing a simple sales and expense forecast, maybe even a profit and loss, so she can plan how to use and develop her resources. She might not need to create detailed cash flow, balance sheet, and business ratios. A simple plan may be just what she needs to get going.

For an example of the very early stages of a plan, review the elements of starting a business plan in the section *Chapter 3: Initial Assessment*. This first stage of a plan focuses only on a few starter elements. The Mission Statement, Keys to Success, Market Analysis, and Break-even Analysis give you a critical head start toward understanding your business.

However, not all start-ups are that simple. Many of them need product development, packaging, retail fittings and signage, office equipment, websites, and sometimes months or even years of payroll before the sales start. Unless you're wealthy enough to finance these expenditures on your own, then you'll need to deal with bank loans or investors or both; and for that you'll need a more extensive business plan. Start-up company or not, the plan has to meet expectations.

One suggestion for getting started is to develop your plan in stages that meet your real business needs. A few key text sections might be enough to discuss the plan with potential partners and team members, as a first phase. You may well want to add a basic sales and expense forecast, leading to profit and loss, as next phase. Adding business numbers helps you predict business flow and match spending to income.

This might be an intermediate plan, incorporating a more extensive outline and business analysis as shown on the following page.

Ultimately, the choice of plan isn't based as much on the stage of business as it is on the type of business, financing requirements, and business objective. Here are some important indicators of the level of plan you'll need, even as a start-up:

- Some of the simpler businesses keep a plan in the head of the owner, but every business has a plan. Even a one-person business can benefit from creating a plan document with ideas written down, because the process is valuable. The exercise of producing a plan is a useful process.

- As soon as a second person is involved, the need for planning multiplies. The plan is critical for communicating values, goals, strategies, and detailed implementation.

- As soon as anybody outside the company is involved, then you have to provide more information. When a plan is for internal use only, you may not need to describe company history and product features, for example. Stick to the topics that add value, that make you think, that help support decisions. When you involve people outside the company, then you need to provide more background information as part of the plan.

- For discussion purposes, text is enough to get a plan started. Try describing your mission, objective, keys to success, target market, competitive advantage, and basic strategies. How well does this cover your business idea?

- Can you live without a sales and expense forecast? Sometimes the one-person business keeps numbers in its (the owner's) head. However, it's much easier to use tools that can put the numbers in front of you, and add and subtract them automatically. That's where a plan helps.

- Do you really know your market? A good market analysis can help you see opportunities that might not otherwise be obvious. Understand why people buy from you. What are the needs being served? How many people are out there, as potential customers?

- Do you manage significant amounts of inventory? That makes your cash management more complicated, and usually requires a more sophisticated plan. You need to buy inventory before you sell it.

- Do you sell on credit? If you are a business selling to businesses, then you probably do have to sell on credit, and that normally means you have to manage money owed to you by your customers, called accounts receivable. Making the sale is no longer the same thing as getting the money. That usually requires a more sophisticated plan.

- Do you do your taxes on a cash basis, or accrual basis? If you don't know, and you are a very small (one person, maybe 2-3 people) business, then you're likely to be on a cash basis. That makes your planning easier. However, most businesses big enough to work with a CPA and have separate tax statements use accrual accounting because they want to deduct expenses as they are incurred, even if they aren't fully paid for. By the time you are using accrual accounting, you'll probably need more sophisticated cash flow tools, and a more extensive business plan.

- As you approach banks and other lending institutions, expect to provide more detail on personal net worth, collateral, and your business' financial position. Some banks will accept a very superficial business plan as long as the collateral looks good. Others will demand to see detailed monthly projections. No bank can lend money on a business plan alone; that would be against banking law. But a good bank wants to see a good plan.

- If you're looking for venture investment, take a good look at your plan. Professional investors will expect your plan to provide proof, not just promises. They'll want to see market data, competitive advantage, and management track records. They'll want to see robust and comprehensive financial projections. True, you'll hear stories about investors backing new companies without a plan, but those are the exceptions, not the rule.

So, however you cut it, your business plan is very important, even at the early start-up stage, and even if you can keep it in your head. Before you purchase business stationery, telephones, or rent a location, you should do a business plan.

Simplified Business Plan Outline

Outline	Topic	Table	Chart
1.0	Executive Summary	Highlights	
1.1	Objectives		
1.2	Mission		
1.3	Keys to Success		
2.0	Company Summary	Start-up	Start-up
3.0	Product Description		
4.0	Market Analysis Summary	Market Analysis	Market Forecast
4.1	Market Segmentation		
4.2	Target Market Segment Strategy		
4.3	Market Needs		
4.4	Competition and Buying Patterns		
5.0	Strategy and Implementation Summary		Annual Sales
5.1	Competitive Edge		
5.2	Sales Strategy	Sales Forecast	Monthly Sales
6.0	Management Summary		
7.0	Financial Plan		
7.1	Break-even Analysis	Break-even	Break-even
7.2	Projected Profit and Loss	Profit and Loss	
7.3	Projected Cash Flow	Cash Flow	Cash Flow

Realistic Start-up Costs

Businesses spend money before they ever open their doors. Start-up expenses are those expenses incurred before the business is running. Many people underestimate start-up costs and start their business in a haphazard, unplanned way. This can work, but is usually a harder way to do it. Customers are wary of brand new businesses with makeshift logistics.

Use a start-up worksheet to plan your initial financing. You'll need this information to set up initial business balances and to estimate start-up expenses, such as legal fees, stationery design, brochures, and others. Don't underestimate costs.

Figure 4-1 reproduces a typical Start-up table for a home office, service business—in this case a resume writing service. The assumptions used in this illustration show how even simple, service-based businesses need start-up money.

FIGURE 4-1: START-UP COSTS

Start-up Plan	
Requirements	
Start-up Expenses	
Legal	$50
Stationery, etc.	$100
Brochures	$450
Consultants	$100
Insurance	$50
Rent	$0
Research and Development	$0
Expensed Equipment	$500
Other	$500
Total Start-up Expenses	**$1,750**
Start-up Assets Needed	
Cash Balance on Starting Date	$500
Start-up Inventory	$250
Other Current Assets	$25
Total Current Assets	**$775**
Long-term Assets	$0
Total Assets	**$775**
Total Requirements	**$2,525**
Funding	
Investment	
Investor 1	$2,525
Investor 2	$0
Other	$0
Total Investment	**$2,525**
Current Liabilities	
Accounts Payable	$0
Current Borrowing	$0
Other Current Liabilities	$0
Total Current Liabilities	**$0**
Long-term Liabilities	$0
Total Liabilities	**$0**
Loss at Start-up	$1,750
Total Capital	**$775**
Total Capital and Liabilities	**$775**

Start-up table for a hypothetical home office resumé service.

Understand the Risks

I've spent many years as an entrepreneur and working with entrepreneurs. I understand and sympathize with the urge to create something, to build your own and make it work. However, I've also seen the disaster of the business start-up that absorbs more money than it should, and optimistic owners who keep dumping more money into a lost cause, digging themselves deeper into a hole instead of getting out of it.

The following illustrations outline the start-up costs for three different companies. The first, Figure 4-2, shows actual numbers for a successful service company. Figure 4-3 shows a successful product company, and Figure 4-4 shows a failed product company.

Figure 4-5 is a chart of all of these start-up companies. The lines indicate the cumulative balance for each business. This balance stands for how much money is spent or received, and how much money is at risk.

Both the successful and the failed product company launches look the same in the beginning. The successful launch turns upward and generates money, but the unsuccessful launch never does. The service company, in contrast, generates less money but also risks less money.

The chart in Figure 4-5 makes two important points about money at risk in different kinds of businesses:

- Product businesses usually require more investment than service businesses.

- "Bootstrapping" (starting the business without start-up capital) is much harder for product businesses than service businesses.

FIGURE 4-2: SUCCESSFUL SERVICE START-UP

I. Successful Service Example

	Jan	Feb	Mar	Apr	May	Jun	Jul	Aug	Sep	Oct	Nov	Dec
Sales			$1,000	$3,500	$6,000	$8,500	$11,000	$13,500	$16,000	$18,500	$21,000	$23,500
Cost of Sales			$50	$175	$300	$425	$550	$675	$800	$925	$1,050	$1,175
Expenses												
General start-up expenses	$2,500											
Product release PR		$500	$500									
Running operating expenses	$1,500	$1,500	$1,750	$2,375	$3,000	$3,625	$4,250	$4,875	$5,500	$6,125	$6,750	$7,375
Total Expenses	**$4,000**	**$2,000**	**$2,250**	**$2,375**	**$3,000**	**$3,625**	**$4,250**	**$4,875**	**$5,500**	**$6,125**	**$6,750**	**$7,375**
Accounts Receivable			$1,000	$3,500	$6,000	$8,500	$11,000	$13,500	$16,000	$18,500	$21,000	
Deposits												
from Accounts Receivable			$1,000	$3,500	$6,000	$8,500	$11,000	$13,500	$16,000	$18,500	$21,000	
Payments												
Costs of sales	$0	$0	$50	$175	$300	$425	$550	$675	$800	$925	$1,050	$1,175
Expenses	$4,000	$2,000	$2,250	$2,375	$3,000	$3,625	$4,250	$4,875	$5,500	$6,125	$6,750	$7,375
Total Payments	**$4,000**	**$2,000**	**$2,300**	**$2,550**	**$3,300**	**$4,050**	**$4,800**	**$5,550**	**$6,300**	**$7,050**	**$7,800**	**$8,550**
Net Cash	**($4,000)**	**($2,000)**	**($2,300)**	**($1,550)**	**$200**	**$1,950**	**$3,700**	**$5,450**	**$7,200**	**$8,950**	**$10,700**	**$12,450**
Cumulative Cash		**($4,000)**	**($6,000)**	**($8,300)**	**($9,850)**	**($9,650)**	**($7,700)**	**($4,000)**	**$1,450**	**$8,650**	**$17,600**	**$28,300**	**$40,750**

FIGURE 4-3: SUCCESSFUL PRODUCT START-UP

II. Successful Product Example

	Jan	Feb	Mar	Apr	May	Jun	Jul	Aug	Sep	Oct	Nov	Dec
Sales					$50,000	$75,000	$100,000	$125,000	$150,000	$150,000	$150,000	$150,000
Cost of Sales					$10,000	$15,000	$20,000	$25,000	$30,000	$30,000	$30,000	$30,000
Expenses												
General start-up expenses	$4,500											
Product work		$5,000	$5,000									
Packaging work			$5,000	$5,000								
Initial inventory build				$10,000								
Product release PR			$5,000	$5,000	$5,000							
Running operating expenses	$5,000	$5,000	$5,000	$10,000	$10,000	$20,000	$20,000	$20,000	$20,000	$20,000	$20,000	$20,000
Total Expenses	**$9,500**	**$10,000**	**$20,000**	**$30,000**	**$15,000**	**$20,000**	**$20,000**	**$20,000**	**$20,000**	**$20,000**	**$20,000**	**$20,000**
Accounts Receivable					$50,000	$125,000	$175,000	$225,000	$275,000	$300,000	$300,000	$300,000
Deposits												
from Accounts Receivable						$50,000	$75,000	$100,000	$125,000	$150,000	$150,000	
Payments												
Costs of sales	$0	$0	$0	$0	$10,000	$15,000	$20,000	$25,000	$30,000	$30,000	$30,000	$30,000
Expenses	$9,500	$10,000	$20,000	$30,000	$15,000	$20,000	$20,000	$20,000	$20,000	$20,000	$20,000	$20,000
Total Payments	**$9,500**	**$10,000**	**$20,000**	**$30,000**	**$25,000**	**$35,000**	**$40,000**	**$45,000**	**$50,000**	**$50,000**	**$50,000**	**$50,000**
Net Cash		**($9,500)**	**($10,000)**	**($20,000)**	**($30,000)**	**($25,000)**	**($35,000)**	**$10,000**	**$30,000**	**$50,000**	**$75,000**	**$100,000**	**$100,000**
Cumulative Cash		**($9,500)**	**($19,500)**	**($39,500)**	**($69,500)**	**($94,500)**	**($129,500)**	**($119,500)**	**($89,500)**	**($39,500)**	**$35,500**	**$135,500**	**$235,500**

A table comparison of start-up numbers for one service and two product businesses.

FIGURE 4-4: FAILED PRODUCT START-UP

III. Failed Product Example	Jan	Feb	Mar	Apr	May	Jun	Jul	Aug	Sep	Oct	Nov	Dec
Sales					$25,000	$27,500	$30,000	$32,500	$35,000	$37,500	$40,000	$42,500
Cost of Sales					$5,000	$5,500	$6,000	$6,500	$7,000	$7,500	$8,000	$8,500
Expenses												
General start-up expenses	$4,500											
Product work		$5,000	$5,000									
Packaging work			$5,000	$5,000								
Initial inventory build				$10,000								
Product release PR			$5,000	$5,000	$5,000							
Running operating expenses	$5,000	$5,000	$5,000	$10,000	$10,000	$20,000	$20,000	$20,000	$20,000	$20,000	$20,000	$20,000
Total Expenses	$9,500	$10,000	$20,000	$30,000	$15,000	$20,000	$20,000	$20,000	$20,000	$20,000	$20,000	$20,000
Accounts Receivable					$25,000	$52,500	$57,500	$62,500	$67,500	$72,500	$77,500	$47,500
Deposits												
from Accounts Receivable							$25,000	$27,500	$30,000	$32,500	$35,000	$72,500
Payments												
Costs of sales					$5,000	$5,500	$6,000	$6,500	$7,000	$7,500	$8,000	$8,500
Expenses	$9,500	$10,000	$20,000	$30,000	$15,000	$20,000	$20,000	$20,000	$20,000	$20,000	$20,000	$20,000
Total Payments	$9,500	$10,000	$20,000	$30,000	$20,000	$25,500	$26,000	$26,500	$27,000	$27,500	$28,000	$28,500
Net Cash		($9,500)	($10,000)	($20,000)	($30,000)	($20,000)	($25,500)	($1,000)	$1,000	$3,000	$5,000	$7,000	$44,000
Cumulative Cash		($9,500)	($19,500)	($39,500)	($69,500)	($89,500)	($115,000)	($116,000)	($115,000)	($112,000)	($107,000)	($100,000)	($56,000)

FIGURE 4-5: THE START-UP CURVE AND RISK TO INVESTMENT

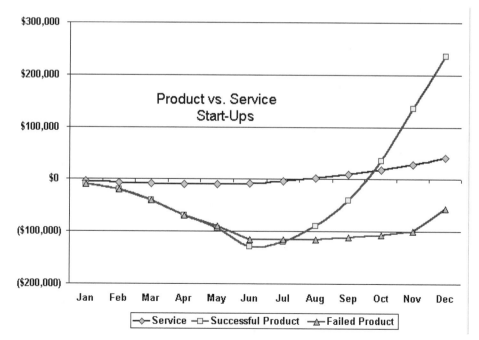

The lines show the cumulative cash positions for a start-up product company and a start-up service company. The product company risks more than the service company.

Friends and Family Funding

If I could make only one point with budding entrepreneurs, it would be that you should know what money you need, and understand that it is at risk. Don't bet money you can't afford to lose. Know how much you are betting.

I'll always remember a talk I had with a man who had spent 15 years trying to make his sailboat manufacturing business work, achieving not much more than aging and more debt. "If I can tell you only one thing," he said, "it is that you should never take money from friends and family. If you do, then you can never get out. Businesses sometimes fail, and you need to be able to close it down and walk away. I wasn't able to do that."

The story points out why the U.S. government securities laws discourage getting business investments from people who aren't wealthy, sophisticated investors. They don't fully understand how much risk there is. If your parents, siblings, good friends, cousins, and in-laws will invest in your business, they have paid you an enormous compliment. Please, in that case, make sure that you understand how easily this money can be lost, and that you make them understand as well.

Although you don't want to rule out starting your company with investments from friends and family, don't ignore some of the disadvantages. Go into this relationship with your eyes wide open.

Licenses, Permits, and Legal Entities

See an Attorney

Make sure you know which legal steps you must take to be in business. I'm not an attorney, and I don't give legal advice. I do strongly recommend working with an attorney to go through the details of your company's legal establishment, licenses, and other items covered here. By including this information in this book, I don't mean to imply you should do it yourself.

The trade-offs involved in incorporation vs. partnership vs. other forms of business are significant. Small problems developed at the early stages of a new business can become horrendous problems later on. The cost of simple legal advice in this regard is almost always worth it. Starting a company should not involve a major legal bill except in special cases. Don't skimp on legal costs.

Licenses and Permits are Usually Local Issues

It's hard to generalize on licenses and permits, because some of these depend on where you are, and some depend on what you do. When in doubt, you should check with local sources. If you don't want to go straight to the local government and ask your questions directly, then ask at a Chamber of Commerce, or Small Business Development Center (SBDC).

For example, many cities have zoning laws that define where you can put retail stores, office space, and industries. Few of these affect the small home-based business, but it's not unusual to have zoning laws prohibit signs on lawns or houses.

Some types of businesses require local or state licenses. This depends on where you are, but businesses including daycare, hair care, food service, and of course bars and nighclubs often require special licenses.

Resale Licenses and Sales Taxes

In states that have sales tax, state authorities manage a system that sets reseller businesses into a special category, so they don't have to pay sales taxes on items they buy for resale. The required paperwork and the state offices that manage it are different in many states, so you'll have to ask state offices for your state as you establish your business.

Taxpayer ID and Employer Numbers

Employer ID numbers (EIN) are assigned by the IRS and state tax authorities. If you don't have employees and you haven't established a corporation, then your Social Security number is your federal taxpayer ID. If you've established a corporation or you have employees, then you must have a federal EIN, which is assigned by the federal IRS. In most states, the state assigns a separate state number.

The Business Entity

The pros and cons of different business formations are worth understanding. They vary by state -- this is not a good area for guesswork, and not a good place to save money, so please go through this with a local attorney you can trust. The following is for background information.

Although the details vary, it starts with the choice between sole proprietorship, partnership, corporation, or the more trendy Limited Liability Company, LLC. Within the corporation classification you have additional choices, between the standard corporation or the small business S corporation.

The Simplest Form is the Sole Proprietorship

The simplest form is the sole proprietorship. Simply put, your business is a sole proprietorship if you don't create a separate legal entity for it. This is true whether you operate it in your own name, or under a trade name. If it isn't your own name, then you register a company name as a "Fictitious Business Name," also called a DBA ("Doing Business As"). Depending on your state, you can usually obtain this through the county government, and the cost is no more than a small registration fee plus a required newspaper ad, for a total of less than $100 in most states.

The main disadvantage of the sole proprietorship is the lack of a separate entity, which means you have personal responsibility for it. If the business fails then its creditors can go after your personal assets.

Tax treatment is quite simple, your profit and loss goes straight through to your personal taxes. Your business income is normally on Schedule C of your tax return. This can be good or bad for your tax situation, depending on where you stand with other income.

Partnerships

Partnerships are harder to describe because they change so much. They are governed by state laws, but a Uniform Partnership Act has become the law in most states. That act, however, mostly sets the specific partnership agreement as the real legal core of the partnership, so the legal details can vary widely. Usually the income or loss from partnerships pass through to the partners, without any partnership tax. The agreements can define different levels of risk, which is why you'll read about some partnerships that have general partners and limited partners, with different levels of risk for each. The agreement should also define what happens if a partner withdraws, buy and sell arrangements for partners, and liquidation arrangements if that becomes necessary.

If you think a partnership might work for your business, make sure you do this right. Find an attorney with experience in partnerships, and check for references of present and past clients. This is a complicated area and a mistake in the agreement will cause a lot of problems.

Corporations

Corporations are either the standard C corporation or the small business S corporation. The C corporation is the classic legal entity of the vast majority of successful companies in the United States. Most lawyers would agree that the C corporation is the structure that provides the best shielding from personal liability for owners, and provides the best non-tax benefits to owners. This is a separate legal entity, different from its owners, which pays its own taxes. Most lawyers would also probably agree that for a company that has ambitions of raising major investment capital and eventually going public, the C corporation is the standard form of legal entity.

The S corporation is used for family companies and smaller ownership groups. The clearest distinction from C is that the S corporation's profits or losses go straight through to the S corporation's owners, without being taxed separately first. In practical terms, this means that the owners of the corporation can take their profits home without first paying the corporation's separate tax on profits, so those profits are taxed once for the S owner, and twice for the C owner. In practical terms the C corporation doesn't send its profits home to its owners as much as the S corporation does, because it usually has different goals and objectives. It often wants to grow and go public, or it already is public. In most states an S corporation is owned by a limited number (25 is a common maximum) of private owners, and corporations can't hold stock in S corporations, just individuals.

Corporations can switch from C to S and back again, but not often. The IRS has strict rules for when and how those switches are made. You'll almost always want to have your CPA, and in some cases your attorney, guide you through the legal requirements for switching.

LLC (Limited Liability Company)

Be careful with this one, because the LLC form is different for different states, with advantages in some states that aren't relevant in others. An LLC is usually a lot like an S corporation, a combination of some limitation on legal liability and some favorable tax treatment for profits and transfer of assets. This is a newer form of legal entity, and often harder to establish than a corporation.

Why would you establish an LLC instead of a corporation? That's a tough legal question, not one we can answer here. In general, the LLC has to be missing two of the four characteristics of a corporation (limited liability, centralized management, continuity of life, and free transferability of ownership interest). Still, with the advisability and advantages varying from state to state, here again, this is a question to take to a good local attorney with small business experience.

Business Names, Trademarks, Copyrights, etc.

The two concerns for start-up business names are the legal requirements, and the commercial use. We are talking about the name of your business, in this section, not your trademarks, or service marks, logos, or slogans. We are not attorneys, we do not give legal advice, so be sure to check with an attorney early on as you build your business. Trademark law protects product names, logos, trade names, even some slogans as trademarks or service marks. Copyright law protects works or art, fiction, movies, art, sculpture, and other creative works. Business law, however, does not fully guarantee you the exclusive use of your business name. To get close to exclusivity, you have to be first, you have to be national, and you have to be alert.

Owning and Establishing a Business Name

The most common misunderstanding about business names is about registering, protecting, and reserving business names. You can't reserve a business name completely, you can't have exclusive use. Think of a business name as a lot like a personal name, in that the first or oldest John Smith cannot claim exclusive use of that name. He can't make all the other John Smiths change their names. So too, the first Smith's Restaurant can't stop all other Smith Restaurants from using that same name. McDonald's Hamburgers can't make McDonald's Hardware Store change its name, and McDonald's Hardware Store in Manhattan can't sue McDonald's Hardware Store in San Francisco.

However, just as you have rights to your own identity, so does your company. One John Smith can sue another John Smith for using his identity, having bills sent to the wrong address, or purposely confusing people. McDonald's Hamburgers can sue just about anybody trying to use McDonald's for a business selling fast foods.

The confusion starts because business names are registered by different authorities in different places, and on different levels.

- The first and simplest business name is your own name, which might be enough for John Smith using Smith Consulting or hosting Smith's Restaurant. This kind of business name normally requires no additional paperwork, although most business owners end up registering a name anyhow to establish their legal claim to it.

- The second normal common level of business names is called DBA (for "Doing Business As") or Fictitious Business Name, which gives an individual the right to operate under a business name with signs, bank accounts, checks, and so on. These are generally registered and legalized by county governments within states. There might be a McDonald's Hardware Store as a DBA in many counties within a given state, and across many different states. To register a business with a fictitious business name, call your county government for details. You can expect that you'll have to visit an office in the county government, pay a fee of less than $100, and do some legal advertising, also less than $100, probably using forms you can fill out in the same office. Somebody will probably look up the registry to make sure that yours is the first business in the county with that name. Details will actually vary depending on which county you're in.

- The third level is the corporation, regardless of its various corporate entities. Whether they are S Corporations, C Corporations, LLCs, or whatever, a corporation is registered at the state level and no two can have the exact same name in each state. However, there is no guarantee that there won't be many businesses registered as McDonald's Hardware Store in several counties in a state, and a corporation registered as McDonald's Hardware Corporation. This kind of duplication happens. To establish a corporation, you can use national services such as

www.corporate.com,

or a local attorney. The corporate forms will go to the state, and details will depend on which state you're in.

Even though duplicate business names are very possible, and quite common, you do still have the right to protect and defend you own business name, once you've built the business around it. The key to this is confusion and confusing identity. As we said above, one John Smith can sue another John Smith for purposely confusing their identities. So too, McDonald's Hamburgers can and should sue anybody who starts a new restaurant named McDonald's serving fast foods.

On this point, when one business is confused with another, being first matters. When somebody tries to establish a second McDonald's Hardware where it would confuse people with the first, then the first

McDonald's has a legal right to prevent it. If the second store puts up a sign, then the first store should take quick legal action to stop it. The longer the first store ignores the second, the better the case of the second store. When the whole mess goes to court, the first one to use the name is likely to win, but if the first one sat quietly while the other one built the name, then there is more doubt. An existing business should always watch out for people using the same or confusingly similar names, because the sooner it complains, the better for its legal arguments.

Researching Whether a Name is Available

So you see you can't absolutely guarantee that nobody has the name you want, but you can at least try. The fastest and simplest way to start researching a name is to do an Internet search. Search about half a dozen of your favorite searchers and see whether or not the name you're considering is already taken. You don't want to name a business with a name that can cause problems later, because it confuses you with other businesses. That's obvious, but how do you research a name to make sure there won't be a conflict? There is no single sure way, but here are some suggestions:

- Search the Web. Start with your favorite searches and see whether anything turns up on the company name you're considering. You can also go to the U.S. Patent and Trademark Office website

  www.uspto.gov/

  or KnowX.com

  www.knowx.com

  or similar searcher sites.

- Search the Internet domain names. There are several searchers that offer access to the "whois" database of Internet sites. The most traditional site for this is the one at Network Solutions

  http://www.networksolutions.com/en_US/whois/index.jhtml

- See an attorney. Since you probably want to talk to an attorney about the correct business entities and other start-up matters, you may also ask your attorney about checking on business names. Generally you want to do your own check first to catch any obvious conflicts.

Ultimately, you really protect your business name only by using it. Corporations are registered by states, and factitious business names are registered in counties. Registering a name doesn't really protect it though, because the same name could legally exist in many other states, many other counties.

You could be Acme Corporation in Illinois and legally own that corporation in that state, but there could be another Acme Corporation in every other state, and every one of them is legal until you win a lawsuit proving that they are trading on the commercial interests you own. When you really get protection is when you use that name, and therefore when you find somebody else using it you can prove that you had it first, so they are trading on your name. There are lots of McDonald's restaurants around, and McDonald's can't stop them from using that name if they had it early enough, and especially if they aren't pretending to be a fast food hamburger joint. The attempt to confuse is very important.

Choosing a Business Name

The choice of a business name is very important, worth taking time to develop. Don't end up with a name that you can't live with. Look for something that describes your business, is easy to explain, fits on the signs, and works.

Chapter 5:

DESCRIBE YOUR COMPANY

This is a good time to explain your company and some of its underlying strategy, such as competitive edge and value proposition, as well as establishing base-line numbers for your plan.

I find switching modes like this, from numbers to text and back, helps keep the process fresh as you develop your plan. This chapter will cover a table or two, either past performance or start-up costs, depending on your specific plan.

You're probably noticing by now that developing a business plan doesn't really happen in a straight logical order of steps. It isn't really a sequential process. For example, you looked at your market numbers first while doing the Initial Assessment, *Chapter 3: Initial Assessment*, and will again as you focus on more detail for the Market Analysis topic. You'll probably visit those numbers again as you do the Industry Analysis. In coming chapters you'll project your sales, personnel, and profits, but you'll probably have to revise those numbers when you look at your balance sheet and cash flow.

If you are starting a business, please go now to *Chapter 4: Starting a Business* dedicated to issues in starting a business. I don't want to interrupt the flow of the plan with that discussion at this point, particularly for those who are working on an ongoing business. However, if you are starting a business, and haven't read *Chapter 4*, please read that chapter now and then return here.

Company Information

As discussed earlier in *Chapter 2: Pick Your Plan*, my recommended business plan outline includes a chapter topic on your company, right after the Executive Summary. I pointed out then that you may not need to include this chapter if you are writing an internal plan. However, any outsiders reading your plan will want to know about your company before they read about products, markets, the rest of the story.

Summary Paragraph

Start the chapter with a good summary paragraph that you can use as part of a summary memo or a loan application support document. Include the essential details, such as the name of the company, its legal establishment, how long it's been in existence, and what it sells to what markets.

Legal Entity / Ownership

In this paragraph, describe the ownership and legal establishment of the company. This is mainly specifying whether your company is a corporation, partnership, sole proprietorship, or some other kind of legal entity, such as a limited liability partnership. You should also explain who owns the company, and, if there is more than one owner, in what proportion.

If your business is a corporation, specify whether it is a C (the more standard type) or an S (more suitable for small businesses without many different owners) corporation. Also, of course, specify whether it is privately owned or publicly traded.

Many smaller businesses, especially service businesses, are sole proprietor businesses. Some are legal partnerships. The protection of incorporating is important, but sometimes the extra legal costs and hassles of turning in corporate tax forms with double-entry bookkeeping are not worth it. Professional service businesses, such as accounting or legal or consulting firms, may be partnerships, although that mode of establishment is less common these days. If you're in doubt about how to establish a start-up company, consult a business attorney.

Locations and Facilities

Briefly describe offices and locations of your company, the nature and function of each, square footage, lease arrangements, etc.

If you are a service business, you probably don't have manufacturing plants anywhere, but you might have Internet services, office facilities, and telephone systems that are relevant to providing service. It is conceivable that your Internet connection, as one hypothetical case, might be critical to your business.

If you're a retail store, then your location is probably a critical factor, so explain the location, traffic patterns, parking facilities, and possibly customer demographics as they relate to the specific location (your Market Analysis goes elsewhere, but if your shopping center location draws a particular kind of customer, note that here).

If you are manufacturing, then you may have different facilities for production, assembly, and various offices. You may have manufacturing and assembly equipment, packing equipment, docks, and other facilities.

Depending on the nature of your plan, its function and purpose, you may want to include more detail about facilities as appendices attached to your plan.

For example, if your business plan is intended to help sell your company to new owners, and you feel that part of the value is the facilities and locations, then you should include all the detail you can. If you are describing a manufacturing business to bankers or investors, or anybody else trying to value your business, make sure you provide a complete list and all necessary detail about capital equipment, land, and building facilities. This kind of information can make a major difference to the value of your business. On the other hand, if your business plan is for internal use in a small company with a single office, then this topic might be irrelevant.

Think Strategically

One of the most valuable benefits of developing a business plan is thinking in depth about your company. You started that as part of *Chapter 3: Initial Assessment*, as you entered drafts of your objectives, mission statement, and keys to success. A standard plan also includes sections in the strategy chapter that provide deep background for strategy. This is a good point for developing those texts.

Value Proposition

Value-based marketing is a useful conceptual framework. The value proposition is benefit offered less price charged, in relative terms. For example, the auto manufacturer, Volvo, has for years offered a value proposition based on the value of safety, at a price premium. A more detailed discussion of this framework can be found in *Chapter 17: Strategy Is Focus*.

Competitive Edge

So what is your competitive edge? How is your company different from all others? In what way does it stand out? Is there a sustainable value there, something that you can maintain and develop over time? The classic competitive edges are based on proprietary technology protected by patents. Sometimes market share and brand acceptance are just as important, and know-how doesn't have to be protected by patent to be a competitive edge.

For example, Apple Computer for years used its proprietary operating system as a competitive edge, while Microsoft used its market share and market dominance to overcome Apple's earlier advantage. Several manufacturers used proprietary compression to enhance video and photographic software, looking for a competitive edge.

The competitive edge might be different for any given company, even between one company and another in the same industry. You don't have to have a competitive edge to run a successful business—hard work, integrity, and customer satisfaction can substitute for it, to name just a few examples—but an edge will certainly give you a head start if you need to bring in new investment. Maybe it's just your customer base, as in the case with Hewlett-Packard's relationship with engineers and technicians, or it's image and awareness, such as with Compaq. Maybe it is the quality control and consistency of IBM.

The most understandable of the competitive edges are those based on proprietary technology. A patent, an algorithm, even deeply entrenched know-how, can be solid competitive edges. In services, however, the edge can be as simple as having the phone number 1 (800) SOFTWARE, which is an actual case. A successful company was built around that phone number.

Baseline Numbers

While we're focusing on the company description, let's establish the starting numbers that form the basis of your cash flow and balance sheet in *Chapters 13-16*. For ongoing companies, your starting balance for the future is the last balance from the past.

Past Performance for Ongoing Companies

Past performance explained here is for ongoing companies. If you are a start-up business, skip to the section called **Start-up Costs for Start-up Companies**. Figure 5-1 shows a sample listing of recent financial results for an ongoing company. Generally three years is good enough. You should have these numbers as part of your standard business accounting.

FIGURE 5-1: PAST PERFORMANCE TABLE

Past Performace	2001	2002	2003
Sales	$3,773,889	$4,661,902	$5,301,059
Gross Margin	$1,189,495	$1,269,261	$1,127,568
Gross Margin %	31.52%	27.23	21.27
Operating Expenses	$752,083	$902,500	$1,052,917
Collection Period (days)	48	35	41
Inventory Turnover	6.88	7.97	7.41
Balance Sheet			
Current Assets	**2001**	**2002**	**2003**
Cash	$23,341	$44,090	$55,432
Accounts Receivable	$302,738	$273,694	$395,107
Inventory	$375,605	$475,689	$651,012
Other Current Assets	$19,904	$18,956	$25,091
Total Current Assets	$721,588	$812,429	$1,126,642
Long-term Assets			
Capital Assets	$255,098	$289,887	$351,435
Accumulated Depreciation	$35,988	$42,890	$51,661
Total Long-term Assets	$219,110	$246,997	$299,774
Total Assets	$940,698	$1,059,426	$1,426,416
Capital and Liabilities			
	2001	**2002**	**2003**
Accounts Payable	$189,566	$191,854	$223,897
Current Borrowing	$120,000	$11,000	$90,000
Other Current Liabilities	$9,870	$69,659	$15,000
Subtotal Current Liabilities	$319,436	$272,513	$32,897
Long-term Liabilities	$0	$0	$284,862
Total Liabilities	$319,436	$272,513	$613,759
Paid-in Capital	$400,000	$548,908	$500,000
Retained Earnings	$168,116	$221,262	$238,005
Earnings	$53,146	$16,743	$74,652
Total Capital	$621,262	$786,913	$812,657
Total Capital and Liabilities	$940,698	$1,059,426	$1,426,416
Other Inputs	**2001**	**2002**	**2003**
Payment Days	21	16	16
Sales on Credit	$2,302,072	$2,983,617	$2,987,128
Receivables Turnover	7.6	10.9	7.56

Important past performance items can be typed into the past performance worksheet. They are used for comparing past performance to projected future, and to establish your starting balances.

Ongoing companies need to include a summary of company history, as a topic in your text. If you are an ongoing company, then you'll need to present financial results of the recent past, and this text section is where you explain them.

Explain why your sales and profits have changed. If you've had important events like particularly bad years or good years, or new services, new locations, new partners, etc., then include that background here. Cover the founding of the company, important events, and important changes.

Your first consideration is the needs of your reader. This isn't a history assignment. Give the reader of the business plan the background information he or she needs to understand your business.

For your financial analysis as an ongoing company, you will want to make sure you have some very important highlights of your company's past financial performance, as shown in the previous table.

Start-up Costs for Start-up Companies

The start-up company should include a start-up table instead of the past performance table. Figure 5-2 is a simple example.

Start-up Expenses

The first portion of the sample start-up table estimates start-up expenses. Make, sure first of all, that you understand expenses, which are different from assets. You can check with the glossary for a detailed definition of expenses, but basically your start-up expenses are like those shown in the example. Start-up expenses are only those expenses incurred before the start of the plan. If they come after the start of the plan, they belong in the profit and loss table in the appropriate month. In the example, the total is $18,350.

The table shows some common types of start-up expenses, such as legal costs, stationery, and brochures. One category that frequently generates questions is the so-called "expensed equipment," which is used for office equipment such as computers and telephones that the tax authorities allow a business to report as expenses. While these purchases might normally be assets, they are expensed because that reduces taxable income, and the government allows using them as expenses instead of assets.

Product development expenses occasionally cause confusion because some people want to make them assets, but they are almost always expenses. The trouble is that although you'd like to think of product expense as developing future assets, that's not the normal tax treatment.

Starting Assets

The second portion of the sample start-up table estimates the assets your business will have at start-up, including starting cash, inventory (except for service companies), and others. The example shows just two categories, cash and other short-term assets, because it was taken from a service company that had no starting inventory requirements. Office furniture, shelving and signage are often start-up assets. The total in the example is $32,000.

Don't confuse expenses and assets. Assets are goods and documents that have transferable value. Assets make the company's balance sheet look better. However, given a choice, most companies prefer to deduct their purchases as expenses rather than store them up as assets.

FIGURE 5-2: START-UP TABLE

Start-up Plan	
Requirements	
Start-up Expenses	
Legal	$1,000
Stationery, etc.	$3,000
Brochures	$5,000
Consultants	$5,000
Insurance	$350
Rent	$0
Research and Development	$0
Expensed Equipment	$3,000
Other	$1,000
Total Start-up Expenses	**$18,350**
Start-up Assets Needed	
Cash Balance on Starting Date	$25,000
Start-up Inventory	$0
Other Current Assets	$7,000
Total Current Assets	**$32,000**
Long-term Assets	$0
Total Assets	**$32,000**
Total Requirements	**$50,350**
Funding	
Investment	
Investor 1	$20,000
Investor 2	$20,000
Other	$10,000
Total Investment	**$50,000**
Current Liabilities	
Accounts Payable	$350
Current Borrowing	$0
Other Current Liabilities	$0
Total Current Liabilities	**$350**
Long-term Liabilities	$0
Total Liabilities	**$350**
Loss at Start-up	($18,350)
Total Capital	**$31,650**
Total Capital and Liabilities	**$32,000**

Use the start-up worksheet to plan your initial financing.

For example, in the United States a computer purchase can be treated either as an asset or an expense, depending on conditions set forth in federal tax law. When you can choose, you normally want to expense your purchases because then you can deduct those expenses from income. This is why we have "expensed equipment" among the expenses.

Your starting cash is your most critical input. Don't expect to get it right the first time without adjustments. Normally you start by putting a simple educated guess into this cell, typing in an amount equal to what you think should be your business checking account bank balance when you start. After that, you continue working with other tables in your plan, including sales forecast, personnel, and profit and loss, developing estimates for the values in those tables. If you are like most start-ups, as you refine your estimates you'll discover that your Cash Flow table has a negative balance. If you do have this negative balance, that's an indication of typical negative cash flow of start-up companies. To complete your plan, you'll have to go back to the Start-up table and increase the estimate for starting cash until the starting cash is enough to eliminate any negative balances in the cash flow projections for the following months. For example, if your cash flow indicates a negative balance of $-8,000 in the worst month, and your original estimate of starting cash was $15,000, then you would need to increase your estimated starting cash by $8,000 to cover the estimated deficit in the cash flow for the first few months. That would require a starting cash balance of $23,000 ($15K + $8K). In the example the starting cash is $25,000 instead of $23,000 because that's a round number and adds a slight cash buffer.

Ultimately the cash in the starting balance comes from the money you raise as loans and investments. If you need more cash, you need to raise more money. If you raise more money, then you need to increase your cash. The starting cash is often an important logical check, which you increase or decrease to make your balance correct. In the example, this company is raising $50,350 as a combination of loans and investments, and it has a total of $50,350 combined between start-up expenses and start-up assets, so its start-up table is correctly balanced. If it had raised $100,000, but you only had $50,350 in assets and expenses, then it would have lost $49,650 as accounted for funding. It could correct that situation by putting an extra $49,650 into its starting cash, which will increase the assets by $49,650.

Important: The cash you want to have in the bank at start-up is different from the money raised to start the business. The total money raised must match what was spent as expenses and assets. The cash at start-up is one of the assets. If you increase the amount of money raised, then you have to increase the start-up assets, usually by increasing the starting cash.

You have to fund start-up expenses as well as starting assets.

The Start-up Requirements

The total start-up requirements, which is shown in the middle of the table, is the sum of start-up expenses and start-up assets. This is the money you've decided you need—by estimating start-up expenses and start-up assets—to start the business. The "left to finance" amount shows up as a positive number only when you haven't provided enough funding to finance both expenses and assets. If it shows as a zero, you may have exactly the right amount, or too much.

You can tell that you have not accounted for all your incoming financing by looking at the "loss at start-up" value in the lower portion of Figure 5-2. That should be the same number as total start-up expenses (except negative). If it is more negative than start-up expenses are positive, then you have brought in funds that haven't been accounted for. You can fix that by adding more money into your starting cash to account for the additional financing.

Start-up Funding

The third portion of the table contains your estimates for start-up funding, including investments, loans, and unpaid bills.

Investment is money that you or your investors sink into the business for good. You don't expect to get it back. Borrowing is money loaned to the business—including loans as simple as purchases with credit cards and unpaid bills, called unpaid expenses. Loans can be unpaid expenses, short-term loans, or long-term loans. You need to invest and borrow enough money to equal the start-up expenses and start-up assets.

Loss at Start-up

Your loss at start-up should be exactly equal to your start-up expenses, but in the opposite direction. In the example, the start-up expenses total $18,350, so the loss at start-up should be exactly -$18,350. This is correct accounting. These are expenses taken against future income, and you have no income, so you have a loss. This is normal, since the vast majority of start-up companies start with a loss.

The rule of accounting is that assets are equal to investment plus loans. That is the same as capital being equal to assets minus liabilities, which is also your company's net worth. In order to make your balance correct as you start your company, you must recognize a loss at start-up that you can calculate as whatever number it takes to make capital equal to assets minus liabilities. For example, if you have $32,000 in assets and $350 in liabilities, your capital should be $31,650 (assets less liabilities). If you invested $50,000 in this case but your capital is only $31,650, then your loss at start-up has to be $18,350. The original $50,000 investment minus the $18,350 loss at start-up gives you the correct number for capital, $31,650 (assets are equal to capital plus liabilities). Your loss at start-up should normally be equal to start-up expenses, but it will be calculated as whatever number it takes to make investment and borrowing equal to start-up assets. This makes your balance correct at the start.

If your loss at start-up is greater than your start-up expenses, this means that you haven't accounted for all of the money you raised in investments and liabilities. Remember, all the money has to be accounted for as either expenses or assets. If your loss at start-up is less than your start-up expenses, you haven't raised enough money to meet your funding requirements.

To reduce the loss at start-up, you can do several things:

- Reduce start-up expenses.

- Increase start-up assets. Normally you increase these by increasing cash. This happens often while you're developing a plan, because you discover cash needs by estimating future cash flow. Remember, when you decide you need more cash, you have to increase both funding and starting cash.

- Decrease investment or borrowing.

Remember, however, that you must show investment and borrowing to match the total of your start-up expenses and start-up assets. If you just add funding without changing the resulting cash, then every dollar of additional funding, beyond the amount required, increases your loss at start-up, which isn't correct.

Text: Start-up Explanations

Summarize your start-up plan. Explain the list of start-up expenses, which are expenses you make before you start the business in the first month. After the expenses, you list the assets you want to have in the company as it starts. For a service company that would be cash in the bank account, and possibly short-term assets such as equipment. Service companies rarely have starting inventory. Then you show how you intend to finance both the expenses and the initial assets, which usually means investment or borrowing.

Summary

You should include a good company description, especially if you're developing a plan to be shown to people outside the company.

Don't stop with just legal formation and history; include some strategic topics, such as competitive edge and value proposition.

You need one of two tables, either start-up or past performance, to establish a starting balance for your projected cash flow and balance sheet.

A standard business plan includes company background information, history, and basic descriptions.

Chapter 6:

WHAT YOU SELL

This step in the process is much more important for a plan going to external readers, the banks or investors, than for internal plans. A complete business plan describes what you sell: either products, services, or both.

This part of the plan is mainly description. Sometimes it will include tables that provide more details, such as a bill of materials or detailed price lists. More frequently, however, this section is mainly text. It normally appears in the plan after the company description, but before the market analysis.

Start with a Summary Paragraph

Every section in a business plan should have an opening paragraph that describes the rest of the section. These summary paragraphs can also be used quite effectively in summary memos and loan application support documents. Readers may frequently skip the details, but only when they have an effective summary. It should be a clear and concise single paragraph that can be merged into the executive summary page. For this section, what do you sell, and to whom?

Detailed Description

The previous topic was the summary, so in this topic, you need to provide more detail. List and describe the products or services you sell. For each business offering, cover the main points, including what the product or service is, how much it costs, what sorts of customers make purchases, and why. What customer need does each product or service line fill? You might not want or need to include every product or service in the list, but at least consider the main sales lines.

It is always a good idea to think in terms of customer needs and customer benefits as you define your product offerings, rather than thinking of your side of the equation—how much the product or service costs, and how you deliver it to the customer.

As you list and describe your sales lines, you may run into one of the serendipitous benefits of good business planning, which is generating new ideas. Describe your product offerings in terms of customer types and customer needs, and you'll often discover new needs and new kinds of customers to cover. This is the way ideas are generated.

Competitive Comparison

Use this topic for a general comparison of your offering as one of several choices a potential buyer can make. There is a separate topic, in the market analysis section, for detailed comparison of strengths and weaknesses of your specific competitors.

In this topic you should discuss how your product lines and retail offerings compare in general to the others. For example, your outdoor store might offer better ski equipment than others, or perhaps it is located next to the slopes and caters to rental needs. Your jewelry store might be mid-range in price but well known for proficiency in appraisals, remounts, and renovation. Your hobby shop has by far the largest selection of model trains and airplanes.

In other words, in this topic you want to discuss how you are positioned in the market. Why do people buy from your business instead of from others in the same market? What do you offer, at what price, to whom, and how does your mix compare to others? Think about specific kinds of benefits, features, and market groups, comparing where you think you can show the difference. Describe the important competitive features of your products and/or services. Do you sell better features, better price, better quality, better service, or some other factor?

Sourcing and Fulfillment

In this section, you want to explain your product sourcing and the cost of fulfilling your service. Manufacturers and assemblers should present spreadsheet output showing standard costs and overhead. Distributors should present discount and margin structures. Service companies should present costs of fulfilling service obligations.

For example, sourcing is extremely important to a manufacturing company. Your vendors determine your standard costs and hold the key to continued operation. Analyze your standard costs and the materials or services you purchase as part of your manufacturing operation. Look for strengths and weaknesses.

Manufacturing companies want to have ample information about resource planning and sourcing of vital materials, especially if you are preparing a plan for outsiders, such as bankers or investors, or for business valuation. In this case, you may have additional documentation you can copy and attach as appendices, perhaps even contracts with important suppliers, standard cost breakdowns, bills of materials, and other information.

Where materials are particularly vital to your manufacturing, you might discuss whether second sources or alternative sources are available, and whether or not you use them or maintain relationships with them. This is also a good time to look at your sourcing strategy, and whether or not you can improve your business by improving your product sourcing.

But sourcing is not just for product-based companies. For example, a professional service company, such as an accounting practice, medical practice, law practice, management consulting firm, or graphic design firm, is normally going to provide the service by employing professionals. In this case, the cost is mainly the salaries of those professionals. Other service businesses are quite different. The travel agency provides a service through a combination of knowledge, rights, and infrastructure, including computer systems and databases.

The Internet provider or telephone company provides a service by owning and maintaining a network of communications infrastructure. A restaurant is a service business whose costs are a combination of salaries (for kitchen and table waiting) and food costs.

Technology

In this section, explain how technology affects your business, the products you sell, the means you use to sell them, and the needs of the customers you serve.

In some cases this might be a change in scanning technology, retail point-of-sale systems, or even video displays. In others, technology changes the nature of the goods or services you sell, such as cellular phones or high-density videos that didn't even exist a few years ago. Do you want to include the Internet? Will a website change the way you do business?

Sometimes technology can be vital to a service company, such as the case of the Internet provider that uses wireless connections as a competitive edge, or the local company that offers conference rooms for video conferencing. An accounting practice might gain a competitive advantage from proprietary software or wide-area network connections to its clients. A medical laboratory might depend completely on certain expensive technologies for medical diagnostics. A travel agency might depend on its connection to an airline reservation system.

Technology can be critical to a manufacturing business in at least two ways: first, the technology involved in assembly or manufacturing, such as in the manufacture of computer chips; and second, the technology incorporated in your product, such as proprietary technology that enhances the value of the product. In either case, technology can be a critical competitive edge. If you are writing a plan for outsiders, then you need to describe the technology and how well or thoroughly you have the technology protected in your business, through contracts, patents, and other protection.

Technology might be a negative factor, something to be included in a plan because a threat should be dealt with. For example, that same travel agency that depends on a computerized reservation system might also note growing competition from Internet reservations systems available to consumers who prefer to buy direct.

Not all businesses depend on technology. Technology might also be irrelevant for your business. If so, you can delete this topic if it doesn't seem important.

Future Products

Now you want to present your outlook for future products or services. Do you have a long-term product strategy? How are products developed? Is there a relationship between market segments, market demand, market needs, and product development?

Here again, what you include depends on the nature of your plan. In some cases future products are the most important point for investors looking to buy into your company's future. On the other hand, a bank is not going to lend you money for product development or hopes for future products; so in a plan accompanying a loan application, there would probably be much less stress on this point.

You may also need to deal with the issue of confidentiality. When a business plan includes sensitive information on future products, then it should be carefully monitored, with good documentation of who receives copies of the plan. Recipients might reasonably be asked to sign nondisclosure statements and those statements should be kept on file.

Sales Literature

It is generally a good idea to include specific pieces of sales literature and collateral as attachments or appendices to your plan. Examples would be copies of advertisements, brochures, direct mail pieces, catalogs, and technical specifications. When a plan is presented to someone outside the company, sales literature is a practical way to both explain your services and present the look and feel of the company.

If it is relevant for your business, you should also use this topic to discuss your present situation regarding company literature and your future plans. Is your sales literature a good match to your services and the image your company wants to present? How is it designed and produced? Could you improve it significantly, or cut the cost, or add additional benefits?

Summary

Depending on the purpose of your plan, you should provide good, practical information on the products or services you sell. Give your plan readers what they will need to evaluate the plan. Make sure they understand the need you serve, how well you satisfy that need, and why your customers buy from you instead of somebody else. Ideally, the descriptions in this chapter make your sales forecast seem realistic and even conservative.

Chapter 7:

MANAGEMENT TEAM

A management team and bringing people together is a lot more than just resumes and venture capital. It is what makes a company work or not work.

Planning for People

For example: It's a sunny March Friday in Western Oregon, which is rare; so rare, in fact, that the boss decides to have office pizza for lunch.

The controller is a former history major, Phi Beta Kappa into grad school, who discovered midway through her 30s that she really liked making numbers work. As people gather in the main room around the pizza, she announces that all should enjoy her hair that day "because I am having a rare good hair day." Everybody laughs.

The head of tech support turns the attention to the "krinkly hair" of the marketing manager. Everybody laughs again. There are jokes about the pizza and the root beer.

The product manager demonstrates ballroom dancing steps in preparation for his upcoming wedding, and somebody thinks to turn the music-on-hold up, through the phones, as accompaniment.

The documentation manager emerges from her sunny office in the back and announces that she has a new couch in her office so people can escape from all the administration in the front.

These people seem happy. The technical support manager really likes to explain to people on the telephone; the documentation manager loves teaching and writing. The admin department includes a college student and a soccer mom, both of whom understand the accounting system very well and usually forgive it its flaws. The office manager, a former teacher, says managing this diversity is nothing compared to dealing with a classroom full of adolescents. The product manager and marketing manager both earned their business degrees while working part-time in tech support, and joined full-time as soon as they graduated. These people like their jobs and they like each other. They work together well.

Flash back to the same company four years earlier, with a totally different staff. Then, the controller was worried sick about the integrity of the computer system. The technical support person was tired of technical support and upset that the controller had a better computer. The sales manager spent half of her day settling disputes between the controller and the technical support person.

In other words, the jobs need to be done and the people need to match their job functions and preferences. A manufacturing company can't survive without a production manager, a software company can't live without technical support, and most companies also need office management and administration.

If we jump straight into personnel plans and resumes and business jargon related to the management team, we can inadvertently forget that there is something much more vital and alive than just looking good for investors. A company is where its employees come together most every day, for the major part of the day. If it isn't a good place to work, then it won't be successful. Keep this in mind as you plan your management and develop this part of your plan.

Cover the Bases in Text

Chapter Summary

The management chapter starts, like the other chapters, with a good summary. You may want to use that summary as part of a summary memo or loan application document, so cover the main points. Consider what you'd say about your management if you only had one or two paragraphs to say it.

Make sure you cover the basic information first. That would include how many employees the company has, how many managers, and how many of the managers are founders. Is your team complete, or are there gaps still to be filled? Is your organizational structure sound, with job descriptions and logical responsibilities for all the key members?

Particularly with start-up companies, you may not have the complete team as you write the plan. In that case, be sure to point out the gaps and weaknesses and how you intend to fill them.

Organizational Structure

The organizational structure of a company is what you frequently see as an organizational chart, also known as an "org chart." If you have access to an organizational chart graphic, that works really well at this point. If not, you can just use the text to describe the organizational structure in words, without a chart.

Make sure you explain how job descriptions work and how the main company functions are divided up. Are your organizational lines drawn clearly? Is the authority properly distributed? Do you have jobs that include responsibility without authority? Do your resources seem in line with your organizational needs?

Management Backgrounds

List the most important members of the management team. Include summaries of their backgrounds and experience, using them like brief resumes. Describe their functions with the company. Resumes should be attached to the back of a plan.

Management Gaps

You may have obvious gaps in management, especially in start-up companies, but even in ongoing companies. For example, the manufacturing company without a production manager has some explaining to do, and the computer company without a service department has some problems. It is far better to define and identify a weakness than to pretend it doesn't exist. Specify where the team is weak because of gaps in coverage of key management functions. How will these weaknesses be corrected? How will the more important gaps be filled?

Other Considerations

Applicability depends on your company. Some questions that should be answered include: Do any managers or employees have "noncompete" agreements with competitors? Who is on your board of directors? What do the members contribute to the business? Who are your major stockholders? What is their role in management?

Develop Your Numbers

At this point you should normally include a personnel table to project personnel costs, including direct compensation and indirect costs. The indirect costs include vacation pay, sick pay, insurance benefits, education, and of course, payroll taxes and some other costs. There are different terms for all of this, but my favorite is "personnel burden," which is a cost over and above the direct wages and salaries.

Home Offices

If you are working as a sole proprietor in a home office, you should still include your own compensation as part of your business plan. What you pay yourself should be added into the profit and loss as an expense. However, in this case you don't really need to include payroll burden, because these additional expenses are irrelevant until you include additional employees.

Two Personnel Variations

As with the sales forecast in *Chapter 10: Forecast Your Sales*, a good personnel plan varies according to your business and business plan needs. You may want a simple list of names, titles, or groups, each of which is assigned a monthly cost. This model is shown in Figure 7-1.

FIGURE 7-1: STANDARD PERSONNEL PLAN

Personnel	Oct	Nov	Dec	2004	2005	2006
Partners	$12,000	$12,000	$12,000	$144,000	$175,000	$200,000
Consultants	$0	$0	$0	$0	$50,000	$63,000
Editorial/Graphic	$6,000	$6,000	$6,000	$18,000	$22,000	$26,000
VP Marketing	$5,000	$5,000	$5,000	$20,000	$50,000	$55,000
Sales People	$0	$0	$0	$0	$30,000	$33,000
Office Manager	$2,500	$2,500	$2,500	$7,500	$30,000	$33,000
Secretarial	$1,750	$1,750	$1,750	$5,250	$20,000	$22,000
Other	$0	$0	$0	$0	$0	$0
Subtotal	$27,250	$27,250	$27,250	$194,750	$377,000	$434,006

The standard personnel plan is a simple list of names, titles, or categories. The sum transfers into your profit and loss statement. This illustration shows the last three months and subsequent two years of a sample plan.

The simpler model totals all payroll only. It is perfectly appropriate for a lot of small businesses. You can use each of the lines in the table to describe specific individuals, or groups and departments. When you have the list complete, just add up the totals for personnel costs in your Profit and Loss *Chapter 14: The Bottom Line*. Multiply that total times your burden rate—say 15 or 20 percent—to calculate your personnel burden. The burden goes into the profit and loss as a separate line.

Figure 7-2 shows the more detailed personnel plan that divides the rows into categories, such as sales and marketing, general and administrative, and so forth. The detailed model totals the planned payroll for each department, then calculates total payroll.

FIGURE 7-2: DETAILED PERSONNEL PLAN

Personnel	Oct	Nov	Dec	2004	2005	2006
Production						
Manager	$3,000	$3,000	$3,000	$36,000	$40,000	$42,000
Assistant	$1,000	$1,000	$1,000	$12,000	$13,000	$14,000
Technical	$2,000	$2,000	$2,000	$24,000	$27,500	$27,500
Fulfillment	$1,500	$1,500	$1,500	$18,000	$22,000	$50,000
Subtotal	$7,500	$7,500	$7,500	$90,000	$102,500	$133,500
Sales and Marketing						
Manager	$6,000	$6,000	$6,000	$72,000	$76,000	$85,000
Technical Sales	$5,000	$5,000	$5,000	$60,000	$63,000	$80,000
Salesperson	$2,500	$2,500	$2,500	$30,000	$55,000	$64,000
Salesperson	$2,500	$2,500	$2,500	$30,000	$50,000	$55,000
Subtotal	$16,000	$16,000	$16,000	$192,000	$244,000	$284,000
General and Administrative						
President	$5,500	$5,500	$5,500	$66,000	$69,000	$95,000
Finance	$0	$0	$0	$0	$29,000	$30,000
Admin Assistant	$2,000	$2,000	$2,000	$24,000	$26,000	$28,000
Clerical	$0	$0	$0	$0	$0	$15,000
Subtotal	$7,500	$7,500	$7,500	$90,000	$124,000	$168,000
Other Personnel						
Programming	$3,000	$3,000	$3,000	$36,000	$40,000	$44,000
Other Technical	$0	$0	$0	$0	$30,000	$33,000
Other	$0	$0	$0	$0	$0	$0
Subtotal	$3,000	$3,000	$3,000	$36,000	$70,000	$77,000
Total People	11	11	11	11	13	14
Total Payroll	$34,000	$34,000	$34,000	$408,000	$540,500	$662,500
Payroll Burden	$4,760	$4,760	$4,760	$57,120	$81,075	$106,000
Total Payroll Expenditures	$38,760	$38,760	$38,760	$465,120	$621,575	$768,500

The more detailed personnel plan shown here divides personnel expenditures into classifications including production, sales and marketing, general and administrative, and other.

For either the simple or detailed personnel table, you also want to calculate a payroll burden as a percentage of the total, and make sure to include the personnel burden assumption in your list of general assumptions. Personnel burden is the extra costs of payroll taxes and benefits.

The payroll assumptions in this model will also be used for the other financial projections. The Profit and Loss (also called income statement) will use personnel plan numbers.

GATHERING
INFORMATION

*A good plan will include useful
information about your market, your
customers, and the business you're
in.*

Chapter 8:

THE BUSINESS YOU'RE IN

*In addition to the information you've already developed, you also
need to explain the type of business you're in; not just your company,
but the business environment you'll be operating in. This is one step
in a business plan's comprehensive market analysis.*

You'll be expected to explain the general state of your industry
and the nature of the business, especially if your plan is going
outside your company to banks or investors.

Whether you're a service business, manufacturer, retailer,
or some other type of business, you should do an Industry
Analysis, describing:

- Industry Participants.
- Distribution Patterns.
- Competition.

This chapter will describe these topics in more detail.

Industry Analysis

A complete business plan discusses industry economics,
participants, distribution patterns, factors in the competition,
and whatever else describes the nature of this business to
outsiders.

This chapter emphasizes the enormous impact of the Internet
on the state of business information. Finding information isn't
really the problem any more, after the information explosion
and the huge growth in the Internet during the 1990s. Even 10
or 15 years ago, dealing with information was more a problem
of sorting through it all than of finding raw data. That generality
is more true every day.

There are websites for analysis, financial statistics,
demographics, trade associations, and just about everything
you'll need for a complete business plan. We'll look at that in
this chapter after going through some of the topics to cover. I'll
also include some of the old-fashioned reference works, just in
case you really need them.

Industry Participants

You can't easily describe a type of business without describing the nature of the participants. There is a huge difference between an industry like long-distance telephone trunk services, in which there are only a few huge companies in any one country, and one like dry cleaning, in which there are tens of thousands of smaller participants.

This can make a big difference to a business and a business plan. The restaurant industry, for example, is what we call "pulverized" which, like the dry cleaning industry, is made up of many small participants. The fast food business, on the other hand, is composed of a few national brands participating in thousands of branded outlets, many of them franchised.

Economists talk of consolidation in an industry as a time when many small participants tend to disappear and a few large players emerge. In accounting, for example, there are a few large international firms whose names are well known and tens of thousands of smaller firms. The automobile business is composed of a few national brands participating in thousands of branded dealerships. In computer manufacturing, for example, there are a few large international firms whose names are well known, and thousands of smaller firms.

Distribution Patterns

Explain how distribution works in this industry. Is this an industry in which retailers are supported by regional distributors, as is the case for computer products, magazines, or auto parts? Does this industry depend on direct sales to large industrial customers? Do manufacturers support their own direct sales forces, or do they work with product representatives?

Some products are almost always sold through retail stores to consumers, and sometimes these are distributed by distribution companies that buy from manufacturers. In other cases, the products are sold directly from manufacturers to stores. Some products are sold directly from the manufacturer to the final consumer through mail campaigns, national advertising, or other promotional means.

In many product categories there are several alternatives, and distribution choices are strategic. Encyclopedias and vacuum cleaners were traditionally sold door-to-door, but are now also sold in stores and direct from manufacturer to consumer through radio and television ads.

Many products are distributed through direct business-to-business sales, and in long-term contracts such as the ones between car manufacturers and their suppliers of parts, materials, and components. In some industries companies use representatives, agents, or commissioned salespeople.

Technology can change the patterns of distribution in an industry or product category. The Internet, for example, is changing the options for software distribution, books, music, and other products. Cable communication is changing the options for distributing TV, movies, music, games, and high speed Internet access.

The Distribution Patterns topic may not apply to most service companies, because distribution is normally about physical distribution of specific physical products. If you are a restaurant, graphic artist, professional services practice, architect, or some other service that doesn't involve distribution, just delete this topic.

For a few services, distribution may still be relevant. A phone service or cable provider, or an Internet provider, might describe distribution related to physical infrastructure. Some publishers may prefer to treat their business as a service rather than a manufacturing company, and in that case distribution may also be relevant.

Competition

Explain the nature of competition in this market. This topic is still in the general area of describing the industry, or type of business. Explain the general nature of competition in this business, and how the customers seem to choose one provider over another. What are the keys to success? What buying factors make the most difference—Price? Product features? Service? Support? Training? Software? Delivery dates? Are brand names important?

In the computer business, for example, competition might depend on reputation and trends in one part of the market, and on channels of distribution and advertising in another. In many business-to-business industries, the nature of competition depends on direct selling, because channels are impractical. Price is vital in products competing with each other on retail shelves, but delivery and reliability might be more important for materials used by manufacturers in volume, for which a shortage can affect an entire production line.

In the restaurant business, for example, competition might depend on reputation and trends in one part of the market, and on location and parking in another.

In many professional service practices the nature of competition depends on word of mouth, because advertising is not completely accepted. Is there price competition between accountants, doctors, and lawyers? How do people choose travel agencies or florists for weddings? Why does someone hire one landscape architect over another? Why choose Starbucks, a national brand, over the local coffee house? All of this is the nature of competition.

Main Competitors

List the main competitors. What are the strengths and weaknesses of each? Consider their products, pricing, reputation, management, financial position, channels of distribution, brand awareness, business development, technology, or other factors that you feel are important. In what segments of the market do they operate? What seems to be their strategy? How much do they impact your products, and what threats and opportunities do they represent?

Finding Information

You'll end up getting almost everything you need on the Internet, using the World Wide Web. As it turns out, a great deal of business information and small business or entrepreneurial help is readily available. Always start first on the Internet. Market research firms and industry experts publish much of their information in websites, and in trade and business magazines. Reference sites index these magazines, many offer the texts online, and if not, then libraries stock them. Trade associations publish many listings and statistics in their websites as well as in hard copy publications. Public stock laws require detailed reporting of financial results, and stock market information sources compile industry statistics from financial reports.

If you have a personal computer, you have most of what you need to access the information on the Internet. These services offer computerized versions of publication indices, statistical abstracts, and even complete text of published articles that are available online. In some cases, you can download information from a remote database into your computer and dump it in a convenient format directly into your business plan.

If you aren't already online, I urge you to get your Internet access, and learn how to use it. There is no substitute for the facility to logon to the Internet and communicate with other people who have questions, advice, and similar interests. The Internet offers an amazing array of information and services. As you read through the more specific suggestions to follow, you can assume that most all of them have websites available.

As alternatives use university libraries, professional information brokers, and US government publications.

Business Plan Websites

Palo Alto Software maintains an Internet website that offers free downloadable sample plans, tips, outlines, and discussions of topics related to developing a business plan. Look for them at:

www.bplans.com

FIGURE 8-1: PALO ALTO SOFTWARE'S BUSINESS RESOURCE WEBSITE, BPLANS.COM

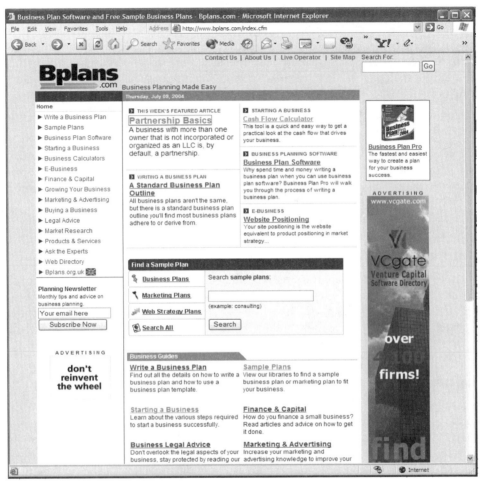

The Bplans.com website is intended to be a valuable business information source, including business planning information, market information, articles, sample plans, and links to other resources.

This site includes suggested links to other sources of small business information, including the Small Business Administration (SBA), Small Business Development Centers (SBDCs), and many other valuable sites. It is stocked with the latest available information, and references to information, that might be available elsewhere.

Figure 8-2 shows Palo Alto Software's main website, as it looked when this book was revised. The website address is:

www.paloalto.com

FIGURE 8-2: PALO ALTO SOFTWARE'S MAIN WEBSITE

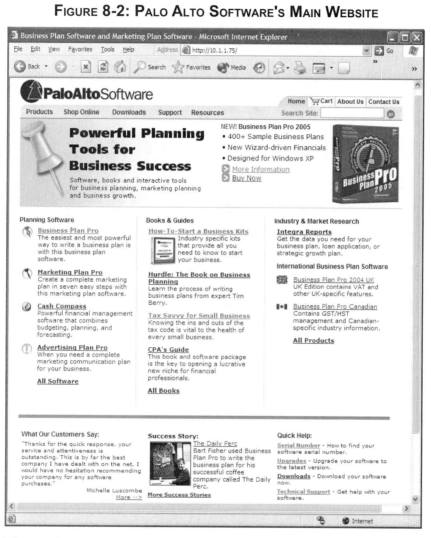

The Palo Alto Software website is intended to provide valuable product information to our customers, including business planning resources, an online store, and links to sample plans and other sources of information.

Both our main website and **www.bplans.com** are linked to our "**Ask the Experts**" team. This team of business planning experts from around the country, responds to general questions about business planning, entrepreneuring, and marketing planning. You can post your question and receive an answer as an email reply. You can search among the more than 1,800 answers currently available in the database.

Government Sites

We describe the U.S. Census Bureau site in the sections on market analysis, *Chapter 9: Know Your Market* and *Chapter 11: Market.*

Visit the Small Business Administration (SBA) website at:

www.sba.gov

Figure 8-3 shows their home page.

FIGURE 8-3: SBA WEBSITE

The Small Business Administration Internet site offers a wealth of free information and links to other sources as well.

Web Search Engines

Another excellent lead is Yahoo's small business information listing. From the main page at Yahoo!, choose Business and Economy, then use the Yahoo! search for small business information. The specific URL is:

www.yahoo.com/Business_and_Economy/Business_to_Business/Small_Business_Information

Excite's competition is a small business information page at:

http://local.excite.com/small_business/index.html

Each one of these websites lead to further links and more information. Be aware that websites frequently change content, and their URL addresses. So be diligent and thorough in your searches.

Trade Associations

Many industries are blessed with an active trade association that serves as a vital source of industry-specific information. Such associations regularly publish member directories and the better ones publish statistical information that track industry sales, profits, economic trends, etc.

If you don't know which trade associations apply to your industry, search the Internet in Yahoo, Excite, and other search engines. Look for the website of the trade association for your industry. Ask at the reference section of your library for listings of industry associations. Ask someone else in the same industry. Consult an industry-specific magazine. Look in the readers guide or business index (in the following section, **Business Publications**) or *Ayer's Directory*, published by Gayle Publishers of Philadelphia, which lists periodicals. You can also look for association listings in *Information U.S.A.*, published by Viking Press.

For example, the National Shoe Retailers Association publishes Business Performance Report, a statistical review of more than 1,700 independent shoe retail companies. They sell it to members or nonmembers. It covers men's, women's, children's, and family shoe companies, and includes financials and other information.

Industry Data

Evaluate the risk associated with your business venture. Every industry has a series of financial and business ratios, collected and collated over time. Compare your plan and its computed ratios to your Industry average. Try these sources, among others, for industry data and financial ratios:

- Integra Information **www.integrainfo.com**
- Risk Management Association **www.rmahq.org**

Business Publications

Business magazines are an important source of business information. Aside from the major general-interest business publications (*Business Week, Wall Street Journal*, etc.) there are many publications that look at specific industries.

Specialization is an important trend in the publishing business. Dingbats and Widgets may be boring to the general public, but they are exciting to Dingbat and Widget manufacturers who read about them regularly in their specialized magazines. The magazines are an important medium for industry-specific advertising, which is important to readers as well as advertisers.

The editorial staffs of these magazines have to fill the space between the ads. They do that by publishing as much industry-specific information as they can find, including statistics, forecasts, and industry profiles. Paging through one of these magazines can sometimes produce a great deal of business forecasting and economic information.

Several good reference sources list magazines, journals, and other publications. They also offer indices to published articles, which you can use to search for the exact references you need. These will be kept in the reference section of most libraries:

- *Readers Guide to Periodical Literature* indexes popular magazines. Published by H.W. Wilson of New York. Available in most library reference sections.
- *Business Periodicals Index*, also published by H.W. Wilson of New York. Indexes business magazines and journals only.
- *The Magazine Index*, published by Information Access Co.

Use the indices to identify published information that might help your business plan. When you find an index listing for an article that forecasts your industry or talks about industry economics or trends, jot down basic information on the publication and ask the library for a copy of the publication.

Reference Libraries

Reference librarians follow reference sources as a profession. They are excellent sources of good advice and tips on reference materials that may help you provide the information your business plan requires. Online, try the James J. Hill library at

www.hillsource.org.

We have found Predicast *Sourcebooks* particularly useful on several occasions. These summarize forecasts that have appeared in any of several hundred business magazines and journals. The presentation focuses on the most important forecast information, and provides the magazine citation—date of publication, page number, etc.—as background.

Small Business Administration (SBA)

The United States Small Business Administration (SBA) is best known for its small business loans. However, it also provides business training, business information, and business services including workshops, counseling, publications, and videotapes. It has program offices in every state, the District of Columbia, the Virgin Islands, and Puerto Rico. It has business development specialists stationed in more than 100 field offices nationwide. We noted its website in Figure 8-3.

The SBA publishes more than 50 business booklets and information products. These products are free, but the SBA suggests a small donation for most of them. They answer many frequently asked questions and provide important information for business owners and would-be business owners.

If you don't have Internet access, you can find out about SBA business development programs and services by calling the SBA Small Business Answer Desk at 1-800-UASKSBA (1-800-827-5722). The answer desk "hotline" provides an information and referral service staffed by the organization's office of business initiatives, education, and training. In Washington D.C. the local number is (202) 205-7151. It operates during normal office hours five days a week.

Small Business Development Centers (SBDC)

Small business development centers (SBDCs) are funded in part by the Small Business Administration (SBA) and also work with local colleges and some other funding agencies. Every state has at least one SBDC, and most states have offices in several cities. The SBDCs are an excellent resource for businesses, offering high quality professional advice at very low prices. SBDCs also work closely with local colleges to provide courses in business planning, bookkeeping, employee management, sales, marketing, and other vital subjects. SBDCs also publish books, surveys, and studies, and in some cases even audio tapes, videotapes, and workshops. Palo Alto Software works with SBDCs to provide software and seminar courses related to business planning.

Service Corps of Retired Executives (SCORE)

The SBA sponsors the Service Corps of Retired Executives (SCORE), which includes more than 13,000 volunteers who provide training and one-to-one counseling at no charge, in offices all over the country. You can find out about SCORE at:

www.score.org

U. S. Census Bureau

The United States Census Bureau, part of the Department of Commerce, has a wealth of information available for business and educational purposes. I refer to it, specifically and with examples, in the market analysis portion of *Chapter 9: Know Your Market*. Most of the Census Bureau's reports cover the entire United States and summarize data for the nation. However, the Bureau also publishes information on states, counties in states, and even cities within counties. Among the more valuable special reports are city and county reports that list the number of business establishments by type of establishment. These are special reports available directly from the Bureau and also from some libraries and electronic database services. Many of these reports are also available through online services. The Census has an electronic edition called CENDATA. It also has an Internet website at:

www.census.gov

Finding Business Assistance

New businesses, small businesses, and business planning are good for the economy. Governments, higher education institutions, and business organizations know that and try to help businesses as much as possible. For you and your business, there is probably a great deal of help available.

SBDCs and SCORE

We've listed the SBA, SCORE, and SBDCs in the previous section as sources of information. Both SCORE and the SBDCs are also sources of real business assistance. They both exist to help people in small business and entrepreneurs. Not all services are free, but those that aren't free are priced way below market value. For business assistance, go there first. You can get local addresses for SBDCs on our website.

You can find local addresses for SCORE at their website.

In these pages, I only describe the United States organizations offering help to small business and start-ups. In other markets, similar organizations exist. Check with your chambers of commerce and industry organizations, government development organizations, and business schools.

Consultants, Accountants, and Attorneys

Consultants, accountants, and attorneys are in the first line of business assistance. They aren't really the main focus of this chapter, however, and not because they aren't, in general, excellent sources of information. We have the utmost respect for the value of professional advice. In this discussion, however, we deal with relatively low-cost sources of business assistance, such as development agencies, local night schools, and online information services. We don't have a lot to add to the general doctrine of how to choose a good business professional. Let the buyer beware. A good business professional is always worth the money, if you have the money. Unfortunately, not all professionals are good, and it's hard to know who's good until you've committed money.

Always try to get some good references on professionals—other clients, satisfied clients—before you use them, and don't forget to check their references. Furthermore, it is not always true that with business consultants you get what you pay for. In our experience, there is not always a direct correlation between the fees charged and the value provided.

The SBA says consultants "can be a great asset to a small business owner. A business consultant's fees typically range between $25 and $250 an hour. If you decide to retain the services of a consultant, make sure he/she is reputable and be certain that you understand the fee schedule up front."

Business Organizations

Explore what's available through local business organizations such as the Chamber of Commerce. Many have entrepreneurial interest groups, such as a new enterprise forum or industry associations.

Schools and Colleges

Many local community colleges work directly with the SBA to house the Small Business Development Centers (SBDCs) discussed as part of the government resources in the previous section. The community college/SBDC combination is often an excellent resource for workshops, classes, and even business consulting, all of it with experts whose job involves helping small businesses and start-ups, funded at least in part by the school and the government. Call your local community college and ask about business classes.

Libraries

Libraries regularly carry business periodicals and business books. Reference sections have staff able to help you find what you need. Look for magazine indices, trade association and government publications.

Banks

Banks are often involved in local development activities, and even when they don't directly offer business help (some do), they will at least know where else you can go for help. The SBA says "many bank officers have a broad understanding of finance, business operations, and the local economic climate. Do not be afraid to ask your banker questions."

State Development Agencies

Most states have development agencies of one kind or another. They also offer information related to small businesses and start-ups, and can be a valuable resource. Check with your other resource providers about state agencies. You can also look in your telephone directory for government agencies under the state category.

Trade Associations

Trade associations can be an excellent source of good information for some industry start-ups. Use your library directory of trade associations to explore associations related to your industry.

Publications

Many publications specialize in your industry, and others specialize in small businesses and start-ups. Explore libraries, bookstores, and magazine directories for publications for your specific industry.

Summary

We are in a brave new world of too much information, not too little. It will be hard for you to sort through all the information you'll find on your business or your industry, hard to summarize, hard to decide what is most important. As you do, keep in mind that the business plan is supposed to guide decisions. It is not a school report or even a graduate thesis. If it doesn't have a business purpose—which might be describing the industry for bank or investor, or for your own team, for example—then you shouldn't include it.

Chapter 9:

KNOW YOUR MARKET

What's the first thing, the most essential element, you need in business? No, not a plan: **you need customers.**

In Chapter 3: Initial Assessment, *you took a good first look at whether or not your business has (or will have) enough customers to keep it healthy. For the next step, you need to go further into a market analysis. It doesn't have to be academic, necessarily, and it doesn't have to be a huge project that stalls your planning process. What you want, ultimately, is to know your customers.*

Practical Market Research

Some of the best market research is simple, practical, and even obvious. You don't get it from reference sections in libraries, or even from the Internet. Get it from real people, particularly customers or potential customers. Here are some practical examples.

Study Similar Businesses

Always take a look at other businesses similar to your own, as a very good first step. If you're looking at starting a new business, you may well be starting one similar to one you already know. If you're doing a plan for an existing business, you are even more likely to know the business well. Even so, you can still learn a lot by looking at other similar businesses.

- Look at existing, similar businesses.

   If you are planning a retail shoe store, for example, spend some time looking at existing retail shoe store businesses. Park across the street and count the customers that go into the store. Note how long they stay inside, and how many come out with boxes that look like purchased shoes. You can probably even count how many pairs of shoes each customer buys. Browse the store and look at prices. Look at several stores, including the discount shoe stores and department store shoe departments.

- **Find a similar business in another place.**

  If you are planning a local business, find a similar business far enough away that you won't compete. For the shoe store example, you would identify shoe stores in similar towns in other states. Call the owner, explain your purpose truthfully, and ask about the business.

- **Scan local newspapers for people selling a similar business.**

  Contact the broker and ask for as much information as possible. If you are thinking of creating a shoe store and you find one for sale, you should consider yourself a prospective buyer. Maybe buying the existing store is the best thing. Even if you don't buy, the information you gain will be very valuable. Why is the owner selling? Is there something wrong with the business? You can probably get detailed financial information.

- **Shop the competition.**

  If you're in the restaurant business, patronize your competition once a month, rotating through different restaurants. If you own a shoe store, shop your competition once a month, and visit different stores.

Talk to Customers

If you're considering starting a new business, talk to potential customers. In the shoe store example, talk to people coming out of the stores. Talk to your neighbors, talk to your friends, talk to your relatives. Ask them how often they buy shoes, what sizes, where, at what price, and whatever else you can think of. If you're starting a restaurant, landscape architecture business, butcher shop, bakery, or whatever, talk to customers.

At most business schools, when they teach business planning, students have to do a market survey as part of the plan. The plan isn't complete unless they go out and ask a credible number of people what they want, why, where they get it, how much they pay, and so forth. Although you may not go through the formality of a customer survey for your business, this information is vital.

At Palo Alto Software, we frequently put a customer survey on two of our websites on the Internet. People who are browsing the Internet looking for materials and information on business plans can visit us at:

www.paloalto.com

www.bplans.com

One of the sites does no selling, but provides free information, including free downloadable sample plans, outlines, and discussions, including answers to several hundred specific questions about details of developing a business plan. We sometimes ask people stopping by our websites to answer a few quick questions that concern us. The invitation promises just a few questions, and promises also that we won't ask their names or email addresses, and we won't follow up with sales information. When we do, we get about 300 responses a month, which provides us with valuable information about the concerns people have as they consider writing a business plan.

If you have an ongoing business, the process of developing a plan should include talking to customers. Take a step away from the routine, dial up some of your customers, and ask them about your business. How are you doing? Why do they buy? How do they feel about your competitors? It is a good idea to take a customer to lunch once a month, just to keep yourself in touch.

Potential Customers

Most business plans contain an analysis of potential customers. We saw that in *Chapter 3: Initial Assessment*, as part of the initial assessment. As an essential first step, you should have a good idea of how many potential customers there are. The way you find that out depends on your type of business. For example, a retail shoe store needs to know about individuals living in a local area, a graphic design firm needs to know about local businesses, and a national catalog needs to know about households and companies in an entire nation.

Good sources depend on what you need. Government and commercial statistics are usually more than enough, but for some plans you may end up purchasing information from professional publishers or contract researchers.

For general demographic data about a local area, if you have no easier source, ask the reference desk at a local library. A local university library is even better, particularly a business library. Chambers of Commerce usually have general information about a local market. In the United States, there is the federal government's U.S. Census Bureau. Nowadays the quickest route to the census bureau is the Internet website at:

www.census.gov

The official statistics are good for business information as well. You should be able to find a count of local businesses with some measure of size, such as sales or employees. The U.S. Census Bureau has a lot of information on businesses. You can also find free information at the Chamber of Commerce and probably at a local library.

Before the Internet became so prevalent, I frequently turned to vendors of mailing lists for general information about people and types of business. The mailing list vendors often have catalogs listing total numbers of types of people and types of business. For example, to find out how many attorneys or CPA offices there are in the United States, I might look at the lists for sale at a list broker.

Magazines provide another good source of demographics. If you're selling to computer stores, for example, call *Computer Retail Week* and *Computer Reseller News* and ask both publications for a media kit. The media kit is intended to sell pages of advertising to potential advertisers. They are frequently full of demographics on the readers. For information on any specific type of business, get the media kits for the magazines that cater to those types of businesses as readers.

Just browsing the Census Bureau website while preparing this draft, it took me about 10 minutes to discover that my home county has 378 general contractors, of which 360 have fewer than 20 employees and the remaining 18 have between 20 and 100. There are 238 legal businesses in my county, of which only 12 have more than 20 employees. Also, following the shoe store example, there are 32 shoe stores in the county, none of them having more than 20 employees. There are 111,000 households in the county, 61 percent of them owner occupied, and an average of 2.49 people per household. Some 22 percent of adults in the county are college graduates, and the median household income is $26,000. All of this information was available for free at the U.S. Census Bureau website, listed above.

Know the Customers

Aside from just counting the customers, you also want to know what they need, what they want, and what makes them buy. The more you know about them, the better. For individuals as customers, you probably want to know their average age, income levels, family size, media preferences, buying patterns, and as much else as you can find out that relates to your business. If you can, you want to divide them into groups according to useful classifications, such as income, age, buying habits, social behavior, values, or whatever other factors are important. For the shoe store example, shoe size is good, but you might also want activity preferences and even—if you can find it—psychographics.

Psychographics divides customers into cultural groups, value groups, social sets, motivator sets, or other interesting categories that might be useful for classifying customers. For example, in literature intended for potential retailers, First Colony Mall of Sugarland, Texas, describes its local area psychographics as including "25% Kid & Cul-de-Sacs (upscale suburban families, affluent), 5.4% Winner's Circle (suburban executives, wealthy), 19.2% Boomers and Babies (young white-collar suburban, upper middle income), and 7% Country Squires (elite ex-urban, wealthy)." Going into more detail, it calls the Kids & Cul-de-Sacs group "a noisy medley of bikes, dogs, carpools, rock music and sports." The Winner's Circle customers are "well-educated, mobile, executives and professionals with teenaged families. Big producers, prolific spenders, and global travelers." The Country Squires are "where the wealthy have escaped urban stress to live in rustic luxury. No. 4 in affluence, big bucks in the boondocks."

SRI Consulting Business Intelligence (SRIC-BI), formerly provides another example. Its VALS service (values and lifestyles) offers information on U.S. customers classified according to the value sets shown in Figure 9-1. Customers and potential customers are divided into groups, including innovators, achievers, experiencers, and others. More information about that is available from SRIC-BI from their website at:

www.sric-bi.com/VALS/types.shtml

Their email is vals@sric-bi.com, and the main telephone number is (650) 859-4600.

FIGURE 9-1: SRIC-BI's VALS PSYCHOGRAPHICS

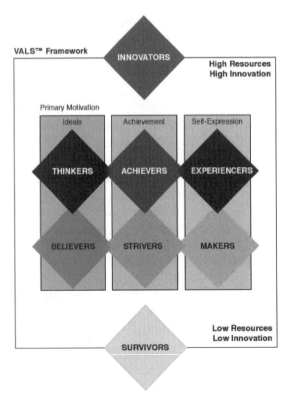

The diagram illustrates SRIC-BI's values and lifestyles psychographics research that divides the U.S. market into various types of potential customers.

Internet Research for Business Plans

I'm old enough to remember when gathering information was a problem. Business consultants could make money just collecting the kind of information you need for a good business plan market analysis. These days, however, the problem is more sorting through all the information than it is gathering information. The World Wide Web on the Internet has completely changed practical business research.

This is far too large a topic to cover in this book, but it is also vital to modern business. By the time you're looking at developing a business plan, I think you should know how to use the World Wide Web on the Internet.

New search engines and new searching techniques appear all the time, so please try to stay current.

At the very least, know how to find the Yahoo! main page, shown in Figure 9-2, and sort through its catalog of business information at:

www.yahoo.com

As you click on any of the underlined words, the view opens up to more information and more specifics.

FIGURE 9-2: THE YAHOO INTERNET CATALOG

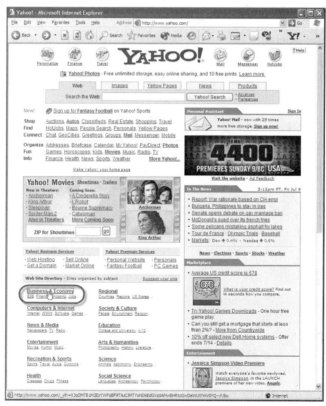

The Yahoo! site (www.yahoo.com), probably the best-known Internet navigational aid, sorts and catalogs the World Wide Web according to logical categories.

Another search engine for business information is Excite. Figure 9-3 shows their main search page at:

www.excite.com

FIGURE 9-3: SEARCHING THE NET WITH EXCITE

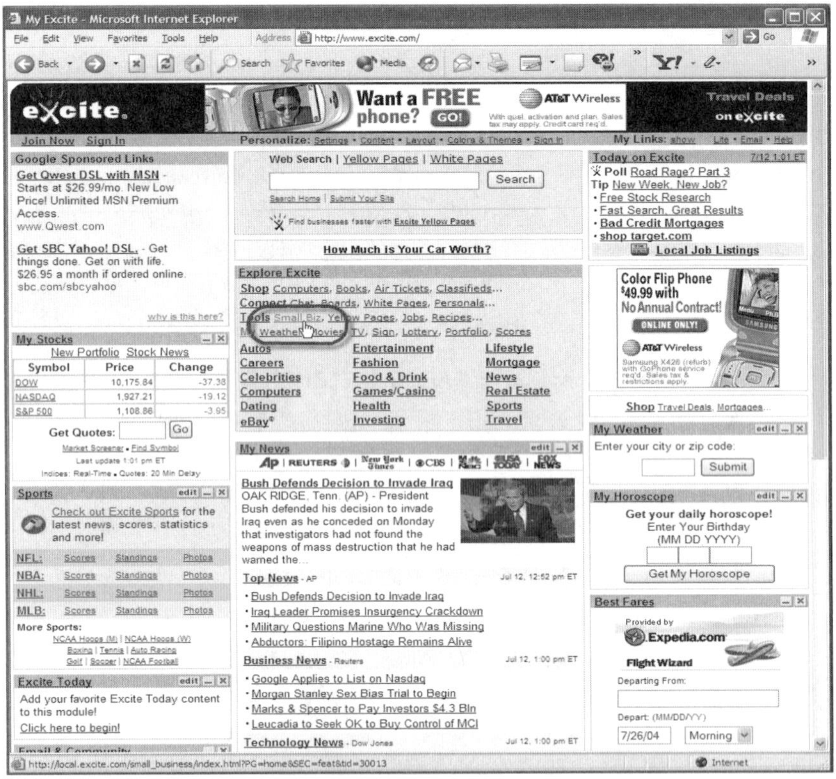

The Excite Internet search engine at www.excite.com is another leading Internet search site that you can use to help you locate market and business information.

Summary

Projecting market growth is particularly important when your plan is related to finding investors or supporting a loan application, because market growth enhances the implied value of your business.

Cite growth rates in terms that fit the available information, whether growth in the number of potential customers, projected dollar sales, meals served, website projects, tax reporting hours, yards to landscape, or whatever you have.

Chapter 10:

FORECAST YOUR SALES

The next step is developing your sales forecast. Don't fear—it isn't as hard as most people think. Think of your sales forecast as an educated guess. Forecasting takes good working knowledge of your business, which is much more important than advanced degrees or complex mathematics. It is more art than science.

Whether you have business training or not, don't think you aren't qualified to forecast. If you can run a business, then you can forecast its sales. Most people can guess their own business' sales better than any expert device, statistical analysis, or mathematical routine. Experience counts more than any other factor.

If you've been following along with this book, you've been through some Internet sites and other information sources to know your customers and your industry. You were probably thinking about your sales forecast while you went through that information. The research for a good forecast is almost always harder than the final process of actually making the detailed educated guesses. You've probably already done the research.

Sales Forecast - Simple

When the research is already done, the mechanics of sales forecasting are relatively simple.

Break your sales down into manageable parts, and then forecast the parts. Guess your sales by line of sales, month by month, then add up the sales lines and add up the months.

Figure 10-1 gives you an example of a simple value-based sales forecast which estimates total dollar value for each category of sales.

FIGURE 10-1: SIMPLE SALES FORECAST

Sales	May	Jun	Jul	Aug
Retainer Consulting	$20,000	$20,000	$20,000	$20,000
Project Consulting	$30,000	$40,000	$20,000	$10,000
Market Research	$8,000	$15,000	$10,000	$5,000
Strategic Reports	$0	$0	$0	$0
Other	$0	$0	$0	$0
Total Sales	$58,000	$75,000	$50,000	$35,000
Direct Costs	May	Jun	Jul	Aug
Retainer Consulting	$2,500	$2,500	$2,500	$2,500
Project Consulting	$5,000	$6,500	$3,500	$1,500
Market Research	$6,000	$10,000	$6,000	$4,000
Strategic Reports	$0	$0	$0	$0
Other	$0	$0	$0	$0
Subtotal Direct Cost of Sales	$13,500	$19,000	$12,000	$8,000

This example of a value-based sales forecast includes simple price and cost forecasts to calculate projected sales and direct cost of sales. (Note: This illustration displays only four months of the twelve-month table).

Sales Forecast - Detailed

Forecasting is usually easier when you break your forecast down into components. As an example, consider a forecast that projects $1,000 in sales for the month, compared to one that projects 100 units at $10 each for the month. In the second case, when the forecast is price x units, as soon as you know the price is going up, you also know that the resulting sales should also increase. Thinking of the forecast in components is easier.

Figure 10-2 shows a units-based sales forecast. It takes assumptions for sales in units, then the assumed average prices, and multiplies them to calculate sales dollar values. Then it takes assumptions for unit costs and uses them, along with unit sales assumptions above, to calculate direct cost of sales.

FIGURE 10-2: DETAILED SALES FORECAST

Unit Sales	May	Jun	Jul	Aug
Systems	85	115	145	190
Service	200	200	200	200
Software	150	200	250	330
Training	145	155	165	170
Other	160	176	192	240
Total Unit Sales	740	846	952	1130

Unit Prices	May	Jun	Jul	Aug
Systems	$2,000	$2,000	$2,000	$1,859
Service	$75	$69	$58	$46
Software	$200	$200	$200	$200
Training	$37	$35	$39	$41
Other	$300	$300	$300	$300

Sales	May	Jun	Jul	Aug
Systems	$170,000	$230,000	$290,000	$347,510
Service	$15,000	$13,800	$11,600	$9,200
Software	$30,000	$40,000	$50,000	$66,000
Training	$5,365	$5,425	$6,435	$6,970
Other	$48,000	$52,800	$57,600	$72,000
Total Sales	$268,365	$342,025	$415,635	$501,680

Direct Unit Costs	May	Jun	Jul	Aug
Systems	$1,700	$1,700	$1,700	$1,700
Service	$30	$30	$30	$30
Software	$120	$120	$120	$120
Training	$11	$11	$11	$11
Other	$90	$90	$90	$90

Direct Cost of Sales	May	Jun	Jul	Aug
Systems	$144,500	$195,500	$246,500	$323,000
Service	$6,000	$1,200	$12,000	$12,000
Software	$18,000	$24,000	$30,000	$39,600
Training	$1,595	$1,705	$1,815	$1,870
Other	$14,400	$15,840	$17,280	$21,600
Subtotal Direct Cost of Sales	$184,495	$238,245	$307,595	$398,070

The sales forecast multiplies unit forecasts by price and cost forecasts to calculate projected sales and cost of sales. (Note: This illustration displays four months only of the twelve-month table).

Graphics as Forecasting Tools

Business charts are much more than just pretty pictures; they are excellent tools for understanding and estimating numbers. You should always create charts to illustrate your sales forecast, then use them to evaluate the projected numbers. When you view your forecast on a business chart, does it look real? Does it make sense? It turns out that most people sense the relative size of shapes better than they sense numbers, so we see a sales forecast differently when it shows up in a chart. Use the power of the computer to help you visualize your numbers.

For example, consider the monthly sales chart shown in Figure 10-3. You can look at this chart and immediately see the ebbs and flows of sales during the year. Sales go up from January into April, then down from Spring into Summer, then up again beginning in September. When you look at a chart like that, you should ask yourself whether that pattern is correct. Is that the way your sales go?

FIGURE 10-3: MONTHLY SALES FORECAST CHART

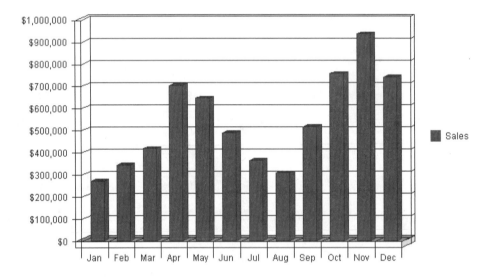

This chart shows planned sales for each month of the first 12 months.

The next chart, in Figure 10-4, shows a comparison of three years of annual sales. Here again, you can sense the relative size of the numbers in the chart. If you knew the company involved, you'd be able to evaluate and discuss this sales forecast just by looking at the chart. Of course you'd probably want to know more detail about the assumptions behind the forecast, but you'd have a very good initial sense of the numbers already.

FIGURE 10-4: ANNUAL SALES FORECAST CHART

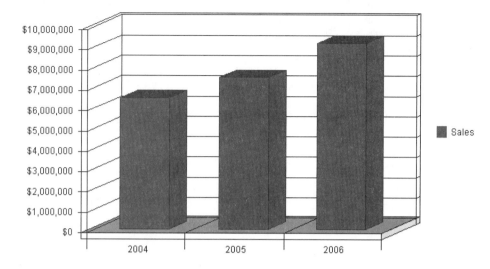

This chart shows the sales forecast for each year of the three-year sales forecast.

Explain Forecast and Related Background

Although the charts and tables are great, you still need to explain them. A complete business plan should normally include some detailed text discussion of your sales forecast, sales strategy, sales programs, and related information. Ideally, you use the text, tables, and charts in your plan to provide some visual variety and ease of use. Put the tables and charts near the text covering the related topics.

In my recommended business plan text outline, the discussion of sales goes into Strategy and Implementation. You can change that to fit whichever logic and structure you use. In practical terms, you'll probably prepare these text topics as separate items, to be gathered into the plan as it is finished.

Sales Strategy

Somewhere near the sales forecast you should describe your sales strategy. Sales strategies deal with how and when to close sales prospects, how to compensate sales people, how to optimize order processing and database management, how to maneuver price, delivery, and conditions.

How do you sell? Do you sell retail, wholesale, discount, mail order, phone order, online? Do you maintain a sales force? How are sales people trained, and compensated? Don't confuse sales strategy with marketing strategy. Sales close the deals that marketing opens.

To help differentiate between marketing strategy and sales strategy, think of marketing strategy as the broader effort of generating sales leads and sales strategy as the effort to bring those sales leads into the system as sales transactions. Marketing can affect image, awareness and propensity to buy, while sales involves getting the order.

Forecast Details

Your business plan text should summarize and highlight the numbers you have entered in the Sales Forecast table. Make sure you discuss important assumptions in enough detail, and that you explain the background sufficiently. Try to anticipate the questions your readers will ask. Include whatever information you think will be relevant.

Sales Programs

Use this topic to list the specific information related to sales programs in your Milestones table, with the specific persons responsible, deadlines, and budgets. How is this strategy to be implemented and measured? Do you have concrete and specific plans?

Business plans are about results, and generating results depends in part on how specific you are in the plan. For anything related to sales that is supposed to happen, include it here and list the person responsible, dates required, and budgets. All of that will make your business plan more real.

How Many Years?

I believe a business plan should normally project sales by month for the next 12 months, and annual sales for the following three years. This doesn't mean businesses shouldn't plan for a longer term than just three years, not by any means. It does mean, however, that the detail of monthly forecasts doesn't pay off beyond a year, except in special cases. It also means that the detail in the yearly forecasts probably doesn't make sense beyond three years. It does mean that you still plan your business for 5, 10, even 15-year time frames; just don't do it within the detailed context of a business plan.

Summary

A sales forecast is hard for many people because they are unsure of how to forecast. Don't worry, if you know your business, you can give an educated guess of future sales. Remember, one thing harder than forecasting is running a business without a forecast.

FORECASTING

Forecasting is more art than science, a combination of good research, logic, simple math, and educated guessing. It's hard to forecast, but it's harder to run a business without forecasting.

Chapter 11:

MARKET

The market segmentation concept is crucial to market assessment and market strategy. Divide the market into workable market segments—age, income, product type, geography, buying patterns, customer needs, or other classifications. Define your terms, and define your market.

Market Segmentation is Critical

Segmentation can make a huge difference in understanding your market. For example, when a local computer store business defines "high-end home office" and "high-technology small business" as its customer segments, its segmentation says a lot about its customers. The segmentation helps the company plan focus on the different types of potential customers.

When I was consulting for Apple Computer in the middle 1980s, we divided the markets into workable categories, including home, education, small business, large business, and all others. Some other groups in Apple also focused on government as a specific market segment. As you define the segment you point toward an understanding of the market. In the 1970s, I knew a company that was selling candy bars through retail channels. They segmented the market in a way that defined a range of products as "oral satisfacters" (their term, not mine). That included candy, cookies, soft drinks, and bagged chips. The segmentation helped the marketers understand their real competition, which wasn't just other candy bars, but also other products targeting the same customer money. That understanding of competition improved the marketing and sales programs.

In today's business it's easy to see segmentation in action. Consider the different tone, content, and media for ads that sell products to kids, compared to those that sell the same product to parents. Car companies change their advertising substantially from one type of program to another. Stand-up comedian Richard Klein used to joke about the beer company ads that changed the style of the music to match the audience. He complained that he kept getting the country music version, but he liked the blues version better. The company that did those ads used the styles of music to address different target customer groups.

In developing segmentation, consider what factors make a difference in the purchasing, media, and value patterns of your target groups. Does age matter in choice of restaurants, or is style and food preference more important? Is income level a key factor? Education? I suspect some restaurants will sell more meals to college graduates than others. Is this because of education, age, or income levels?

In your initial assessment you may have already developed your first basic Market Analysis worksheet for analyzing potential customers. It will help you define your market and understand your key market segments. As you complete your market analysis, look at your segmentation critically and strategically. Is this the best segmentation? Be sure to revise and polish your numbers.

Market Analysis

As part of the business plan, you should generate enough information to develop a basic Market Analysis table. Figure 11-1 gives you an example of a list of market segments, implemented as a spreadsheet table. Each segment is a group of customers that are classified according to the market segments you define.

FIGURE 11-1: MARKET ANALYSIS TABLE

Potential Customers	Growth	Total Customers
Consumer	2%	12,000
Small Business	5%	15,000
Large Business	8%	33,000
Government	-2%	36,000
Education	0%	19,000
Total	2.78%	115,000

This table shows a simple classification of market segments, each segment defined by its total potential customer count and its estimated growth rate.

You can create a simple market analysis by estimating the number of potential customers for each segment and the growth rate, as shown in this example. Once you have those numbers, it should be a simple step to develop the corresponding chart in Figure 11-2.

FIGURE 11-2: MARKET ANALYSIS CHART

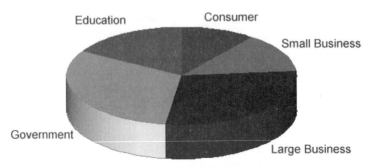

This simple pie chart shows the potential market as the plan starts. The different segments of the pie show the relative sizes of different target market groups.

Filling Out the Text

After you find out about your market for a business plan, you also want to communicate that knowledge to the readers of your plan. Keep your explanations clear and concise. The depth of detail in market analysis will depend a lot on the type of plan. You may not need to provide a complete market study in a plan developed for internal use, when all of your team knows the market well. Maybe you'll just cite the type of customers you attract, and the part of town you serve. The market analysis section in a business plan is the section that is most likely to require research for information from outside your business, while most others require thinking and analysis of factors within your business.

This is a good point to add a word of caution about the level of detail required. Remember that planning is about making good decisions, applying focus and enforcing priorities. A business plan doesn't have to include a market analysis suitable for a Ph.D. candidate in market research. Planning is not about testing your knowledge. If you are looking for investment, then you may have to use this section to display your wisdom and understanding of your industry, but don't overdo it. If you are planning an internal plan and have no audience other than your own team, I recommend enough market research to make sure you're not missing key points.

The value of information is limited by its impact on decisions. If more market information is not going to help you do something better, then don't bother.

Begin With a Summary

Your market section should begin with a simple summary. You should generally describe the different groups of target customers included in your market analysis and refer briefly to why you are selecting these as targets. You may also want to summarize market growth, citing highlights of some growth projections, if you have this information available.

Assume that this paragraph might be included in a loan application or summary memo, so you need it to summarize the rest of the section. What information would be most important if you had only one brief topic to include about your market? A good technique is to skip this topic until you have finished the rest of the section. Then go back to the summary to write the highlights.

Explain your Segmentation

Make sure to explain and define the different segments in your table, particularly since you refer to them and they are the basis of your strategy. What distinguishes small business from large business, if this is part of your segmentation? Do you classify them by sales, number of employees, or some other factor? I've seen segmentations that define customers by the channels they buy in, as in the retail customer compared to the wholesale or direct customer, also compared to the Internet download customer. Have you defined which segment is which, and why?

As you deal with segmentation, you should also introduce the strategy behind it and your choice of target markets. Explain why your business is focusing on these specific target market groups. What makes these groups more interesting than the other groups that you've ruled out? Why are the characteristics you specify important? This is more important for some businesses than others. A clothing boutique, for example, might focus on one set of upper-income customers instead of another, for strategic reasons. An office equipment store might focus on certain business types whose needs match the firm's expertise. Some fast food restaurants focus on families with children under driving age. Strategy is focus; it is creative and it doesn't follow pre-written formulas.

Explain Market Needs, Growth, and Trends

All marketing should be based on underlying needs. For each market segment included in your strategy, explain the market needs that lead to this group's wanting to buy your service. Did the need exist before the business was there? Are there other products or services or stores that offer different ways to satisfy this same need? Do you have market research related to this market need? It is always a good idea to try to define your retail offering in terms of target market needs, so you focus not on what you have to sell, but rather on what buyer needs you satisfy. As a shoe store, for example, are you selling shoes or are you satisfying the customer needs for covered feet? Are there really underlying needs, such as style and prestige for fashion footwear, or padding for runners, or jumping for basketball players, that relate to selling shoes? Are kids buying status with their basketball shoes?

Understand and explain market trends. What factors seem to be changing the market, or changing the business? What developing trends can make a difference? Market trends could be changes in demographics, changes in customer needs, a new sense of style or fashion, or something else. It depends on what business you are in.

For example, a building supply store might note the trend toward remodeling older homes instead of buying new homes, or a trend toward more rooms in larger houses, despite smaller families, because of home offices, dens, and exercise rooms.

A grocery store might note a trend toward Asian foods or spicier foods, or toward fresher, healthier foods, or development of a new shopping area in a different part of town.

A credit and investment counselor might note demographic trends; for example, as baby boomers age, this leads them more toward the need for estate planning and retirement planning.

Look to market trends as a way to get ahead of the market, to know where it is going before it gets there. You should also understand and explain market growth in each segment. Ideally you cite experts, a market expert, market research firm, trade association, or credible journalist.

Summary

Projecting market growth is particularly important when your plan is related to finding investors or supporting a loan application, because market growth enhances the implied value of your business.

Cite growth rates in terms that fit the available information, whether growth in the number of potential customers, projected dollar sales, meals served, website projects, tax reporting hours, yards to landscape, or whatever you have.

Whenever you can, relate the growth rates cited in expert forecasts to the growth in potential customers that you included in the market analysis table.

Chapter 12:

EXPENSE BUDGET

Budgets are plans. They are spending plans, activity plans, sales plans, marketing plans, all linked to the disciplines of careful projection and resource allocation.

Simple Math, Simple Numbers

The math of the expense budget is very simple. The content takes work, but not the design of the table. It's built on common sense and reasonable guesses, without statistical analysis, mathematical techniques, or any past data. The mathematics are also simple, sums of the rows and columns.

In the following example, rows are horizontal, columns are vertical. Each line of expense occupies a row, and months and years occupy columns. The source spreadsheet hides the monthly columns for March through October, for the purpose of illustration, so you can see the annual total. Those other months are there, even if they don't show. The total expense row sums the individual expense rows. The annual expense column sums the months for each row, including the total rows.

As you develop a budget, think of it as the part of your plan you can most easily control. Consider your plan objectives, your sales and marketing activities, and how you'll relate your spending to your strategy. Remember as you budget that you want to prioritize your spending to match your priorities in sales and target marketing. The emphasis in your strategy should show up in your actual detailed programs. That's your budget.

FIGURE 12-1: SIMPLE EXPENSE BUDGET

Marketing Expense Budget	Jan	Feb	Nov	Dec	2004
Advertising	$15,000	$15,000	$20,000	$10,000	$150,000
Catalogs	$2,000	$3,000	$2,000	$2,000	$25,000
Websites	$3,000	$11,800	$8,000	$5,000	$113,300
Promotions	$0	$0	$15,000	$0	$16,000
Shows	$0	$0	$0	$0	$20,200
Literature	$0	$7,000	$0	$0	$7,000
Promotions	$0	$0	$0	$0	$1,000
Seminars	$1,000	$0	$0	$0	$31,000
Service	$2,000	$1,000	$500	$250	$10,250
Training	$5,000	$5,000	$5,000	$5,000	$60,000
Other	$1,000	$1,000	$1,000	$1,000	$12,000
Total Sales/Marketing Expenses	$29,000	$43,800	$51,500	$23,250	$445,750

An expense budget can be as simple or complex as you wish, but greater detail in your plan will give you more information about, and more control over, how you spend your money.

Budgeting is About People More Than Numbers

Managing the budget numbers can be simple, but managing a budget takes people, not spreadsheets. While budget numbers are simple, budget management isn't. To make a budget work, you need to add real management:

1. **Understand that it's about people:** Successful budgeting depends on people management more than anything else. Every budgeted item must be "owned" by somebody, meaning that the owner has responsibility for spending, authority to spend, and the belief that the spending limit is realistic. People who don't believe in a budget won't try to implement it. People who don't believe that it matters won't worry about a budget either.

2. **Budget "ownership" is critical:** To "own" a budget item is to have the authority to spend and responsibility for spending. Ideally a budget management system makes plan-vs.-actual results visible to a group of managers, so that there is peer pressure that rewards budgeting successes and penalizes budgeting failures.

3. **Budgets need to be realistic:** Nobody really owns a budget item until they believe the budget amount is realistic. You can't really commit to a budget you don't believe in.

4. **It's also about following up:** Unless the people involved know that somebody will be tracking and following up, they won't honor a budget. Publishing budget plan and actual results will make a world of difference. Rewards for budget success and penalties for budget failures can be as simple as peer group managers sharing results.

The Budgeting Process

A budgeting process that brings people directly into the involvement and ownership of the budget is strongly recommended. Here's a simple step-by-step way to increase the importance of budgeting and implementation within your business.

1. **The budget preliminary meeting:** Start your budgeting process with a preliminary meeting that brings your main managers together. Discuss strategy and priorities, realistic amounts, and the planning process. Distribute a simple template and ask each manager to prepare a proposed budget for his or her area. Ask the managers to create a proposal that includes monthly numbers, and descriptions of the programs and activities involved.

2. **Budget development:** Allow a period for managers to develop their budgets, working with the standard template. Enforce deadlines for preliminary proposal and revisions. Consolidate the proposed budgets into a single budget table that lists all of the proposed programs and activities. **In most cases the total of all proposals will be 2-3 times the real amount your company can spend.** Share that consolidated table with all managers. Share with them the difference between proposed budgets and actual spending limits, and ask them to think about it.

3. **Budget discussion:** Bring your managers back together with the budget table. Ideally you set up a conference room with a projector and the consolidated proposed budget table. Then you go through the budget, item by item, and pare it down to a realistic amount. Your managers will be together in a group, so they will have to defend different proposals, and as they do they will build up their personal commitments and their ownership of budget items and programs. They will explain why one program is more valuable than another, they will argue about relative value, and they will increase the level of peer-group commitment.

When this process works well, you have a more accurate, more realistic, and more useful budget. You also have a high level of commitment from your managers, who are now motivated to implement the budget as well as possible.

Your Budget and Milestones Work Together

As you develop your budget, keep in mind your business plan milestones. That's where you set specific goals, dates, responsibilities, and budgets for your managers. It makes a plan concrete. Make sure your budget matches your milestones.

Ideally, every line in a budget is assigned to somebody who is responsible for managing that budget. In most cases you'll have groups of budget areas assigned to specific people, and a budgeting process that emphasizes commitment and responsibility. You'll also need to make sure that everybody involved knows that results will be followed up.

The ideal plan relates the budgets to the Milestones table which we will discuss in more detail in *Chapter 18: Make it Real.* The Milestones table takes all the important activities included in a business plan and assigns them to specific managers, with specific dates and budgets. It also tracks completion of the milestones and actual results compared to planned results.

FIGURE 12-2: MILESTONES TABLE

| Business Plan Milestones | | Planned | | | | Actual | Actual | Date | Budget |
Milestone	Manager	Date	Department	Budget	Actual Date	Budget	Variance	Variance
Corporate Identity	TJ	12/17/2003	Marketing	$10,000	1/15/2004	$12,004	(29)	($2,004)
Seminar Implementation	IR	1/10/2004	Sales	$1,000	12/27/2003	$1,000	14	$0
Business Plan Review	RJ	1/10/2004	GM	$0	1/23/2004	$500	(13)	($500)
Upgrade Mailer	IR	1/16/2004	Sales	$5,000	2/12/2004	$1,000	(27)	$4,000
New Corporate Brochure	TJ	1/15/2004	Marketing	$5,000	1/15/2004	$5,000	1	$0
Delivery Vans	SD	1/25/2004	Service	$12,500	2/26/2004	$0	(32)	$12,500
Direct Mail	IR	2/16/2004	Marketing	$3,500	2/25/2004	$1,000	(9)	$2,500
Advertising	RJ	2/16/2004	GM	$115,000	3/6/2004	$100,000	(18)	$15,000
X4 Prototype	SG	2/25/2004	Product	$2,500	2/25/2004	$1,000	0	$1,500
Service Revamp	SD	2/25/2004	Product	$2,500	2/25/2004	$2,500	0	$0
Presentations - 6	IR	2/25/2004	Sales	$0	1/10/2004	$1,000	46	($1,000)
X4 Testing	SG	3/6/2004	Product	$1,000	1/16/2004	$0	49	$1,000
New Accounts - 3	SD	3/17/2004	Sales	$0	3/17/2004	$2,500	0	($2,500)
L30 Prototype	PR	3/26/2004	Product	$2,500	4/11/2004	$15,000	(16)	($12,500)
Tech2004 Expo	TB	4/12/2004	Marketing	$15,000	1/25/2004	$1,000	77	$14,000
VP Sales/Marketing Hired	JK	6/11/2004	Sales	$1,000	7/25/2004	$5,000	(44)	($4,000)
Mailing System	SD	7/25/2004	Service	$5,000	7/14/2004	$7,654	11	($2,654)
Other				$0				
Totals				$181,500		$156,158	10	$25,342

Using the Milestones table will assign responsibility and authority to the expense budget plans.

The Budget Will be Part of Profit and Loss

As you build your expense budget you are also creating your projected profit and loss. The profit and loss includes sales, costs of sales, and expenses.

With the way business numbers work, your expense budget will eventually become part of your Profit and Loss table which we'll see in *Chapter 14: The Bottom Line*. If you're using a personal computer with spreadsheet or business plan software, you should expect to see automatic linking so the expense budget is absorbed into the Profit and Loss table.

Figure 12-3 shows a simple profit and loss, with the expense budget showing as the expenses portion of the larger statement.

This first example is a simple budget that doesn't divide expenses into categories. This is ideal for smaller businesses with only a few employees. By the time you have workgroups and a slightly larger business, however, you'll probably end up dividing expenses into categories such as sales and marketing expenses, administrative expenses, and other expenses. This next example shows how that might look when it's brought into the income statement.

FIGURE 12-3: STANDARD PROFIT AND LOSS STATEMENT

Pro Forma Profit and Loss	Oct	Nov	Dec	2004
Sales	$85,000	$90,000	$55,000	$592,000
Cost of Sales	$24,000	$25,000	$19,000	$159,000
Other	$0	$0	$0	$0
Total Cost of Sales	$24,000	$25,000	$19,000	$159,000
Gross Margin	$61,000	$65,000	$36,000	$433,000
Gros Margin Percent	71.76%	72.22%	65.45%	73.14%
Operating Expenses				
Advertising/Promotion	$3,000	$3,000	$3,000	$36,000
PR	$2,500	$2,500	$2,500	$30,000
Travel	$7,500	$7,500	$7,500	$90,000
Misc.	$500	$500	$500	$6,000
Payroll Expense	$27,250	$27,250	$27,250	$194,750
Leased Equipment	$500	$500	$500	$6,000
Utilities	$1,000	$1,000	$1,000	$12,000
Insurance	$300	$300	$300	$36,000
Rent	$1,500	$1,500	$1,500	$18,000
Depreciation	$0	$0	$0	$200
Payroll Burden	$4,760	$4,760	$4,760	$30,100
Contract/Consultants	$0	$0	$0	$0
Other	$0	$0	$200	$200
Total Operating Expenses	$48,810	$48,810	$49,010	$459,250
Earning Before Interest and Taxes	$12,190	$16,190	($13,010)	$6,350
Interest Expense - Current	$400	$400	$400	$3,600
Interest Expense - Long-term	$417	$417	$417	$5,000
Taxes Incurred	$2,843	$3,843	($3,457)	($563)
Net Profit	$8,530	$11,530	($10,370)	($1,688)
Net Profit/Sales	10%	12.81%	-18.85%	-0.29%

This illustration shows the standard income statement (profit and loss). This is a partial snapshot, showing only three months of a 12-month table.

FIGURE 12-4: DETAILED PROFIT AND LOSS STATEMENT

Pro Forma Profit and Loss	Oct	Nov	Dec	2004
Sales	$754,505	$934,341	$739,799	$5,962,247
Direct Cost of Sales	$565,402	$714,295	$567,100	$4,356,077
Production Payroll	$14,500	$7,500	$7,500	$119,791
Other	$500	$500	$500	$5,751
Total Cost of Sales	$580,402	$722,295	$575,100	$4,481,619
Gross Margin	$174,103	$212,046	$164,699	$1,480,628
Gross Margin %	23.08%	22.69%	22.26%	24.83%
Operating Expenses				
Sales and Marketing Expenses				
Payroll	$32,000	$16,000	$16,000	$303,856
Ads	$15,000	$20,000	$10,000	$138,570
Catalog	$2,000	$2,000	$2,000	$25,395
Mailing	$22,000	$8,000	$5,000	$113,569
Literature	$0	$0	$0	$6,401
Seminar	$0	$0	$0	$31,000
Service	$500	$500	$250	$10,296
Training	$450	$450	$450	$5,550
Total Sales and Marketing Expenses	$78,950	$61,950	$33,700	$671,837
Sales and Marketing %	10.46%	6.63%	4.56%	11.27%
General and Administrative Expenses				
Payroll	$15,000	$7,500	$7,500	$13,500
Payroll Burden	$10,320	$4,760	$4,760	$93,840
Depreciation	$1,094	$1,105	$1,116	$12,681
Leased Equipment	$2,500	$2,500	$2,500	$30,000
Utilities	$750	$750	$750	$9,000
Insurance	$500	$500	$500	$6,000
Rent	$7,000	$7,000	$7,000	$84,000
Other	$545	$550	$556	$6,331
Total General and Administrative Expenses	$37,709	$24,665	$24,682	$376,852
General and Administrative %	5.00%	2.64%	3.34%	6.32%
Other Expenses				
Other Payroll	$3,000	$3,000	$3,000	$36,000
Contract/Consultants	$125	$125	$125	$1,500
Other	$0	$0	$0	$0
Total Other Expenses	$3,125	$3,125	$3,125	$37,500
Other %	0.41%	0.33%	0.42%	0.63%
Total Operating Expenses	$119,784	$89,740	$61,507	$1,086,189
Profit Before Interest and Taxes	$54,319	$122,306	$103,192	$394,439
Interest Expense Current	$1,033	$2,533	$1,533	$15,133
Interest Expense Long-term	$2,511	$2,489	$2,466	$29,628
Taxes Incurred	$10,155	$23,457	$19,838	$69,935
Net Profit	$40,619	$93,827	$79,354	$279,742
Net Profit/Sales	5.38%	10.04%	10.73%	4.69%

This illustration shows the more detailed profit and loss analysis that divides operating expenses into categories. This is a partial snapshot, showing three months of a 12-month table.

Summary

Regardless of which budget style you choose, you make very important choices as you plan your profit and loss. This is where you plan your expenses. You are estimating expenditures across the business, from rent and overhead to marketing expenses such as advertising, sales commissions, and public relations. Decisions you make here are as important as the mathematics are simple. Your sum of expenses ultimately determines your company's profitability. This is the business plan equivalent to budgeting, as you set your sights on the levels of expenditures you expect your company will need.

FINANCIAL
ANALYSIS

The financials aren't as hard as you think, particularly if you have the patience to follow the steps. A good plan includes sales, cash flow, profits, and related financials.

Chapter 13:

ABOUT BUSINESS NUMBERS

A business plan depends on both words and numbers. You can't describe a business in words alone, and the numbers don't work without the words. In this chapter, we go through the basics of how the numbers come together.

Allow me to tell a personal story about words and numbers, and why you need both to make a complete plan.

In 1974, I switched from general journalism, writing for United Press International from Mexico City, to business journalism, writing for Business International and McGraw-Hill World News.

With the switch, I found myself covering business and economics instead of general news, writing for (among others) *Business Week* and *Business Latin America*. At this point, because I thought it would be nice to have some idea what I was writing about, I went to the local graduate school at night for courses in general economics, accounting, finance, and marketing.

As I learned about macroeconomics, and how to read financial statements, I discovered that the truth in business is almost always a combination of words and numbers and can't be explained by either one without the other. For example, when a Central American government announced a new federal budget that it said was going to both develop growth and reduce inflation, the numbers said that was a contradiction. You can't do both; you can do one or the other. You could only see that by dealing with both words and numbers.

A business plan is like that, too. You can't describe a plan without both text and tables, both words and numbers. The single most important analysis in a business plan is a cash flow plan, because cash is the most critical element in business.

With the way the numbers work, however, you can't do a cash flow plan without looking at the income statement and balance sheets as well.

You really can't do the income statement without looking at sales, cost of sales, personnel expenses and other expenses, so you need those too.

And you'd have trouble doing a sales forecast without understanding your market, so a market analysis is recommended.

And then you have the break-even as part of the initial assessment, and tables for business ratios, general assumptions, and other numbers. Step by step, the business plan becomes a collection of tables and charts around the text.

Numbers Tell the Story

Although cash is critical, people think in terms of profits instead of cash. We all do. When you and your friends imagine a new business, you think of what it would cost to make the product, what you could sell it for, and what the profits per unit might be. We are trained to think of business as sales minus costs and expenses, which equals profits.

Unfortunately, we don't spend the profits in a business. We spend cash. Profitable companies go broke because they had all their money tied up in assets and couldn't pay their expenses. Working capital is critical to business health. Unfortunately, we don't see the cash implications as clearly as we should, which is one of the best reasons for proper business planning. We have to manage cash as well as profits.

Cash vs. Profits – Example

One of the best ways to understand the dilemma of cash vs. profits is to follow an otherwise-profitable company going broke because it can't meet its obligations. This is a quick and simple example. It also leads us into the relationship between income statement, balance sheet, and cash.

Start with $100, which we'll call capital. At the beginning of this exercise, your balance sheet has assets of $100—the money—and capital of $100. Assets are equal to capital plus liabilities. A summary of the simple financial statement at this point is shown in Figure 13-1.

FIGURE 13-1: STARTING NUMBERS

	Income			Balance
Sales	$0	Assets		
Cost of Sales	$0		Bank Balance	$100
Profit	$0	Total		$100
		Liabilities		
		Capital		
			Paid-In	$100
			Earnings	
		Total		$100

The simple financials show a hypothetical widgets business as it starts.

If you buy a widget for $100 and sell it for $150, you should end up with $50 profit, which is what your income statement covers. Sales minus costs are profit. You should have $150 in the bank. Now your balance sheet shows the same $100 in original capital plus $50 in earnings, which are equal to the $150 you have in cash as an asset. Figure 13-2 shows you how the financials work after the sale.

Buy another widget for $100 and sell it again for $150, and now you have $200 in the bank. Do it again, you have $250 in the bank. Your income statement shows sales of $450, cost of sales of $300, and profit of $150.

Figure 13-3 shows your income statement and balance sheet at this point.

FIGURE 13-2: SELL A WIDGET

	Income			Balance
Sales	$150	Assets		
Cost of Sales	$100		Bank Balance	$150
Profit	$50	Total		$150
		Liabilities		
		Capital		
			Paid-In	$100
			Earnings	$50
		Total		$150

Figure 13-2 shows how the company looks after its first sale.

FIGURE 13-3: SELL THREE WIDGETS

	Income			Balance
Sales	$450	Assets		
Cost of Sales	$300		Bank Balance	$250
Profit	$150	Total		$250
		Liabilities		
		Capital		
			Paid-In	$100
			Earnings	$150
		Total		$250

In Figure 13-3 your business has sold 3 units and made $150 profit. In theory it has $250 in the bank.

Adding Some Realism

Now go back a step and make the situation more realistic. For example, most sales of products to businesses go on terms, with the money due in 30 days. So if you sold that widget on credit, you don't have $150 in the bank. You still have $50 in your bottom line, but now you have nothing in the bank. Instead, a customer owes you $150, which is what we call "Accounts Receivable."

Compare Figure 13-4 to Figure 13-2. This is what really happens to the huge number of businesses that sell to other businesses.

Knowing you can buy a widget for $100 and sell it for $150, you get your widget supplier to sell to you on the same terms you sell, net 30, instead of for cash. Now you have $100 that you owe to suppliers, which is called "Accounts Payable." You also have $100 worth of widget in inventory.

This gives you the case in Figure 13-5, in which you are now poised to sell another widget and make more profit.

You have an extra $100 in assets (the widget in inventory) and an extra $100 as liabilities (Accounts Payable), so you are still in balance. Also, you still have no money.

FIGURE 13-4: SELLING ON TERMS

	Income			Balance
Sales	$150	Assets		
Cost of Sales	$100		Bank Balance	$0
Profit	$50		Accounts Receivable	$150
		Total		$150
		Liabilities		
		Capital		
			Paid-In	$100
			Earnings	$50
		Total		$150

Sales and profits are the same as in Figure 13-2, but you sold on credit, so now you have no money in the bank.

FIGURE 13-5: BUYING ON TERMS

	Income			Balance
Sales	$150	Assets		
Cost of Sales	$100		Bank Balance	$0
Profit	$50		Accounts Receivable	$150
			Inventory	$100
		Total		$250
		Liabilities		
			Accounts Payable	$100
			Total liabilities	$100
		Capital		
			Paid-In	$100
			Earnings	$50
		Total		$250

Business looked good in Figure 13-4, so you borrowed the money to buy another widget and continue.

Figure 13-6 shows the financial picture after the same sales as in Figure 13-3, but with sales to businesses on credit and purchase of inventory on credit as a short-term debt.

Now the case is more like what you have with real business numbers, in which you have to manage your cash very carefully, and the amounts sitting in inventory and accounts receivable are significant.

FIGURE 13-6: NUMBERS MOUNT UP

	Income			Balance
Sales	$450	Assets		
Cost of Sales	$300		Bank Balance	$0
Profit	$150		Accounts Receivable	$450
			Inventory	$100
		Total		$550
		Liabilities		
			Accounts Payable	$100
			Short-term debt	$200
			Total liabilities	$300
		Capital		
			Paid-In	$100
			Earnings	$150
		Total		$550

You have the same sales and profits as in Figure 13-3, but the balance sheet is more complex.

FIGURE 13-7: WORKING CAPITAL

	Income			Balance
Sales	$450	Assets		
Cost of Sales	$300		Bank Balance	$300
Profit	$150		Accounts Receivable	$450
			Inventory	$100
		Total		$850
		Liabilities		
			Accounts Payable	$100
			Short-term debt	$200
			Total liabilities	$300
		Capital		
			Paid-In	$400
			Earnings	$150
		Total		$850

In this illustration the business has enough working capital to survive the unexpected.

More Realism: Working Capital

Even in the case of Figure 13-6, the example is completely unrealistic. Where are the running expenses, such as rent, salaries, telephones, or even advertising those widgets? How would they affect the cash situation? How far would we get if we couldn't pay the rent or the telephone bill while waiting for customers to pay us? Furthermore, what supplier would give us a widget on credit when we have no history and no assets? What bank would loan us money in this situation? Banks do loan against inventory and receivables, but only to a certain percentage of total value. What was missing here, all along, was working capital.

Important: In strict accounting terms, working capital is equal to short-term assets minus short-term liabilities. In real terms, however, working capital is the glue that holds your cash flow together. Get it into the bank before you need it, or you won't survive the unexpected.

Figure 13-7 goes back to the beginning of this whole example and does it right, with enough capital in the beginning to finance the company.

Instead of starting with $100 as capital, this business looks a lot better with a starting capital of $400. With this additional capital from the start, buying on credit and borrowing against assets is more realistic. In Figure 13-6 the working capital of $250 just wasn't enough, but in this scenario, working capital is up to $550. Now it has a proper input of working capital at the beginning. With even the barest of business plans, we could tell that $100 wasn't enough to get this business going.

I hope the theoretical examples make the concepts clear. If you followed these illustrations, you can see some enormous implications for running a business.

Important: Every dollar in accounts receivable means a dollar less in cash. Every dollar of inventory is a dollar less in cash. Every dollar of accounts payable is a dollar more in cash.

A Real Case Example

Now let's look at the implications in a real case. The real case is a computer store in a medium-sized local market.

The first chart, in Figure 13-8, shows a representative sample business plan cash flow for 12 months, given standard assumptions for sales, costs, expenses, profits, and cash management. The sample company is profitable and growing. It sells about $6 million annually, produces about 8 percent net profit on sales, and is self-supporting.

The chart shows a 12-month projection of cash resources. The lighter of the two sets of bars represent the checkbook balance at the end of each month, and the other represents the cash flow, which is how much the balance changes in a month. The first set of bars should never drop below zero, because if your checkbook balance is less than zero, then you are bouncing checks. The mathematics doesn't care, but the banks do. The cash flow bars, on the other hand, can drop below zero without major problems, as long as the balance stays above zero. For example, if a company's balance was $10,000 at the end of January, and its February cash flow is a negative $5,000, then the balance at the end of February is $5,000 and the cash flow is -$5,000. The lighter bar stays positive, but the darker one is negative.

FIGURE 13-8: AS THE CASH CASE STARTS

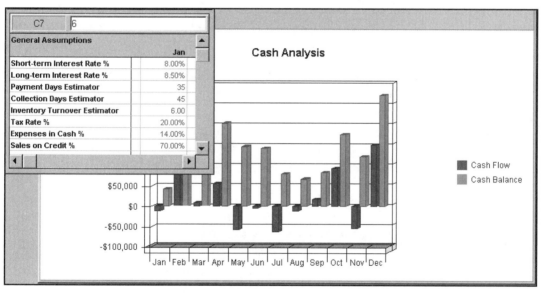

With the first take of the cash case, the business looks good and the cash plan is acceptable.

In Figure 13-9, only one assumption has changed: that same company now waits an extra 15 days, on average, to receive money from customers on invoices presented. The average wait, which is called "collection days," goes from 45 days to 60 days.

FIGURE 13-9: CHANGING COLLECTION DAYS ONLY

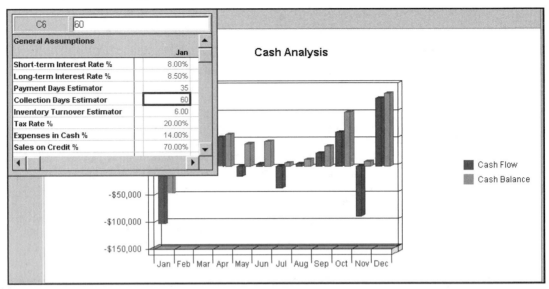

A single change, from 45 to 60 days, makes a huge difference in the cash flow.

Nothing else changes - no new employees, no change in costs, no additional expenses.

No other changes except waiting on average an extra 15 days before receiving money owed from their customers. As stated earlier, accountants call money owed by customers "Accounts Receivable."

Notice here the critical importance of cash and the critical difference between cash and profits. With this single change in assumptions, the company is still as profitable as it was, down to the last dollar. Now, however, its projected bank balance in January is more than $50,000 below zero. Therefore, the company needs more than $50,000 in additional financing. This is new money needed, new investment or new borrowing. The problem can't be solved by reducing expenses or increasing sales.

Companies go out of business for problems like these. Even otherwise-healthy companies can go under for lack of cash. This kind of projection can kill a company if it sneaks up by surprise, but can be easily managed when there is a plan for it. This is an eloquent argument for good business planning.

In the third case, shown in Figure 13-10, we set the collection days back to the original assumption of 45 days, but change the assumption for inventory. Where previously it kept an average of two month's worth of inventory on hand, in this changed assumption it now keeps three months of inventory on hand. Accountants call this Inventory Turnover. The changed assumption creates an inventory turnover rate of 4, instead of the previous rate of 6. The collection days are back to 45 in this next scene, but inventory turnover went from 6 to 4, which means keeping more inventory on hand.

The implications of Figure 13-10 are massive. This is still a profitable company, but it has a critical financial problem. You see how the cash balance bar falls to more than $600,000 below zero in November. That means that this company needs new money, new loans or new capital investment to make up its cash deficit, even though it is still profitable. This is hard to swallow until you see it happen in real business, but it is the truth and it will happen.

Profits are not cash.

FIGURE 13-10: CHANGING INVENTORY ONLY

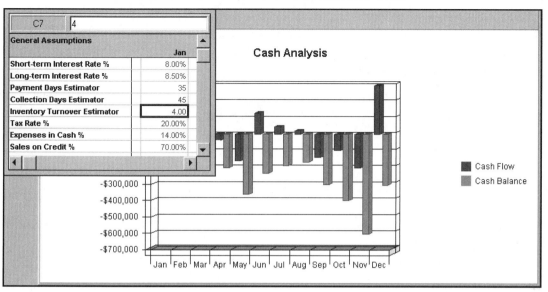

The change in inventory turnover shows the cash balance is now well below zero.

A Graphical View

As you can see from the examples, the numbers in a normal business analysis, and in a business plan, are very interrelated. In previous chapters we did the sales forecast and personnel plan, which then reappeared in the income statement, also called the profit and loss. You can see from the examples how the income statement links to the balance sheet. We'll go into cash flow and balance in following chapters, but the point here is that the assumptions and estimates in the standard business plan tables link up to each other in a complex system of relationships. You can see how these relationships work in Figure 13-11.

FIGURE 13-11: LOGIC OF BUSINESS STATEMENTS

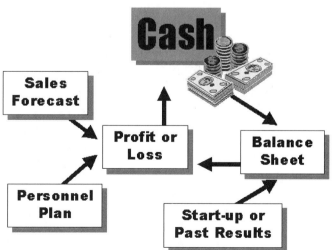

The business plan tables and charts should be linked together to reflect the practical realities of business numbers.

Linking the Numbers

As the chart suggests and the previous examples show, there is a logical link between the business numbers in a standard analysis.

- Your sales forecast table should show sales and cost of sales. The same numbers in the sales forecast are the ones you use in the profit and loss table.

- As with sales, you should normally have a separate personnel plan, but the numbers showing in that table should be the same numbers that show up for personnel costs in your profit and loss table.

- Your profit and loss table should show the same numbers as the sales forecast and personnel plan tables in the proper areas. It should also show interest expenses as a logical reflection of interest rates and balances of debt.

- Your cash flow reflects your profit or loss, plus changes in balance sheet items and non-cash expenses such as depreciation, which are on the profit and loss table. The changes in the balance sheet are critical. For example, when you borrow money, it doesn't affect the profit or loss (except for interest expenses later on), but it makes a huge difference to your checking account balance.

- The balance sheet has to reflect the profit and loss and the cash flow tables.

- Your business ratios should calculate automatically, based on the numbers in the sales forecast, profit and loss, personnel plan, cash flow, and balance sheet tables.

Summary

Use the charts along with the tables to illustrate and enhance your analysis. For example, keeping the Cash Flow chart visible while changing assumptions gives you an instant picture of whether or not you have exceeded available cash resources as you plan your operations.

FINANCIAL ANALYSIS

The financials aren't as hard as you think, particularly if you have the patience to follow the steps. A good plan includes sales, cash flow, profits, and related financials.

Chapter 14:

THE BOTTOM LINE

The familiar phrase "the bottom line," often used as synonymous with the conclusion or the underlying truth, is actually taken from the standard Income Statement in accounting, which subtracts costs and expenses from sales and shows profits as the bottom line of the statement.

Now that you have projected sales and cost of sales (discussed in *Chapter 10: Forecast Your Sales*) and personnel expenses (*Chapter 7: Management Team*), you're probably starting to think about comparing expenses to your sales.

Expenses start with personnel. Then you have rent, utilities, equipment, and probably some advertising, maybe commissions, public relations, and other expenses.

What we're leading to is profits. Profits are what is left over after you start with sales, then subtract cost of sales, expenses, and taxes.

The Income statement is the same as the Profit and Loss statement. They are also called "pro forma income" or "pro forma profit and loss." The pro forma income is the same as a standard income statement except that the standard statement shows real results from the past, while a pro forma statement is projecting the future.

Figure 14-1 shows a simple income statement. The format and math starts with sales at the top. This example doesn't divide operating expenses into categories.

First, subtract cost of sales from sales. This gives you gross margin, an important ratio for comparisons and analysis. Acceptable gross margin levels depend on the industry. According to the 1997 Financial Statement Studies of Robert Morris Associates, an average shoe store has a gross margin of 42 percent. A hat manufacturer has a gross margin of 30 percent, and a grocery store about 20 percent.

The more detailed Profit and Loss is shown in Figure 14-2.

This example divides operating expenses into standard categories, including Sales and Marketing expenses and General and Administrative expenses. It provides a clearer picture of the business expenses and what they stand for, but for some cases the extra detail may not be relevant.

Summary

Your profit and loss statement is where you budget and forecast your expenses. You also absorb the more important numbers of your sales forecast and personnel plan, to create a planned bottom line for profit. This is educated guessing. Keep it on a computer so you can revise often as the business changes.

FIGURE 14-1: STANDARD PROFIT AND LOSS STATEMENT

Pro Forma Profit and Loss	Oct	Nov	Dec	2004
Sales	$85,000	$90,000	$55,000	$592,000
Cost of Sales	$24,000	$25,000	$19,000	$159,000
Other	$0	$0	$0	$0
Total Cost of Sales	$24,000	$25,000	$19,000	$159,000
Gross Margin	$61,000	$65,000	$36,000	$433,000
Gros Margin Percent	71.76%	72.22%	65.45%	73.14%
Operating Expenses				
Advertising/Promotion	$3,000	$3,000	$3,000	$36,000
PR	$2,500	$2,500	$2,500	$30,000
Travel	$7,500	$7,500	$7,500	$90,000
Misc.	$500	$500	$500	$6,000
Payroll Expense	$27,250	$27,250	$27,250	$194,750
Leased Equipment	$500	$500	$500	$6,000
Utilities	$1,000	$1,000	$1,000	$12,000
Insurance	$300	$300	$300	$36,000
Rent	$1,500	$1,500	$1,500	$18,000
Depreciation	$0	$0	$0	$200
Payroll Burden	$4,760	$4,760	$4,760	$30,100
Contract/Consultants	$0	$0	$0	$0
Other	$0	$0	$200	$200
Total Operating Expenses	$48,810	$48,810	$49,010	$459,250
Earning Before Interest and Taxes	$12,190	$16,190	($13,010)	$6,350
Interest Expense - Current	$400	$400	$400	$3,600
Interest Expense - Long-term	$417	$417	$417	$5,000
Taxes Incurred	$2,843	$3,843	($3,457)	($563)
Net Profit	$8,530	$11,530	($10,370)	($1,688)
Net Profit/Sales	10%	12.81%	-18.85%	-0.29%

This illustration shows the standard income statement (profit and loss). This is a partial snapshot, showing only three months of a 12-month table.

FIGURE 14-2: DETAILED PROFIT AND LOSS STATEMENT

Pro Forma Profit and Loss	Oct	Nov	Dec	2004
Sales	$754,505	$934,341	$739,799	$5,962,247
Direct Cost of Sales	$565,402	$714,295	$567,100	$4,356,077
Production Payroll	$14,500	$7,500	$7,500	$119,791
Other	$500	$500	$500	$5,751
Total Cost of Sales	$580,402	$722,295	$575,100	$4,481,619
Gross Margin	$174,103	$212,046	$164,699	$1,480,628
Gross Margin %	23.08%	22.69%	22.26%	24.83%
Operating Expenses				
Sales and Marketing Expenses				
Payroll	$32,000	$16,000	$16,000	$303,856
Ads	$15,000	$20,000	$10,000	$138,570
Catalog	$2,000	$2,000	$2,000	$25,395
Mailing	$22,000	$8,000	$5,000	$113,569
Literature	$0	$0	$0	$6,401
Seminar	$0	$0	$0	$31,000
Service	$500	$500	$250	$10,296
Training	$450	$450	$450	$5,550
Total Sales and Marketing Expenses	$78,950	$61,950	$33,700	$671,837
Sales and Marketing %	10.46%	6.63%	4.56%	11.27%
General and Administrative Expenses				
Payroll	$15,000	$7,500	$7,500	$13,500
Payroll Burden	$10,320	$4,760	$4,760	$93,840
Depreciation	$1,094	$1,105	$1,116	$12,681
Leased Equipment	$2,500	$2,500	$2,500	$30,000
Utilities	$750	$750	$750	$9,000
Insurance	$500	$500	$500	$6,000
Rent	$7,000	$7,000	$7,000	$84,000
Other	$545	$550	$556	$6,331
Total General and Administrative Expenses	$37,709	$24,665	$24,682	$376,852
General and Administrative %	5.00%	2.64%	3.34%	6.32%
Other Expenses				
Other Payroll	$3,000	$3,000	$3,000	$36,000
Contract/Consultants	$125	$125	$125	$1,500
Other	$0	$0	$0	$0
Total Other Expenses	$3,125	$3,125	$3,125	$37,500
Other %	0.41%	0.33%	0.42%	0.63%
Total Operating Expenses	$119,784	$89,740	$61,507	$1,086,189
Profit Before Interest and Taxes	$54,319	$122,306	$103,192	$394,439
Interest Expense Current	$1,033	$2,533	$1,533	$15,133
Interest Expense Long-term	$2,511	$2,489	$2,466	$29,628
Taxes Incurred	$10,155	$23,457	$19,838	$69,935
Net Profit	$40,619	$93,827	$79,354	$279,742
Net Profit/Sales	5.38%	10.04%	10.73%	4.69%

This illustration shows the more detailed profit and loss analysis that divides operating expenses into categories. This is a partial snapshot, showing three months of a 12-month table.

This page intentionally blank.

FINANCIAL ANALYSIS

The financials are not as hard as you think, particularly if you have the patience to follow the steps. A good plan includes sales, cash flow, profits, and related financials.

Chapter 15:

CASH IS KING

So, as we looked at business numbers in the previous two chapters, we focused on the critical difference between cash and profits. This chapter looks at how to plan for cash in a business plan, understanding the critical elements that affect cash flow. You don't want to be one of those businesses that goes broke even while producing profits.

Basic Cash Planning Example

Let's start again with a simple example. Compared to the examples in the previous chapter, Figure 15-1 looks at the business from a completely different point of view; money coming in and money flowing out. Sales and profits are out of the picture, (although sales influences money in and costs and expenses influence money out).

FIGURE 15-1: BASIC CASH PLAN

Sources of Cash	Start	Jan	Feb	Mar
Cash Sales	$0	$0	$0	$0
From Receivables	$0	$0	$0	$0
New Loans	$0	$0	$100	$100
New Investments	$400	$0	$0	$0
Total Inflow	$400	$0	$100	$100
Expenditures	Start	Jan	Feb	Mar
Interest Payments	$0	$0	$0	$0
Purchase Widgets	$0	$100	$100	$100
Pay Payables	$0	$0	$0	$100
Pay Loans	$0	$0	$0	$0
Total Cash Out	$0	$100	$100	$200
Cash Flow	$400	($100)	$0	($100)
Cash Balance	$400	$300	$300	$200

This sample shows examples of incoming cash and expenditures for our sample company.

In this very simple model, your sources of money are cash sales, payments from receivables, new loan money, and new investment. Your expenditures include buying widgets in cash, paying interest, paying bills as they come due (i.e. paying accounts payable), and paying off loans.

Even at this basic level, you can see the potential complications and the need for linking the numbers up with a computer. Your estimated receipts from accounts receivable must have a logical relationship to sales and the balance of accounts receivable. Likewise, your payments of accounts payable have to relate to the balances of payables and the costs and expenses that created the payables. Vital as this is to business survival, it is not nearly as intuitive as the sales forecast, personnel plan, or income statement. The mathematics and the financials are more complex.

A More Realistic Example

The cash plan can get complicated quickly when you deal with a more realistic business example. In the following illustrations, we're going to look at the cash planning for the company whose cash balances were described in *Chapter 13: About Business Numbers*. This was the company whose cash flow varied widely, depending on cash assumptions.

Beginning Assumptions

With Figures 15-2 and 15-3 we set the starting points, which are the projected income and the starting balance. We see a simple example of business income, which we'll use as a first step for planning cash. Sales hit a peak in May. The example already divides sales between cash sales and sales on credit. We also have a simplified version of wages and operating expenses so that we can focus on the cash plan instead of the income statement.

FIGURE 15-2: SAMPLE CASE INCOME STATEMENT

Income Statement	Jan	Feb	Mar	Apr	May	Jun
Cash Sales	$81	$103	$125	$151	$193	$146
Sales on Credit	$188	$240	$292	$352	$451	$340
Total Sales	$269	$343	$417	$503	$644	$486
Direct Cost of Sales	$185	$250	$309	$400	$503	$368
Personnel Cost of Sa	$10	$10	$10	$10	$10	$10
Other Cost of Sales	$1	$1	$1	$1	$1	$1
Total Cost of Sales	$196	$261	$320	$411	$514	$379
Gross Margin	$73	$82	$97	$92	$130	$107
Operating Expenses						
Wages and Salaries	$44	$44	$44	$44	$44	$60
Depreciation	$1	$1	$1	$1	$1	$1
Other Operating Expe	$25	$40	$28	$41	$47	$35
EBIT	$3	($3)	$24	$6	$38	$11
Interest	$3	$3	$4	$5	$5	$4
Taxes	$0	($1)	$4	$0	$7	$1
Net Profit	$0	($5)	$16	$1	$26	$6

This table shows some of the more important assumptions related to the cash plan for a sample company (numbers displayed in thousands).

FIGURE 15-3: SAMPLE CASE STARTING BALANCE

Assets	Start
Current Assets	
Cash Balance	$55
Accounts Receivable	$395
Inventory	$251
Other Current Assets	$25
Subtotal	$726
Long-term Assets	$350
Accumulated Depreciation	$50
Subtotal	$300
Total Assets	$1,026
Liabilities	Start
Current Liabilities	
Accounts Payable	$224
Current Notes	$90
Other Current Liabilities	$15
Subtotal	$329
Long-term Liabilities	$285
Total Liabilities	$614
Capital	Start
Paid-in Capital	$500
Retained Earnings	$163
Earnings	$75
Total Capital	$412
Capital and Liabilities	$1,026

This is our example's starting balance sheet.

Cash Flow Breakdown

In the following sections, I will explain the Cash Flow table, row by row, and how the numbers in your Cash Flow have a direct impact on the Balance Sheet, to help you better understand the direct link of one table to another, and how changes in one table directly affect the other.

For the purpose of discussion, we have divided a standard Cash Flow table into separate sections, Cash Received and Expenditures.

Cash Received

Figure 15-4 lists possible cash sources for our sample company. Most of these have balance sheet impact, and several come from the income statement. For now, we'll focus just on the cash flow. After dealing with cash, before we go on to the balance in *Chapter 16: Finish the Financials*, we'll also look briefly at the specific cash flow implications on the balance sheet.

FIGURE 15-4: SAMPLE CASE-CASH RECEIVED

Cash Received	Jan	Feb	Mar	Apr	May	Jun
Cash Sales	$80	$103	$125	$151	$193	$146
From Receivables	$212	$137	$190	$284	$292	$352
From Sale of Other Current Assets	$0	$0	$0	$0	$0	$0
From Sale of Long-term Assets	$0	$0	$0	$0	$0	$0
From New Current Debt	$0	$100	$30	$100	$0	$0
From New Other Current Liabilities	$0	$0	$0	$0	$0	$0
From New Long-term Debt	$0	$0	$100	$0	$0	$0
New Investment	$0	$25	$0	$0	$300	$0
Total Cash Received	$292	$365	$445	$535	$785	$498

In this section of the Cash Flow table, we describe the main sources of cash, such as cash sales and monies received from accounts receivable.

1. The first row, **Cash Sales**, is a simple estimate. It should link with your sales forecast and income statement to avoid inconsistencies. Cash sales plus sales on credit equal total sales. Normally, credit card sales are grouped into cash sales because the business gets the money in a day or two. Cash in this case means cash, check, and credit card, everything except the real sales on credit, which are sales made on terms.

2. The second row, **From Receivables**, is an estimate of the dollar amount received from customers as payments of accounts receivable.

3. The third and fourth rows are **From Sale of Other Current Assets** and **From Sale of Long-term Assets**. Selling current (short-term) or long-term assets is another possible way to generate cash.

4. The next three rows are where you estimate amounts of money coming into the company as new borrowed money. The difference between each of the three is a matter of type of borrowing and terms. The row named **From New Current Debt** is for money you get by borrowing through normal lending institutions, as standard loans, with interest payments. This is also called Short-term Debt. The row named **From New Other Current Liabilities** is for items like accrued taxes and accrued salaries and wages, money owed that will have to be paid, but isn't formally borrowed. Normally there are no interest expenses associated with this row. The row named **From New Long-term Debt** is for new money borrowed on longer terms.

5. The last row, **New Investment**, is for new money coming into the company as investment.

Expenditures

Figure 15-5 is an example of expenditures for our sample company.

FIGURE 15-5: SAMPLE CASE CASH EXPENDITURES

Expenditures	Jan	Feb	Mar	Apr	May	Jun
Cash Spending	$168	$207	$207	$207	$316	$79
Bill Payments	$137	$149	$234	$210	$338	$356
Principal Payments Current Debt	$0	$0	$0	$0	$0	$100
Principal Payments Long-term Debt	$3	$3	$3	$3	$3	$3
New Current Assets	$0	$0	$0	$0	$0	$0
New Long-term Assets	$25	$0	$15	$15	$50	$0
Total Expenditures	$333	$359	$459	$435	$707	$538

This section of the Cash Flow table lists projected expenditures, such as payments on accounts payable and direct payments of wages and salaries.

1. The first and most obvious expenditure is **Cash Spending,** which would normally include payroll and other payments made directly in cash. These items don't go into Accounts Payable to sit and wait for payment. Some companies buy inventory for cash, or pay expenses immediately.

2. The next normal spending is paying bills. Most companies record bills into a list of bills to pay, and then gather bills together to pay vendors every so often. The money owed to vendors in **Bill Payments** is called Accounts Payable. The accounts payable balance is money you owe. Every month, you pay these bills.

3. The next two rows, **Principal Payments Current Debt** and **Principal Payments Long-term Debt,** are for principal payments of debt. When you pay off your loans, you lose cash. In the example, there is a regular payoff of long-term debt, and a single payoff of part of the current (short-term) debt.

4. In the second row from the bottom, you record **New Current Assets.** You'll have to know how much you purchase in new assets in order to estimate your Balance Sheet. While in real life these might also be recorded as Accounts Payable and paid a few weeks later, we make them explicit here as if they were paid immediately in cash. That makes for better cash planning.

5. Finally, in the last expenditure row, purchases of **New Long-term Assets** reduce cash and change the balance sheet amount for the related assets.

Calculating The Cash Balance

When you're done with both sections, add the new sources of cash and subtract the uses of cash, and you have an estimated ending Cash Balance for each month, as shown in Figure 15-6.

FIGURE 15-6: SAMPLE CASE-CASH BALANCE

Cash Received	Jan	Feb	Mar	Apr	May	Jun
Cash Sales	$80	$103	$125	$151	$193	$146
From Receivables	$212	$137	$190	$284	$292	$352
From Sale of Other Current Assets	$0	$0	$0	$0	$0	$0
From Sale of Long-term Assets	$0	$0	$0	$0	$0	$0
From New Current Debt	$0	$100	$30	$100	$0	$0
From New Other Current Liabilities	$0	$0	$0	$0	$0	$0
From New Long-term Debt	$0	$0	$100	$0	$0	$0
New Investment	$0	$25	$0	$0	$300	$0
Total Cash Received	$292	$365	$445	$535	$785	$498
Expenditures	Jan	Feb	Mar	Apr	May	Jun
Cash Spending	$168	$207	$207	$207	$316	$79
Bill Payments	$137	$149	$234	$210	$338	$356
Principal Payments Current Debt	$0	$0	$0	$0	$0	$100
Principal Payments Long-term Debt	$3	$3	$3	$3	$3	$3
New Current Assets	$0	$0	$0	$0	$0	$0
New Long-term Assets	$25	$0	$15	$15	$50	$0
Total Expenditures	$333	$359	$459	$435	$707	$538
Cash Flow	($41)	$6	($14)	$100	$78	($40)
Cash Balance	$14	$20	$6	$106	$184	$144

The full cash plan lets you compare your Sources of Cash with Use of Cash and see the Cash Balance.

Even with this detailed list, we've still missed some other items that might reduce cash. There is nothing in this sample table for owner's draw or dividends. There is no row for interest income, or miscellaneous income. The estimate assumes purchase of assets is done immediately in cash, not using Accounts Payable. This is just a simple example intended to point out the relationships between the different tables, and the dependencies involved in calculating a real cash flow.

Links with Balance Sheet

Even though I cover the balance sheet in the next chapter, I can't talk about cash without relating the cash flow to the balance sheet. The three most important financial statements in a plan, income statement, cash flow, and balance sheet, are linked to each other.

Figure 15-7 shows the sample balance sheet linked to the cash flow in the previous illustration. Most of the rows on this balance are directly affected by the cash flow, and need to change every time the cash changes. To close the circle in this chapter, let's look in detail at the balance:

FIGURE 15-7: RELATED BALANCE SHEET

Assets	Start	Jan	Feb	Mar	Apr	May	Jun
Current Assets							
Cash Balance	$55	$14	$20	$6	$106	$184	$144
Accounts Receivable	$395	$371	$474	$576	$644	$803	$791
Inventory	$251	$333	$445	$546	$610	$787	$556
Other Current Assets	$25	$25	$25	$25	$25	$25	$25
Subtotal	$726	$743	$964	$1,153	$1,385	$1,799	$1,516
Long-term Assets	$350	$375	$375	$390	$390	$440	$440
Accumulated Depreciation	$50	$51	$52	$53	$54	$55	$56
Subtotal	$300	$324	$323	$337	$336	$385	$384
Total Assets	$1,026	$1,067	$1,287	$1,490	$1,721	$2,184	$1,900

Liabilities	Start	Jan	Feb	Mar	Apr	May	Jun
Current Liabilities							
Accounts Payable	$224	$268	$371	$431	$564	$704	$517
Current Notes	$90	$90	$190	$220	$320	$320	$320
Other Current Liabilities	$15	$15	$15	$15	$15	$15	$15
Subtotal	$329	$373	$576	$666	$899	$1,039	$852
Long-term Liabilities	$285	$285	$285	$385	$385	$385	$385
Total Liabilities	$614	$658	$861	$1,051	$1,284	$1,424	$1,237

Capital	Start	Jan	Feb	Mar	Apr	May	Jun
Paid-in Capital	$500	$500	$525	$525	$525	$825	$825
Retained Earnings	$163	$238	$238	$238	$238	$238	$238
Earnings	$75	$0	($5)	$11	$12	$38	$44
Total Capital	$412	$412	$432	$448	$449	$775	$781
Capital and Liabilities	$1,026	$1,067	$1,287	$1,490	$1,721	$2,184	$1,900

The balance sheet should follow from the income statement and the cash flow. Notice how long-term liabilities respond in March to a new loan and a principal payment of an existing loan.

1. The **Cash Balance** row is the balance in your checkbook. You calculate this with the cash flow.

2. **Accounts Receivable** is the money owed to you by customers for sales already made. The balance increases with sales on credit, and decreases with payments of accounts receivable. For any month, the ending balance is the sum of the previous ending balance, plus new sales on credit, minus payments received.

3. Calculate the **Inventory** balance as the previous balance minus direct cost of sales plus new inventory purchases.

4. Calculate **Other Current Assets** as the previous balance plus new assets purchased (from cash expenditures) minus disposal of assets (from cash received).

5. **Long-term Assets** are long-term capital assets, usually plant and equipment. This month's balance is equal to last month's balance plus new assets purchased, minus disposal of assets.

6. **Accumulated Depreciation** decreases the value of the capital assets. This month's balance is last month's balance plus new depreciation, from the income statement.

7. **Accounts Payable** will be last month's balance plus additions (a subset of costs and expenses) minus payments of payables. New payables will include new inventory not paid for when purchased, plus indirect costs of sales not paid as incurred, operating expenses not paid as incurred, and similar items.

8. **Current Notes** (short-term) will be equal to last month's balance plus new borrowing minus principal payments. Interest payments are not included, because they go into the income statement and don't affect the balance. Principal payments and new borrowing should come from the cash flow.

9. **Other Current Liabilities** are things like accrued taxes and accrued salary, liabilities you know you have, but haven't as yet, paid.

10. **Long-term Liabilities** (debt) increases when you borrow and decreases with payment of principal. The balance is going to be last month's balance plus new borrowing as a source of cash (received), minus principal payments as a use of cash (expenditure). In the sample case, the March balance shows a $100 increase for a new loan, minus a $3 decrease for payment of principal, so that the $376 at the end of March is exactly $97 more than the $279 at the end of February.

11. **Paid-in Capital** is money invested. The balance should be last month's balance plus new investment from sources of cash, minus dividends from uses of cash.

12. **Retained Earnings** is the accumulated earnings reinvested in the company, not taken out as dividends. Normally this changes once a year when the annual statements are prepared.

13. **Earnings** are the accumulated earnings since the end of the last year. This month's balance should be equal to last month's balance plus this month's earnings. At the end of the year, with an annual adjustment, earnings still left in the business become retained earnings.

Understanding Cash Flow

Your cash plan is the most critical financial element of your business projections. If it is going to be useful at all, a business plan helps you develop a realistic cash estimate, based on the underlying relationships we explored in the previous chapter. Whenever you change an assumption in sales forecast, personnel plan, profit and loss, or balance sheet, it affects your cash flow.

The examples in this and previous chapters describe the way cash flow works. Profits are very important to cash; the more profits, the better the cash, because profits are sales (that generate cash) minus costs and expenses (that cost cash). What is less obvious is the impact of balance sheet items:

- An increase in assets decreases your cash. A decrease in assets increases cash.

- An increase in liabilities increases cash. A decrease in liabilities decreases cash.

These two principals lead eventually to the impact of receivables, inventory, and payables. As you look at your assumptions for the cash flow, keep in mind that every extra dollar of receivables or inventory as assets is a dollar that you don't have in your cash balance. Every dollar in payables is a dollar that you have in cash, too. Although this simple cash model doesn't show the critical impact as clearly as our examples in the previous chapter, the mathematics and financial principals are the same.

Summary

The cash plan is vital, the most critical financial analysis in the business plan. It has to manage the difference between cash and profits. The cash flow stands between income statement and balance sheet, and brings the two together.

This page intentionally blank.

Chapter 16:

FINISH THE FINANCIALS

If you've really followed through with the cash plan, your financials are almost done. The balance sheet should be completed by the time you have a cash flow working. Business ratios should be almost automatic too, because they draw all of their information from tables you've already finished.

The Balance Sheet

I showed you some basic balance sheets, first in the previous sections, *Chapter 13: About Business Numbers* and *Chapter 15: Cash is King*, because you can't deal with cash without addressing the balance. You've seen then that the Balance Sheet table shows the business' financial position, its assets and liabilities, at a specified time. A standard business plan includes a projected Balance Sheet table for each of the first 12 months in the plan, and for each of the three years.

The ironclad rule of Western double-entry bookkeeping and accounting is that assets are equal to capital and liabilities. This is what balance means.

If you think about it, you'll notice we also used that rule in the Start-up costs section of *Chapter 5: Describe Your Company*. It comes up again with the Balance Sheet table as we use this rule to calculate retained earnings, which makes the balance correct.

Figure 16-1 shows the Balance Sheet table, or pro forma Balance Sheet table. The Balance Sheet table should naturally start with either your start-up costs or your ending balance from the previous year, depending on whether you are a start-up company or an ongoing company. Then, for the first 12 months of your plan, it should give detailed projections of your assets, liabilities, and capital as your business progresses. The calculations for this come mainly from your income statement and cash flow. Between those two statements, plus the beginning balances, your Balance Sheet should be virtually done before you start.

FIGURE 16-1: SAMPLE BALANCE SHEET TABLE

Balance Sheet Assets	Starting Balance	Jan	Feb	Mar	Apr	May	Jun
Current Assets							
Cash Balance	$55	$15	$21	$7	$15	$93	$53
Accounts Receivable	$395	$371	$474	$576	$644	$803	$791
Inventory	$251	$332	$444	$545	$701	$878	$647
Other Current Assets	$25	$25	$25	$25	$25	$25	$25
Subtotal	$726	$743	$964	$1,153	$1,385	$1,799	$1,516
Capital Assets	$350	$375	$375	$390	$390	$440	$440
Accumulated Depreciation	$50	$51	$52	$53	$54	$55	$56
Subtotal	$300	$324	$323	$337	$336	$385	$384
Total Assets	$1,026	$1,067	$1,287	$1,490	$1,721	$2,184	$1,900
Liabilities							
Current Liabilities							
Accounts Payable	$224	$268	$371	$431	$564	$704	$517
Current Notes	$90	$90	$190	$220	$320	$320	$220
Other Current Liabilities	$15	$15	$15	$15	$15	$15	$15
Subtotal	$329	$373	$576	$666	$899	$1,039	$752
Long-term Liabilities	$285	$282	$279	$376	$373	$370	$367
Total Liabilities	$614	$655	$855	$1,042	$1,272	$1,409	$1,119
Capital							
Paid-in Capital	$500	$500	$525	$525	$525	$825	$825
Retained Earnings	($163)	($88)	($88)	($88)	($88)	($88)	($88)
Earnings	$75	$0	($5)	$11	$12	$38	$44
Total Capital	$412	$412	$432	$448	$449	$775	$781
Capital and Liabilities	$1,026	$1,067	$1,287	$1,490	$1,721	$2,184	$1,900

This illustration shows the first six months of the Balance Sheet table for the sample company we used in the previous chapter (numbers displayed in thousands).

Business Ratios

Figure 16-2 shows the Ratios table. This table calculates several ratios that are common in financial analysis.

Ratios are often misunderstood. They aren't magic. Correct, healthy ratios vary from industry to industry, business to business, depending on the nature of the business. *Chapter 8: The Business You're In* lists sources for more information on business ratios, including standards for your type of business. Generally, the most important insight gained from ratios is the change in a ratio over time, rather than the specific number at any given time.

While we do explain the standard financial ratios used here, there are better explanations available in financial management textbooks. Experts will almost always agree on the importance of following changes in a ratio over time, and on the wide variations of standards depending on the type of business.

FIGURE 16-2: THE RATIOS TABLE

Profitability Ratios	2004	2005	2006
Gross Margin	22.55%	26.13%	26.72%
Net Profit Margin	2.76%	5.62%	5.53%
Return on Assets	6.73%	13.76%	12.98%
Return on Equity	19.01%	43.64%	32.77%
Activity Rations			
Accts Receivable Turnover	3.75	3.75	3.75
Collection Days	65	90	90
Inventory Turnover	5.89	3.76	3.86
Accts Payable Turnover	5.9	5.9	5.9
Total Asset Turnover	5.44	2.45	2.35
Debt Ratios			
Debt to Net Worth	1.83	2.17	1.52
Short-term Liab. to Liab.	0.79	0.86	0.91
Liquidity Ratios			
Current Ratio	1.67	1.38	1.37
Quick Ratio	0.67	0.52	0.49
Net Working Capital	$881,815	$682,070	$758,509
Interest Coverage	5.45	7.1	7.1
Additional Ratios			
Assets to Sales	0.41	0.41	0.43
Debt/Assets	65%	68%	60%
Current Debt/Total Assets	51%	59%	55%
Acid Test	-0.28	-0.25	-0.31
Asset Turnover	2.44	2.45	2.35
Sales/Net Worth	6.88	7.77	5.93
Dividend Payout	$0	$0	$0

Most standard business plans include some standard business ratios. You should let the computer calculate them.

Profitability Ratios

- **Gross Margin:** sales minus cost of sales, expressed as a percentage.

- **Net Profit Margin:** net profit divided by sales, as a percentage.

- **Return on Assets:** net profit divided by the total assets.

- **Return on Equity:** also return on investment (ROI). This ratio divides net profit by net worth.

Return on equity or return on investment (ROI) is probably the most important of these ratios. A business is an investment and it should yield profits comparable to alternative investments, unless there is additional compensation (such as salaries for the owners). In theory, at least, if ROI is low, you should sell the business and put your investment money to better use.

Return on assets and the net profit margin provide a good basis for comparison between your company and the rest of the industry. They are also good indicators of company performance from year to year.

Activity Ratios

- **AR Turnover** (accounts receivables turnover): sales on credit divided by accounts receivable. This is a measure of how well your business collects its debts.

- **Collection Days:** accounts receivable multiplied by 360, then divided by annual credit sales is another measure of debt collection and value of receivables. Generally, 30 days is exceptionally good, 60 days is bothersome, and 90 days or more is a real problem. This varies by industry.

- **Inventory Turnover:** cost of sales divided by the average balance of inventory. The higher the turnover, the better for cash flow and working capital requirements.

- **Accounts Payable Turnover:** a measure of how quickly the business pays its bills. It divides the total new accounts payable for the year by the average accounts payable balance.

- **Total Assets Turnover:** sales divided by total assets.

These ratios are generally used to compare a company's performance to the average for its industry. Levels of acceptability tend to vary widely between different industries. For example, large manufacturing companies might have a very low assets turnover, but retail stores should have a high turnover.

Debt Ratios

- **Debt to Net Worth:** total liabilities divided by total net worth.

- **Short-term Liabilities to Liabilities:** short-term debt divided by total liabilities. This is a measure of the depth and term of debt.

Liquidity Ratios

- **Current Ratio:** short-term assets divided by short-term liabilities. This gives a view of a business' cash position and ability to meet short-term commitments.

- **Quick Ratio:** this is the same as the current ratio, except that inventories are first subtracted from short-term assets before they are divided by short-term liabilities. Many financial experts consider this a better measurement of liquidity than the current ratio, because inventory is so often not convertible to real cash in a short period of time.

- **Net Working Capital:** subtract short-term liabilities from short-term assets. This is another measure of cash position.

- **Interest Coverage:** profit before interest and taxes (operating profit) divided by total interest payments. A measure of how much a business is burdened by servicing its own debt.

These are all measures of the overall financial position of a company and its ability to pay its debt. They are very important to bankers and for loan applications. The acid test (included with additional ratios in the following section) is generally considered the best measure of a company's ability to pay all its obligations without problems. Acceptable measures vary by industry. Some industries are quite heavy on plant and equipment assets, and others (for example, service businesses) have few long-term assets.

Additional Ratios

- **Assets to sales:** assets divided by sales.

- **Debt/Assets:** total liabilities divided by total assets.

- **Current Debt/Total Assets:** divides short-term (current) liabilities by total assets.

- **Acid Test:** short-term assets (minus accounts receivable and inventory), divided by short-term liabilities.

- **Asset Turnover:** a repetition of the same ratio (Total Asset Turnover) in activity ratios above.

- **Sales/Net Worth:** total sales divided by net worth.

- **Dividend Payout:** dividends divided by net profit.

Break-even Analysis

You prepared a break-even analysis in *Chapter 3: Initial Assessment.* Now it's time to go back to that and review the numbers. Figure 16-3 shows (again) the standard break-even analysis included in a standard business plan.

FIGURE 16-3: BREAK-EVEN ANALYSIS

Break Even Analysis	
Monthly Units Break-even	1,222
Monthly Sales Break-even	$397,262
Assumptions	
Average Per-unit Revenue	$325.00
Average Per-unit Variable Cost	$248.07
Estimated Monthly Fixed Costs	$94,035.00

This section of the model calculates technical break-even points, based on the assumptions for unit prices, variable costs, and fixed costs.

This is a monthly break-even analysis. It assumes monthly fixed costs, and per-unit sales price and variable costs. It uses the standard break-even formulas detailed below, but suggests some modified assumptions. Where standard fixed costs are supposed to be costs that would be sustained even if the business stopped, we suggest you use operating expenses instead. I suggest this change in standard financial analysis because you are better off knowing break-even points on real operations, rather than on some theoretical calculation of fixed expenses.

Units break-even point formula:

Fixed Cost/(Unit Price - Unit Variable Costs)

Sales break-even point formula:

Fixed Cost/(1-(Unit variable Costs/Unit Price))

The Break-even Chart

The break-even analysis depends on assumptions for fixed costs, unit price, and unit variable costs. These are rarely exact assumptions. This is not a true picture of fixed costs by any means, but is quite useful for determining a break-even point.

The analysis included in the chart in Figure 16-4 shows a general break-even analysis for assumed fixed costs of $94,035, average per-unit revenue of $325, and average per-unit variable cost of $248.

The line on the chart shows profits increasing and crossing the break-even line at approximately 1,222 units.

FIGURE 16-4: BREAK-EVEN CHART

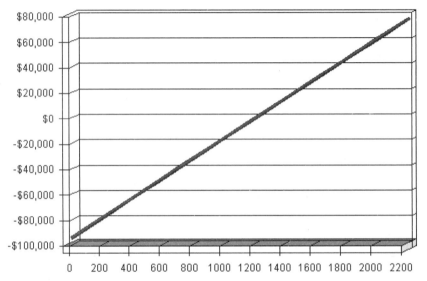

This chart shows the break-even analysis that compares unit sales to profits. It uses data from the table in Figure 16-3.

Refine and Polish the Financials

Your financial tables are interrelated. The sales, personnel forecasts, and assumptions affect the profit and loss, the profit and loss affects cash, and the cash and balance sheet work together.

Summary

Financial analysis is rarely a true step-by-step process. You will probably have to go back through your tables to review the assumptions for realism and accuracy. As you revise assumptions, make sure you constantly check back to keep your cash flow positive.

Chapter 17:

STRATEGY IS FOCUS

With most of the financials now done, it's time to turn to strategy and tactics. You've been developing strategy throughout, I know, because you can't do the numbers without thinking about the strategy. However, now you want to explain your strategy and develop the implementation. If you refer back to the text outline we discussed in Chapter 2: Pick Your Plan, *you probably have several topics still blank in your plan document. But not in your mind. It's time to write your thoughts on strategy and tactics into your text outline.*

Define Overall Strategy

Think of strategy as focus. Of the whole range of possible market segments and the whole range of services and possible sales and marketing activities, which are your main priorities? Avoid making long lists of priorities. More than three or four points makes them more like a laundry list or to-do list than a strategic focus.

The Strategy Pyramid

Imagine a pyramid made of three levels. The top of the pyramid is a single box, which contains a strategy. Strategy is an area of resource focus. In the middle level, you have three or so boxes which contain tactics. In the third level, you have four to six boxes that stand for programs. It would look something like Figure 17-1.

FIGURE 17-1: STRATEGY PYRAMID

Don't get lost in defining strategy and tactics. Make the strategic view work logically.

Your definitions don't have to be exact. A strategy is a main focus, which might be on a specific target market, product opportunity, positioning statement, or some other important or fundamental element.

Tactics are there to implement strategies. For example, if a computer store's strategy is to build long-term relationships with business customers, its tactics might include increasing networking , training, and support.

Programs are specific business activities, each of which has concrete dates and responsibilities, and probably a budget. In the computer store example, programs for the strategy might include upgrade mailings, seminars, installation services, network training and others, each of which is built on specifics.

You don't necessarily do a complete business strategy in a single pyramid. Each fundamental business strategy might be a different pyramid.

One important benefit of the pyramid method is integration and alignment. If your strategy is to focus on one thing, you should be able to trace that strategy into its tactics and, most important, into your actual spending and activity priorities. Compare your pyramid strategy and your specific programs, and ask yourself: do your programs match the emphasis you put on strategy?

The Value Proposition

Value-based marketing is another conceptual framework. Like the pyramid described in the previous topic, it doesn't have to be in your business plan at all, but we add it here because some people find that the framework helps them develop their strategy. Obviously, this has to be a quick treatment. There are textbooks written about value-based marketing, and the business literature on this topic is rich and varied.

This framework begins with defining your business offering as a value proposition. The value proposition is benefit offered minus price charged, in relative terms. The definition encourages you to think in broad conceptual terms, with emphasis on the real benefit offered, rather than the specific tangible. For example, a national fast food chain probably offers the value of convenience and reliability, probably at a slight price premium (at least when compared to the weaker chains). A prestigious local restaurant, on the other hand, is offering a completely different set of benefits (luxury, elegance, and prestige, for example) at a marked price premium. A graphic designer is probably selling benefits related to communication and advertising, not just drawings.

Once you have a value proposition defined, look at your business—and your business plan—in terms of how you:

1. Communicate the business proposition; and

2. Fulfill your promise.

For example, if a computer store's business proposition has to do with reliable service for small business, peace of mind, and long-term relationships, then it probably shouldn't be taking out full-page newspaper advertisements promising the lowest prices in town on brand-name hardware. It probably should communicate that proposition with sales literature that emphasizes how the computer store will become a strategic ally of its clients. It might also think twice about how it handles overdue bills from customers, who might really be holding out for more service or better support. Figure 17-2 shows how the store might lay out its strategy.

Like the pyramid, the framework helps you integrate your planned programs into a logical whole plan.

FIGURE 17-2: SAMPLE STRATEGY PYRAMID

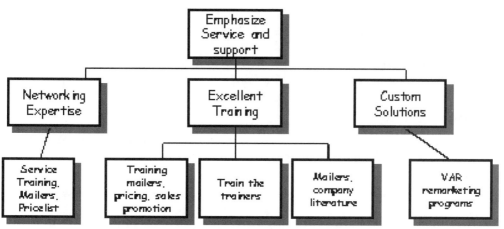

The computer store strategy is to emphasize service and support for its customers.

Define Marketing Strategy

Your marketing strategy normally involves target market focus, emphasis on certain services or media, or ways to position your company and your service uniquely.

Your marketing strategy depends a great deal on which market segments you've chosen as target market groups. You covered this in detail in *Chapter 9: Know Your Market* and *Chapter 11: Market.* You may also have developed strategy using the pyramid or value proposition. Obviously, you want to make sure to preserve the same basic focus and themes.

Aside from the target market strategy, your marketing strategy might also include the positioning statement, pricing, promotion, and whatever else you want to add. You might also want to look at media strategy, business development, or other factors. Strategy is creative, and hard to predict. The material below will give you more ideas.

Positioning Tactics

Positioning Tactics can be a good way to define your marketing strategy. The tactics should include a strategic focus on the most important target market, that market's most important market need, how your product meets that need, what is the main competition, and how your product is better than the competition. Consider this template:

For [target market description] who [target market need], [this product] [how it meets the need]. Unlike [key competition], it [most important distinguishing feature].

For example, the positioning statement for the original *Business Plan Pro®*, in 1994, was: "For the businessperson who is starting a new company, launching new products or seeking funding or partners, *Business Plan Pro®* is software that produces professional business plans quickly and easily. Unlike [name omitted], *Business Plan Pro®* does a real business plan, with real insights, not just cookie-cutter fill-in-the-blanks templates."

Pricing Tactics

You ought to provide detail on product pricing, and relate pricing to strategy. Your value proposition, for example, will normally include implications about relative pricing, and therefore, you should check whether your detailed product-by-product pricing matches the implied pricing in the value proposition. Pricing is also supposed to be intimately related to the positioning statement in the previous topic, since pricing is probably the most important factor in product positioning.

Promotion Tactics

Think of promotion in a broader sense than simply sales promotion. Think of how you spread the word about your business to your future customers. Think of it in the broader context, including the whole range of advertising, public relations, events, direct mail, seminars, and sales literature.

Think strategically. What is your strategy on communicating with people? Do you look for expensive ads in mass media, targeted marketing in specialized publications, or even more targeted with direct mail? Do you have a way to leverage the news media, or reviewers? Do you advertise more effectively through public relations events, trade shows, newspaper, or radio? What about telemarketing, the World Wide Web, or even multilevel marketing?

Are you satisfied with how this is working for you now, or is it a problem area that needs to be addressed? Are you meeting your needs, and in line with your opportunities?

How does your promotion strategy fit with the rest of your strategy? Check for alignment between what you say here and what you say in your strategy pyramid, and your value proposition. As you described market trends and target market segments, did you see ways to improve your promotion strategy?

Define Sales Strategy

Describe sales strategy as different from marketing strategy. To help differentiate between marketing strategy and sales strategy, think of marketing strategy as the broader effort of generating sales leads on a large scale, and sales strategy as the efforts to bring those sales leads into the system as individual sales transactions. Marketing might affect image and awareness and propensity to buy, while sales should close the deals and get the order that marketing opens.

Summary

Sales tactics deal with how and when to close sales prospects, how to compensate sales people, how to optimize order processing and database management, how to maneuver price, delivery, and conditions.

As with your marketing strategy, your sales strategy depends a great deal on which market segments you've chosen as target market groups. Obviously, you don't sell major deals to large companies the same way you sell cereal boxes off grocery store shelves. Think about how you sell in your business. What is your strategy for optimizing your way of selling?

Strategy is focus. You also need tactics to implement the strategy, and tactics require concrete milestones and well defined management responsibilities.

Chapter 18:

MAKE IT REAL

At this point, you've been through the main thinking and analysis. It is time to put some bite into your plan and management by listing specific actions to be taken.

Implementation Milestones

Each action is called a milestone. This is where a business plan becomes a real plan, with specific and measurable activities, instead of just a document. Give it as many milestones as you can think of to make it more concrete. Give each milestone a name, a person responsible, a milestone date, and a budget. Then make sure that all your people know that you will be following the plan and tracking plan-vs.-actual results. If you don't follow up, your plan will not be implemented.

The value of a plan is measured in its implementation.

The Milestones table should be the most important section of the entire business plan. Each marketing and sales-related program you plan should be listed in the table and explained in the related text, along with relevant details. You want to cement your sales strategy with programs that make it real. How is this strategy to be implemented? Do you have concrete and specific plans? How will implementation be measured?

In the sample table in Figure 18-1, you see columns reserved for evaluating the actual results and the difference between plan and actual results, for each program. You can also track actual spending and milestone dates.

Manage Your Summaries

Each of your business plan chapters should begin with a summary paragraph that describes all the high points of the chapter. A good strategy and implementation chapter probably includes several summaries, one for strategy overall, one for marketing strategy, and one for sales strategy. As you develop these summaries, keep in mind that many business plan readers will read only the summaries that begin each chapter. You should make sure to include all the important points that you need to make, even for browsers who don't read every word.

One of the best tactics in preparing a business plan is to write your chapter summaries well enough to use them by themselves as the core of a Summary Memo document. In seeking investment, for example, you will need to have a Summary Memo that describes the complete plan in just a few pages. You should be able to pick out your summary paragraphs and use them to create the Summary Memo.

The Executive Summary is the most important of your chapter summaries. It is the doorway to the rest of the plan. Get it right or your target readers will go no further. The best length is a single page. Emphasize the main points of your plan and keep it brief.

FIGURE 18-1: MILESTONES TABLE

| Business Plan Milestones | | Planned | | | | Actual | Actual | Date | Budget |
Milestone	Manager	Date	Department	Budget		Date	Budget	Variance	Variance
Corporate Identity	TJ	12/17/2003	Marketing	$10,000		1/15/2004	$12,004	(29)	($2,004)
Seminar Implementation	IR	1/10/2004	Sales	$1,000		12/27/2003	$1,000	14	$0
Business Plan Review	RJ	1/10/2004	GM	$0		1/23/2004	$500	(13)	($500)
Upgrade Mailer	IR	1/16/2004	Sales	$5,000		2/12/2004	$1,000	(27)	$4,000
New Corporate Brochure	TJ	1/15/2004	Marketing	$5,000		1/15/2004	$5,000	1	$0
Delivery Vans	SD	1/25/2004	Service	$12,500		2/26/2004	$0	(32)	$12,500
Direct Mail	IR	2/16/2004	Marketing	$3,500		2/25/2004	$1,000	(9)	$2,500
Advertising	RJ	2/16/2004	GM	$115,000		3/6/2004	$100,000	(18)	$15,000
X4 Prototype	SG	2/25/2004	Product	$2,500		2/25/2004	$1,000	0	$1,500
Service Revamp	SD	2/25/2004	Product	$2,500		2/25/2004	$2,500	0	$0
Presentations - 6	IR	2/25/2004	Sales	$0		1/10/2004	$1,000	46	($1,000)
X4 Testing	SG	3/6/2004	Product	$1,000		1/16/2004	$0	49	$1,000
New Accounts - 3	SD	3/17/2004	Sales	$0		3/17/2004	$2,500	0	($2,500)
L30 Prototype	PR	3/26/2004	Product	$2,500		4/11/2004	$15,000	(16)	($12,500)
Tech2004 Expo	TB	4/12/2004	Marketing	$15,000		1/25/2004	$1,000	77	$14,000
VP Sales/Marketing Hired	JK	6/11/2004	Sales	$1,000		7/25/2004	$5,000	(44)	($4,000)
Mailing System	SD	7/25/2004	Service	$5,000		7/14/2004	$7,654	11	($2,654)
Other				$0					
Totals				$181,500			$156,158	10	$25,342

These are the milestones, the heart and core of the business plan.

Long-Term Plan

While you're involved with summaries, consider adding a discussion of long-term plans. How do you expect your company to change over the next 5, 10, or 20 years? What are the important drivers of change? What is your company doing to position itself to manage and even thrive on future growth?

I don't recommend including financial details beyond three years in a business plan. At the most, a brief summary of a five-year plan in text is sufficient. However, this is not because I don't believe in long-term planning. Far from it. Businesses should indeed plan for longer than three years, but the long-term plans running five years or more work better in different formats. They are much less dependent on specific information, and specific business numbers.

Summary

Is your strategy a reflection of your company's strengths and weaknesses? Make it consistent and realistic.

A mediocre strategy implemented well and with consistency will always beat a brilliant strategy never implemented.

Check your plan for consistency throughout. Does your spending reflect your strategy? Do your numbers, including your sales forecast, expense forecast, and personnel plan, reflect your strategy?

Chapter 19:

PLAN FOR IMPLEMENTATION

Some plans are more likely to be implemented than others. Successful implementation starts with a good plan, one that is full of specific information on milestones, managers, responsibilities, dates and budgets. Beyond the plan itself, however, there are other factors also critical to implementation. Are you going to track results, comparing the planned results to the actual results? Are you going to follow up with your management team, making revisions and checking on performance?

Start With a Good Plan

Figure 19-1 shows a view of what it takes to develop and implement a business plan. I call this **planning for implementation**. There are some important factors beyond the plan that are also critical:

1. Is the plan simple? Is it easy to understand and to act on? Does it communicate its contents easily and practically?

2. Is the plan specific? Are its objectives concrete and measurable? Does it include specific actions and activities, each with specific dates of completion, specific persons responsible and specific budgets?

3. Is the plan realistic? Are the sales goals, expense budgets, and milestone dates realistic? Nothing stifles implementation like unrealistic goals.

4. Is the plan complete? Does it include all the necessary elements? Requirements of a business plan vary, depending on the context. There is no guarantee, however, that the plan will work if it doesn't cover the main bases.

Track and Follow Up

Ironically, a good plan alone isn't enough. Figure 19-1 indicates other elements that are also critical. Even a good plan means virtually nothing if somebody doesn't follow up on its concrete and specific milestones or results. A plan won't be implemented unless responsibilities are assigned to specific people, milestones are established and agreed upon, and the people responsible know that somebody will follow up to check on results.

FIGURE 19-1: IMPLEMENTATION ISN'T AUTOMATIC

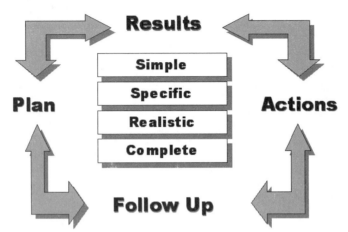

A business plan will be hard to implement unless it is simple, specific, realistic and complete. Even if it is all these things, a good plan will need someone to follow up and check on it.

Keep Your Plan Alive

A business plan is a living document. As you review implementation results with the people responsible, you will often find the need to set new goals and make course corrections. Keep track of the original plan and manage changes carefully. Although changes should be made only with good reason, don't be afraid to update your plan and keep it alive. We recommend using a computer for your financials so you can easily make changes, as described below.

Prescription for Live Planning

1. After your plan starts, as each month closes, make sure you compare the running actual results to the planned sales forecast, balance sheet, profit and loss, and cash flow. Watch what the plan vs. actual comparisons tell you.

2. Note when actual results indicate you need to make changes.

3. When the situation warrants, revise your plan. Make sure that everybody involved knows and understands the revisions.

Plan vs. Actual Management: an Example

Plan vs. actual management is called variance. Tracking and understanding variance is critical to plan implementation. We'll step through an example.

The Starting Sales Plan

The example begins in Figure 19-2 with the sales forecast portion of a finished business plan.

FIGURE 19-2: STARTING SALES PLAN

Unit Sales	Jan	Feb	Mar
Systems	85	115	145
Service	200	200	200
Software	150	200	250
Training	145	155	165
Other	160	176	192
Total Unit Sales	740	846	952
Unit Prices			
Systems	$2,000	$2,000	$2,000
Service	$75	$69	$58
Software	$200	$200	$200
Training	$37	$35	$39
Other	$300	$300	$300
Sales			
Systems	$170,000	$230,000	$290,000
Service	$15,000	$13,800	$11,600
Software	$30,000	$40,000	$50,000
Training	$5,365	$5,425	$6,435
Other	$48,000	$52,800	$57,600
Total Sales	$268,365	$342,025	$415,635

To set the scene, this illustration shows the sales forecast as the business plan is finished.

Actual Results for Sales

In Figure 19-3, we see the actual results for the same company for the first three months of the plan.

FIGURE 19-3: ACTUAL SALES RESULTS

Unit Sales	Jan	Feb	Mar
Systems	63	74	108
Service	168	171	174
Software	174	235	289
Training	156	171	183
Other	162	151	220
Total Unit Sales	723	802	974
Unit Prices			
Systems	$1,783	$1,801	$1,791
Service	$103	$106	$88
Software	$224	$185	$277
Training	$48	$39	$46
Other	$291	$371	$222
Sales			
Systems	$112,329	$133,274	$193,428
Service	$17,304	$18,126	$15,312
Software	$38,976	$43,475	$80,053
Training	$7,488	$6,669	$8,418
Other	$47,142	$56,021	$48,840
Total Sales	$223,239	$257,565	$346,051

The actual sales flow at the end of March shows actual cash flow numbers plus adjustments and course corrections.

Plan vs. Actual Sales

Figure 19-4 shows you the plan vs. actual results (or variance) for our hypothetical company.

FIGURE 19-4: SALES VARIANCE

Unit Sales	Jan	Feb	Mar
Systems	(22)	(41)	(37)
Service	(32)	(29)	(26)
Software	24	35	39
Training	11	16	18
Other	2	(25)	28
Total Unit Sales	(17)	(44)	22
Unit Prices			
Systems	($217)	($199)	($209)
Service	$28	$37	$30
Software	$24	($15)	$77
Training	$11	$4	$7
Other	($9)	$71	($78)
Sales			
Systems	($57,671)	($96,726)	($96,572)
Service	$2,304	$4,326	$3,712
Software	$8,976	$3,475	$30,053
Training	$2,123	$1,244	$1,983
Other	($858)	$3,221	($8,760)
Total Sales	($45,126)	($84,460)	($69,584)

Variance shows plan vs. actual results. Actual results are subtracted from budget results, leaving negative numbers when the sales were less than budget.

As you look at the variance for the sales forecast for the first three months, you should see several important trends:

1. Unit sales of systems are disappointing, well below expectations.

2. The average revenue for systems sales is also disappointing.

3. Unit sales for service are disappointing, but dollar sales are way up.

4. Sales are well above expectations for software and training.

Adjusting the Sales Plan

One of the main advantages of creating a plan on a computer is how easily you can change it. Month by month, as you record your actual results, you can make changes to your plan. Tracking variances is the best way to follow through in order to assure implementation and the success of the business plan.

The Starting Plan for Profit and Loss

Following the sales example in this chapter, Figure 19-5 shows a portion of the profit and loss for the sample company, as it stood in the plan.

FIGURE 19-5: PLANNED PROFIT AND LOSS

Pro Forma Profit and Loss	Jan	Feb	Mar
Sales	$268,365	$342,025	$415,635
Direct Cost of Sales	$184,495	$249,045	$307,595
Production Payroll	$9,500	$9,500	$9,500
Other	$500	$500	$500
Total Cost of Sales	$194,495	$259,045	$317,595
Gross Margin	$73,870	$82,980	$98,040
Gross Margin %	27.53%	24.26%	23.59%
Sales and Marketing Expenses			
Payroll	$24,000	$24,000	$24,000
Ads	$5,000	$5,000	$7,000
Catalog	$2,000	$3,000	$2,000
Mailing	$3,000	$11,800	$5,500
Promo	$0	$0	$0
Shows	$0	$0	$0
Literature	$0	$7,000	$0
PR	$0	$0	$0
Seminar	$1,000	$0	$0
Service	$2,000	$1,000	$1,000
Training	$450	$450	$450
Total Sales & Marketing Expenses	$37,450	$52,250	$39,950

This table shows the gross margin and sales and marketing expense area of the original plan. This is a portion of the full table.

Profit and Loss Actual Results

Figure 19-6 shows the actual results recorded in that portion of profit and loss, after the end of March. Looking at Figure 19-6, the actual results illustration means little without comparison to the original budget in Figure 19-5.

Unfortunately, many businesses also forget to compare the original to the actual. Especially if business is going well—the operation shows a profit, and cash flow is satisfactory—comparisons with the original budget are made poorly or not at all.

FIGURE 19-6: ACTUAL PROFIT AND LOSS RESULTS

Pro Forma Profit and Loss	Jan	Feb	Mar
Sales	$223,239	$257,565	$346,051
Direct Cost of Sales	$141,394	$176,275	$240,051
Production Payroll	$9,308	$9,224	$9,759
Other	$33	$782	$436
Total Cost of Sales	$150,735	$186,281	$250,246
Gross Margin	$72,504	$71,284	$95,805
Gross Margin %	32.48%	27.68%	27.69%
Sales and Marketing Expenses			
Payroll	$23,456	$24,529	$23,871
Ads	$0	$22,674	$7,896
Catalog	$2,200	$3,100	$2,095
Mailing	$1,873	$12,075	$6,621
Promo	$0	$0	$0
Shows	$0	$0	$0
Literature	$0	$0	$6,401
PR	$0	$0	$0
Seminar	$1,000	$0	$0
Service	$0	$3,023	$1,023
Training	$0	$1,000	$500
Total Sales & Marketing Expenses	$28,529	$66,401	$48,407

The illustration shows actual results on the actual worksheet. Note how actual sales, costs, and expenses are different from planned results. This is a portion of the full table.

Profit and Loss Plan vs. Actual

Figure 19-7 shows the variance in expenses. The actual results are subtracted from the budget numbers, leaving negative numbers when the actual spending was more than budget or when the sales or profits were less than budget.

Variances are calculated differently in different portions of the plan.

- In expense rows, variance becomes the **planned amount** minus the <u>actual amount</u>. Lower expenses are a positive variance.

- In the profits and sales areas, variance becomes <u>actual amount</u> minus **planned amount**. In these cases, higher sales are a positive variance.

FIGURE 19-7: PLANNED VS. ACTUAL PROFIT AND LOSS

Pro Forma Profit and Loss	Jan	Feb	Mar
Sales	($45,126)	($84,460)	($69,584)
Direct Cost of Sales	$43,101	$72,770	$67,544
Production Payroll	$192	$276	($259)
Other	$467	($282)	$64
Total Cost of Sales	$43,760	$72,764	$67,349
Gross Margin	($88,886)	($157,224)	($136,933)
Gross Margin %	196.97%	186.15%	196.79%
Sales and Marketing Expenses			
Payroll	$544	($529)	$129
Ads	$5,000	($17,674)	($896)
Catalog	($200)	($100)	($95)
Mailing	$1,127	($275)	($1,121)
Promo	$0	$0	$0
Shows	$0	$0	$0
Literature	$0	$7,000	($6,401)
PR	$0	$0	$0
Seminar	$0	$0	$0
Service	$2,000	($2,023)	($23)
Training	$450	($550)	($50)
Total Sales & Marketing Expenses	$8,921	($14,151)	($8,457)

The illustration shows a portion of the Profit and Loss Variance. March results showed sales below plan and costs above plan, for a large negative variance. Sales and Marketing expenses were also above plan in March, causing another negative variance. This is a portion of the table.

Understanding Variance Analysis

Variance is the frequently-forgotten other half of budgeting. Many businesses, especially the small, entrepreneurial kind, ignore or forget the other half of the budgeting. Budgets are too often proposed, discussed, accepted, and forgotten. Variance analysis looks after-the-fact at what caused a difference between plan vs. actual. Good management looks at what that difference means to the business.

Variance analysis ranges from simple and straightforward to sophisticated and complex. Some cost-accounting systems separate variances into many types and categories. Sometimes a single result can be broken down into many different variances, both positive and negative.

The most sophisticated systems separate unit and price factors on materials, hours worked, cost-per-hour on direct labor, and fixed and variable overhead variances. Though difficult, this kind of analysis can be invaluable in a complex business.

Look for Specifics

This presentation of variances shows how important good analysis is. In theory, the positive variances are good news because they mean spending less than budgeted. The negative variance means spending more than the budget.

Variance Analysis for Sample Company

In our earlier example, the $5,000 variance in advertising in January means $5,000 less than planned was spent, and the $7,000 positive variance for literature in February means $7,000 less than planned was spent. The negative variance for advertising in February and March, and the negative variance for literature in March, show that more was spent than was planned for those items.

Evaluating these variances takes thought. Positive variances aren't always good news. For example, the positive variance of $5,000 in advertising means that money wasn't spent, but it also means that advertising wasn't placed. Systems sales are way below expectations for this same period—could the advertising missed in January be a possible cause? For literature, the positive $7,000 in February may be evidence of a missed deadline for literature that wasn't actually completed until March. If so, at least it appears that the costs on completion were $6,401, a bit less than the $7,000 planned.

Among the larger single variances for an expense item in a month shown on the illustration was the positive $7,000 variance for the new literature expenses in February. Is this good news or bad news?

Every variance should stimulate questions. Why did one project cost more or less? Were objectives met? Is a positive variance a cost saving or a failure to implement? Is a negative variance a change in plans, a management failure, or an unrealistic budget?

A variance table can provide management with significant information. Without this data, some of these important questions might go unasked.

More on Variance

For purposes of example, Figure 19-8 shows the sales table (including costs) in variance mode, for the sales forecast of our hypothetical company. Variance analysis on sales can be very complex. There can be very significant differences between higher or lower sales because of different unit volumes, or because of different average prices.

The units variance shows that the sales of systems were disappointing. In the expenses outlined in Figure 19-7, we see that advertising and mailing costs were below plan. Could there be a correlation between the saved expenses in mailing, and the lower-than-planned sales? Yes, of course there could.

The mailing cost was much less than planned, but as a result the planned sales never came. The positive expense variance is not good for the company.

In systems, the comparison between units variance and sales variance yields no surprises. The lower-than-expected unit sales also had lower-than-expected sales values. Compare that to service, in which lower units yielded higher sales (indicating much higher prices than planned). Is this an indication of a new profit opportunity, or a new trend? This clearly depends on the specifics of your business.

It is often hard to tell what caused differences in costs. If spending schedules aren't met, variance might be caused simply by lower unit volume. Management probably wants to know the results per unit, and the actual price, and the detailed feedback on the marketing programs.

FIGURE 19-8: SALES FORECAST VARIANCE

Unit Sales	Jan	Feb	Mar
Systems	(22)	(41)	(37)
Service	(32)	(29)	(26)
Software	24	35	39
Training	11	16	18
Other	2	(25)	28
Total Unit Sales	(17)	(44)	22
Unit Prices			
Systems	($217)	($199)	($209)
Service	$28	$37	$30
Software	$24	($15)	$77
Training	$11	$4	$7
Other	($9)	$71	($78)
Sales			
Systems	($57,671)	($96,726)	($96,572)
Service	$2,304	$4,326	$3,712
Software	$8,976	$3,475	$30,053
Training	$2,123	$1,244	$1,983
Other	($858)	$3,221	($8,760)
Total Sales	($45,126)	($84,460)	($69,584)
Direct Unit Cost			
Systems	$66	$11	$43
Service	($3)	($5)	$8
Software	$17	$26	$4
Training	$4	($0)	$2
Other	$4	($17)	$13
Direct Cost of Sales			
Systems	$41,555	$70,513	$67,508
Service	$498	$935	$2,912
Software	$55	$1,902	($3,398)
Training	$580	($219)	$141
Other	$413	($361)	$381
Subtotal Direct Cost of Sales	$43,101	$72,770	$67,544

The illustration shows the sales variance, including costs, for the example used in other illustrations in this section.

Measure a Plan by its Implementation

The quality of a business plan is measured, not by the quality of its ideas, its analysis, or presentation, but only by the implementation it causes. It is true, of course, that some business plans are developed only as selling documents to generate financial resources. For these plans, their worth is measured by their effectiveness in selling a business opportunity to a prospective investor. For plans created to help run a business, their worth is measured by how much they help run a business—or, in other words, their implementation.

Summary

Variance analysis is vital to good management. You have to track and follow up on budgets, mainly through variance analysis, or the budgets are useless.

Although variance analysis can be very complex, the main guide is common sense. In general, going under budget is a positive variance, and over budget is a negative variance. But the real test of management should be whether or not the result was good for business.

This page intentionally blank.

Chapter 20:

PRINT AND PUBLISH

So you're about ready to print your plan. Assemble your topics as indicated in the outline in Chapter 2: Pick Your Plan. *Browse through the sample plans and look in the Workbook to get a better sense of the topic sequence. Throughout this book, we have discussed portions of the plan in the order that you work on it, not in the final order it will print.*

Please make sure to run it through a final critical edit. Then make sure to publish it so that commitments made by managers are clearly known and acknowledged. Also make it clear that you will be tracking results, comparing your actual results to the planned results, and discussing the difference.

Publishing = Management

Don't forget the process of publishing within your own company. In this case, publishing means distributing the plan where all the managers can see it.

People who make commitments as part of the plan need to see those commitments on record. They need to know that the plan will be tracked and that the difference between planned and actual results will be calculated and discussed.

Final Edit

Always run a business plan through a final edit. Have you read it over again? Do you have someone who can read it for you? Sometimes you don't see the errors because you are too close to it.

Check the numbers in your charts and tables. Make sure they match each other, and go back and check the references to numbers in the text. For example, your objectives text might set sales objectives of $500,000, but your plan tables show sales projections of $400,000.

Presentation

Presentation is important but only to communicate content. Good charts are dynamite when they make numbers easier to read quickly, and they can be essential when numbers are complex.

Good text formatting should make the text easy to read. Use a legible font and a good mix of section headings and subheadings to make the organization visible. Bullet points are generally easier to read than long paragraphs. Color is good for charts, when it makes numbers easier to understand, but gets in the way when used for text.

Fancy paper, expensive binding, and excessive presentation is not needed. Make the paper whatever quality it takes to make the plan easy to read, avoiding some of the more fibrous papers that end up interfering with the printed content. Make the binding a good coil, or some other binding that will hold up to use, but keep it practical so you impress with content, not expense.

Related Documents

In the process of finding investment financing people normally use a two-to-four-page Summary Memo. It should have the key points, such as competitive edge, market needs, defensibility, and of course track records and resumes of main team members. Focus on real content, not hype, and organize it so that potential investors can understand the main points quickly, then decide whether or not they want to know more.

When looking for loans, you may want to prepare a two-to-four-page document, called a Loan Application. It should include the Executive Summary and company ownership detail as well as financials, such as Profit and Loss and Balance Sheet tables.

Summary

Review your plan from the point of view of the business purpose. Does it cover what you need it to cover? Are there topics the plan's audience will ask about that you haven't covered? Think of the three most important questions you would expect to get from your intended reader. Have you answered them?

FOLLOWING UP

Ultimately, the impact of your plan depends on how you manage and implement it, how it's presented and to whom.

CHAPTER 20:
PRINT AND PUBLISH

CHAPTER 21:
GETTING FINANCED

Chapter 21:

GETTING FINANCED

Contrary to popular belief, business plans do not generate business financing. True, there are many kinds of financing options that require a business plan, but nobody invests in a business plan. Investors need a business plan as a document that communicates ideas and information, but they invest in a company, in a product, and in people.

Correcting Myths About Small Business Financing

Here are some truths to dispel some very common myths:

- Venture capital financing is very rare. I'll explain more later, but assume that very few high-growth plans with high-power management teams are venture opportunities.

- Banks don't finance business start-ups. I'll have more on that later, too. Banks aren't supposed to invest depositors' money in new businesses.

- Business plans don't sell investors.

Where to Look for Money

Where you look for money, and how you look for money, depends on your company and the kind of money you need. There is an enormous difference, for example, between a high-growth high-tech company looking for second-round venture funding and a local retail store looking to finance a branch store. In the following sections of this chapter, I want to talk more specifically about the types of investment and lending available.

Venture Capital

The business of venture capital is often misunderstood. Many start-up companies resent venture capital companies for failing to invest in new ventures or risky ventures. People talk about venture capitalists as sharks—because of their supposedly predatory business practices—or sheep—because they supposedly think like a flock, all wanting the same kinds of deals.

This is not the case. The venture capital business is a business, and the people we call venture capitalists are business people who are charged with investing other people's money. They have a professional responsibility to reduce risk as much as possible. They should not take more risk than is absolutely necessary to produce the risk/return ratios that the sources of their capital ask of them.

Venture capital shouldn't be thought of as a source of funding for any but a very few exceptional start-up businesses. Venture capital can't afford to invest in start-ups unless there is a rare combination of product opportunity, market opportunity, and proven management. A venture capital investment has to have a reasonable chance of producing a tenfold increase in business value within three years. It needs to focus on newer products and markets that can reasonably project increasing sales by huge multiples over a short period of time. It needs to work with proven managers who have dealt with successful start-ups in the past.

If you are a potential venture capital investment, you probably know it already. You have management team members who have been through that already. You can convince yourself and a room full of intelligent people that your company can grow ten times over in three years.

If you have to ask whether your new company is a possible venture capital opportunity, it probably isn't. People in new growth industries, multimedia communications, biotechnology, or the far reaches of high-technology products, generally know about venture capital and venture capital opportunities.

If you are looking for names and addresses of venture capitalists, do a good Web search. Since websites change so often, we don't include specific URLs (website addresses) for specific sites. Use your Internet search capabilities to look for venture capitalists.

The names and addresses of venture capitalists are also available in some annual directories:

The Western Association of Venture Capitalists publishes an annual directory. This organization includes most of the California venture capitalists based in Menlo Park, CA, which is the headquarters for an amazing percentage of the nation's venture capital companies.

Pratt's Guide to Venture Capital Sources is an annual directory available for $625 (at the time of this printing; prices may change) plus shipping. Contact Venture Economics, 40 W. 57th St., 11th Floor, New York, NY 10019, (212) 765-5311.

There may be additional directories available by the time you read this. As always, start with a good Internet search.

"Sort-of" Venture Capital: Angels and Others

Venture capital is not the only source of investment for start-up businesses or small businesses. Many companies are financed by smaller investors in what is called "private placement." For example, in some areas there are groups of potential investors who meet occasionally to hear proposals. There are also wealthy individuals who occasionally invest in new companies. In the lore of business start-ups, groups of investors are often referred to as "doctors and dentists," and individual investors are often called "angels." Many entrepreneurs turn to friends and family for investment.

Your next question, of course, is how to find the "doctors, dentists, and angels" that might want to invest in your business. The discussion in *Chapter 8: The Business You're In* includes some government agencies, business development centers, business incubators, and similar organizations that will be tied into the investment communities in your area. Turn first to the local Small Business Development Center (SBDC), which is most likely associated with your local community college, or the Small Business Administration (SBA) offices in your area. Names and website addresses are also in *Chapter 8*.

You can also find Angel investors with an Internet search. Search for "Angel Investors" in one or more of the more popular Internet searchers and you'll turn up lots of leads. The hard part is sorting through all the various leads to find the good ones.

Important: Be careful dealing with anyone who offers to help you find financing as a service for money. These are shark-infested waters. I am aware of some legitimate providers of business plan consulting, but legitimate providers are harder to find than the sharks.

Commercial Lenders

Banks are even less likely than venture capitalists to invest in, or loan money to, start-up businesses. They are, however, the most likely source of financing for most small businesses.

Start-up entrepreneurs and small business owners are too quick to criticize banks for failing to finance new businesses. Banks are not supposed to invest in businesses, and are strictly limited in this respect by federal banking laws. The government prevents banks from investment in businesses because society, in general, doesn't want banks taking savings from depositors and investing in risky business ventures; obviously when (and if) those business ventures fail, bank depositors' money is at risk. Would you want your bank to invest in new businesses (other than your own, of course)?

Furthermore, banks should not loan money to start-up companies either, for many of the same reasons. Federal regulators want banks to keep money safe, in very conservative loans backed by solid collateral. Start-up businesses are not safe enough for bank regulators and they don't have enough collateral.

Why then do we say that banks are the most likely source of small business financing? Because small business owners borrow from banks. A business that has been around for a few years generates enough stability and assets to serve as collateral. Banks commonly make loans to small businesses backed by the company's inventory or accounts receivable. Normally there are formulas that determine how much can be loaned, depending on how much is in inventory and in accounts receivable.

A great deal of small business financing is accomplished through bank loans based on the business owner's personal collateral, such as home ownership. Some would say that home equity is the greatest source of small business financing.

The Small Business Administration (SBA)

The SBA makes loans to small businesses and even to start-up businesses. SBA loans are almost always applied for and administered by local banks. You normally deal with a local bank throughout the process.

For start-up loans, the SBA will normally require that at least one third of the required capital be supplied by the new business owner. Furthermore, the rest of the amount must be guaranteed by reasonable business or personal assets.

The SBA works with "certified lenders," which are banks. It takes a certified lender as little as one week to get approval from the SBA. If your own bank isn't a certified lender, you should ask your banker to recommend a local bank that is. *Chapter 8: The Business You're In* lists the website and a toll-free telephone number to contact the SBA.

Other Lenders

Aside from standard bank loans, an established small business can also turn to accounts receivable specialists in order to borrow against its accounts receivables.

The most common accounts receivable financing is used to support cash flow when working capital is hung up in accounts receivable. For example, if your business sells to distributors that take 60 days to pay, and the outstanding invoices waiting for payment (but not late) come to $100,000, your company can probably borrow more than $50,000. Interest rates and fees may be relatively high, but this is still often a good source of small business financing. In most cases, the lender doesn't take the risk of payment—if your customer doesn't pay you, you have to pay the money back anyhow. These lenders will often review your debtors, and choose to finance some or all of the invoices outstanding.

Another related business practice is called factoring. So-called factors actually purchase obligations, so if a customer owes you $100,000 you can sell the related paperwork to the factor for some percentage of the total amount. In this case, the factor takes the risk of payment, so discounts are obviously quite steep. Ask your banker for additional information about factoring.

Words of Warning

Don't take private placement, angels, or friends and family as good sources of investment capital just because they are described here or taken seriously in some other source of information. Some investors are a good source of capital, and some aren't. These less established sources of investment should be handled with **extreme caution**.

Never, NEVER spend somebody else's money without first doing the legal work properly. Have the papers done by professionals, and make sure they're signed.

Never, NEVER spend money that has been promised but not delivered. Often companies get investment commitments, will contract for expenses, and then the investment falls through.

Be aware of the risks involved in turning to friends and family for investment. There is no doubt that a significant portion of new businesses turn to friends and family for financial help. Still, taking friends' and family money adds to the risk of a new business, by increasing the penalties of failure. Think of how much worse a business failure might be when you are responsible for losing money of your friends and family. Think also about how many circumstances might cause you to want to give up and close a business, and how that might change when friends and family money is involved. The worst possible time to not have the support of friends and family is when your business is in trouble. You risk losing friends, family, and your business at the same time.

A Business Plan For Lenders

For a plan that is going to be submitted to a bank or other commercial lenders, aim first for a solid business plan describing your business in detail. Use as much past history as you can possibly have available, and make sure to show past financials wherever possible. Banks and other commercial lenders are looking for stability, payment history, and above all, assets pledged as collateral. They expect the business plan to be a good general description of the business.

The SBA wants a business borrower to have a business plan covering the main points described in this book. As a matter of fact, the SBA website links to sample plans including the sample plan at the back of this book, plans developed and archived by the publisher of this book.

Specifics of submitting a plan will vary depending on the lender. Even SBA loans are managed by commercial banks, just guaranteed by the SBA, so specific requirements will be different for each lender.

A Business Plan for Investors

In *Chapter 2: Pick Your Plan*, I said the plan should match the needs of the company. A business plan developed to be shown to investors should by a relatively sophisticated plan, and should include as a matter of course some material that isn't normally necessary for a plan developed for internal planning or for backing up a loan application.

Some of the points that should be included in an investment plan are:

- How much money is planned as investment, for what share in the company.

- Exit strategy showing when investors get money back if all goes according to plan.

- An analysis using discounted cash flow techniques to show projected investor return on investment if the plan is successful.

Submitting a Plan

When you are planning to submit a plan to investors, you should prepare not only a complete plan but also a so-called "Summary Memo." You need to have the plan done before you show the Summary Memo to investors, but, ironically, in many cases they will see only the summary. You should also prepare a one-page cover letter.

The Summary Memo

The summary memo is a document about 5 pages long. It should include paragraphs summarizing the business idea, the backgrounds of the founders, highlights of financial projections, highlights of the potential market, and descriptions of the investment offering and exit strategy. It will be used by investors to decide whether or not they want to see the whole plan.

Formats of summary memos vary. What's important is to make sure that it is clean, easy to read, concise, and contains the required information. Sometimes summary memos are presented as physical documents, sometimes as emails, sometimes as electronic documents.

You should never do a summary memo without a business plan already finished. If the investors like the summary, then they will want to see the entire plan. Make sure you have one ready.

The Cover Letter

The cover letter that goes with a business plan should be one page in most cases, never more than two pages. There are no set formats for cover letters for investment plans, so they generally follow the standards of any other business cover letter. Keep it short, keep the reader interested, be polite, be concise, and look for points that will generate interest in following up.

The Submission Process

There are no set rules for submitting business plans to investors. Sometimes you'll submit a complete business plan, sometimes a Summary Memo. In most cases, even if you submit a short summary, you have to have the complete business plan ready to go as soon as the investors ask for it.

The hardest part of the submission process is finding the right people. Use Internet search, use personal contacts, use local business schools, Small Business Development Centers, old school ties, whatever means you can to find people who might be a good match with your business goals. You won't find investment by mass mailing to long lists of venture capitalists, because professional investors receive too many plans. You need to sort and select potential investors to find a match to your size, business interests, geography, type of business, and so forth.

Ideally, you develop a list through careful searching, and when the search has provided you with a list of useful names, you can print your Summary Memo or loan support documents and send a copy to each of the investors, along with a brief cover letter. In the real world, it is rarely that simple. Ask as many people as you have to in order to find suitable investor prospects.

Providing Information for Investors

Venture capitalists and many other investors look to Net Present Value (NPV) or Internal Rate of Return (IRR) to measure their investment return. If you are developing a business plan for use with investors then you need to know and understand these measurements.

They both start with the concept of the time value of money. What would you choose if you could have $95 today or $100 a year from today? What if you could have $10 today or $100 a year from now? Most people would take the $95 today in the first instance, and the $100 a year from now in the second. This would be regardless of inflation. It illustrates the time value of money, meaning that money now is inherently more valuable than money later.

Net Present Value (NPV)

The Net Present Value (NPV) is a measure of the present value of future cash. To calculate NPV you discount future money at some assumed discount rate. In the following Figure 21-1 you can see two sample investments, both with the same NPV, although very different cash flows. Both are discounted at 10% for calculating NPV.

FIGURE 21-1: NET PRESENT VALUE COMPARISON

NPV / IRR Analysis	2005	2006	2007	2008	2009	2010
Investor Cash Flow 1	($2,000)	$0	$0	$0	$0	$4,578
NPV Discount Rate	10%					
NPV at that rate	$766					
IRR	18.01%					
Investor Cash Flow 2	($2,000)	$750	$750	$750	$750	$750
NPV Discount Rate	10%					
NPV at that rate	$766					
IRR	25.41%					

Both of the investments have NPV of $766, even though one pays regular annual payments of $750, and the other pays nothing until a large payment at the end. Notice how the time value of money changes. The total payout of the first investment is more than that of the second, but because the second's payout starts sooner, they both have equal NPV.

For more background on how the discounting calculation can be done manually, you should consult a finance textbook or search the Web for the term "Net Present Value."

Internal Rate of Return (IRR)

The Internal Rate of Return (IRR) is based on the NPV calculation. It is the discount rate at which the NPV is zero. Notice in Figure 21-2 how the selected cell's formula uses the built-in IRR function to calculate IRR for the first investment option.

FIGURE 21-2: INTERNAL RATE OF RETURN CALCULATION

	B	C	D	E	F	G	H
	C8		fx	=IRR(C5:H5,C6)			
		C	D	E	F	G	H
4	NPV / IRR Analysis	2005	2006	2007	2008	2009	2010
5	Investor Cash Flow 1	($2,000)	$0	$0	$0	$0	$4,578
6	NPV Discount Rate	10%					
7	NPV at that rate	$766					
8	IRR	18.01%					
9							
10	Investor Cash Flow 2	($2,000)	$750	$750	$750	$750	$750
11	NPV Discount Rate	10%					
12	NPV at that rate	$766					
13	IRR	25.41%					

One important point with IRR, as the two investments show, is that although they have equal NPV, they can have very different IRR. That's because the better one generates cash flow sooner.

Another important IRR point is that venture capitalists expect very high IRR on new investments. In recent years venture capital funds have generated overall IRR of 50-100% or better, meaning that the winning deals have to generate IRR of 200% or better. That's a very high return.

Investment Analysis

A business plan for investors should include an investment analysis that lays out the details of investment, valuation, and return on investment. Usually investors want to see either NPV or IRR or both, plus valuation assumptions. Figure 21-3 shows an example.

FIGURE 21-3: SAMPLE INVESTMENT ANALYSIS

	A	N	O	AD	AE	AF	AG
	AG6	=AG21*percent_equity_acquired					
	A	N	O	AD	AE	AF	AG
1	Investment Analysis						
2		Start	2005	2006	2007	2008	2009
3	Initial Investment						
4	Investment	$500,000	$0	$0	$0	$0	$0
5	Dividends	$0	$0	$0	$0	$0	$0
6	Ending Valuation	$0	$0	$0	$0	$0	$3,717,000
7	Combination as Income Stream	($500,000)	$0	$0	$0	$0	$3,717,000
8	Percent Equity Acquired	45%					
9	Net Present Value (NPV)	$1,643,604					
10	Internal Rate of Return (IRR)	49%					
11							
12	Assumptions						
13	Discount Rate	10.00%					
14	Valuation Earnings Multiple		10	10	10	10	10
15	Valuation Sales Multiple		2	2	2	2	2
16							
17	Investment (calculated)	$200,000	$500,000	$250,000	$300,000	$0	$0
18	Dividends		$0	$0	$0	$0	$0
19	Calculated Earnings-based Valuation		$100,000	$50,000	$1,840,000	$3,170,000	$4,190,000
20	Calculated Sales-based Valuation		$3,180,000	$5,720,000	$8,580,000	$10,720,000	$12,330,000
21	Calculated Average Valuation		$1,640,000	$2,885,000	$5,210,000	$6,945,000	$8,260,000

The illustration, taken from Business Plan Pro®, shows an investment analysis presented as part of a business plan.

The investor analysis in the example shows potential investors their potential return on a $500,000 investment. It spells out assumptionsincluding the Calculated Average Valuation at $8,260,000 (in cell AG21 in the illustration), which is the average of 10 times projected earnings (the assumed multiple is in row 14 and the result in row 19), and 2 times projected sales (rows 15 and 20) for 2009, which is five years after the proposed investment. The offer is 45% ownership in the company (cell N8 in the illustration) for $500,000 (cell N4). The amount of money to be received by investors at the end, which is shown in the cell highlighted in the illustration, is $3,717,000. The formula for that very important calculation is shown in the edit bar in the illustration. It multiplies the percent of ownership by the estimated ending valuation.

In this example, investors are supposed to receive $3.7 million five years after investing $500,000. As shown in the illustration, that is an NPV of $1.6 million and an IRR of 49%.

In the real world all of these values are the subject of negotiation. Investors rarely if ever accept the entrepreneurs' assumptions for future sales, valuation, investment amount, or percent of ownership. They do, however, expect the entrepreneurs seeking investment to calculate return on investment and to show their assumptions clearly as they suggest possible returns.

The sample shown here is just one example. The world of investing and start-up businesses doesn't have a set format for presenting this type of information. What's most important is to make sure that the information is available to investors as part of the plan.

The Investment Offering

Investors also want to know how you plan to distribute stock ownership and handle dilution. This is especially important when a start-up needs multiple rounds of financing, but even with a more simple investment plan, the investors want to know what you plan to do with shares. How many shares of stock are there, how many do the founders already own, how many are pledged to employees, and how many will be offered to future investors?

Figure 21-4 shows a sample investment offering, taken from Business Plan Pro®. It shows the investors the plan for stock ownership and dilution through three rounds of investment.

For the investment offering there is no generally accepted single format. What's important is showing investors the details they'll need to evaluate a new business investment opportunity. Most of these details are shown in the table:

- The investment amount proposed, for each of three rounds of financing.

- The equity share offered for each round of financing. The first round investors get 45% of the company, for $500,000, in the example shown in Figure 21-4. Second-round investors get 8% and third-round investors get only 4%.

- The proposed valuation at the end of the investment—the exit—and the timing of the planned exit. In this example the plan assumes the company will have a public offering in 2009, when it will be valued at $8,260,000.

- The expected return on investment for each round of investment. For example, in this sample case if all goes as planned, the first-round investors end up with $2.7 million on a $500,000 investment, after five years. That is an IRR of 40.71%. It is less than the 49% IRR shown in Figure 21-3 because of dilution of additional rounds of investors (see below).

- The numbers of shares owned by founders, and proposed options shares for employees, and shares planned for three different rounds of financing.

- Ownership percentages. For example, in the illustration, the first-round investors own 45% of the company immediately after their investment, but only 33.39% after the third round. This effect is called "dilution" because ownership is diluted as more shares are issued. The founders in this example start with 100% of the company but, as investors join the company, they end up with only 37.1% ownership. This is just one example, but it isn't unusual. Notice that the dilution changes the return on investment of a $500,000 investment for 45% of the company. The difference between return in Figure 21-3 and return shown in Figure 21-4 is caused by the further dilution of ownership through additional rounds of funding.

If you are developing a plan for investors, show them the investment offering, but don't expect them to accept your numbers. Investors will normally use this portion of the plan as a starting point for negotiations. They will question the ownership percentages, the valuation assumptions, and amounts required.

FIGURE 21-4: INVESTMENT OFFERING

Investment Offering Proposed Year:	Seed 2004	Round 1 2005	Round 2 2006	Exit 2009
Valuation, Investment, Shares				
Investment Amount	$500,000	$250,000	$300,000	
Equity Share Offering Percentage	45.00%	8.00%	4.00%	
Valuation	$1,111,111	$3,125,000	$7,500,000	$8,260,000
Investor Exit Payout	$2,758,330	$586,312	$318,141	
Investor Years Until Exit	5	4	3	
Investor IRR	40.71%	23.75%	1.98%	
Share Ownership	**2004**	**2005**	**2006**	**2009**
Founders' Shares	1,000,000	1,000,000	1,000,000	2,000,000
Stock Split Multiple		0	0	2
Stock Options Issued	100,000	200,000	100,000	200,000
Investor Shares Issued	900,000	191,304	103,804	
Price per share	$0.56	$1.31	$2.89	$1.53
Options Holders' Shares	100,000	300,000	400,000	1,000,000
2004 Investors' Shares	900,000	900,000	900,000	1,800,000
2005 Investors' Shares		191,304	191,304	382,609
2006 Investors' Shares			103,804	207,609
Total Shares Outstanding	2,000,000	2,391,304	2,595,109	5,390,217
Equity Ownership Percent	**2004**	**2005**	**2006**	**2009**
Founders' Equity	50.00%	41.82%	38.53%	37.10%
Option Holders' Equity	5.00%	12.55%	15.41%	18.55%
2004 Investors' Equity	45.00%	37.64%	34.68%	33.39%
2005 Investors' Equity		8.00%	7.37%	7.10%
2006 Investors' Equity			4.00%	3.85%
Total Equity	100.00%	100.00%	100.00%	100.00%
Investors' Equity	45.00%	45.64%	46.05%	44.34%
Founders' & Employees' Equity	55.00%	54.36%	53.95%	55.66%

The investment offering shows potential investors the plan for stock ownership including percentage ownership, valuation, dilution, and appreciation.

The Exit Strategy

An exit strategy is a plan for selling ownership in the company. One common exit strategy, for example, is to build the company to be acquired by a larger company sometime in the future. Another is to plan on a public stock offering (IPO). Holding stock in a company isn't interesting to normal investors, what they want is to be able to sell that stock for money. Ultimately, there is no investor return without an exit that turns stock holdings into money.

While not all businesses have exit strategies, and not all business plans include them, when a business plan includes looking for outside investors then it should include an exit strategy. Investors want to see prospective returns.

Summary

Most businesses are financed by home equity or savings as they start. Only a few can attract outside investment. Venture capital deals are extremely rare. Borrowing will always depend on collateral and guarantees, not on business plans or ideas.

SAMPLE PLAN: Acme Consulting

This sample business plan has been made available to users of Business Plan Pro®, business planning software published by Palo Alto Software. Names, locations and numbers may have been changed, and substantial portions of the original plan text may have been omitted to preserve confidentiality and protect proprietary information.

You are welcome to use this plan as a starting point to create your own, but you do not have permission to reproduce, publish, distribute or even copy this plan as it exists here.

Requests for reprints, academic use, and other dissemination of this sample plan should be emailed to the marketing department of Palo Alto Software at marketing@paloalto.com. For product information visit our Website: www.paloalto.com or call: 1-800-229-7526.

Acme Consulting
Table of Contents

1.0 Executive Summary

Acme Consulting will be formed as a consulting company specializing in marketing of high-technology products in international markets. Its founders are former marketers of consulting services, personal computers, and market research, all in international markets. They are founding Acme to formalize the consulting services they offer.

Business Plan Highlights

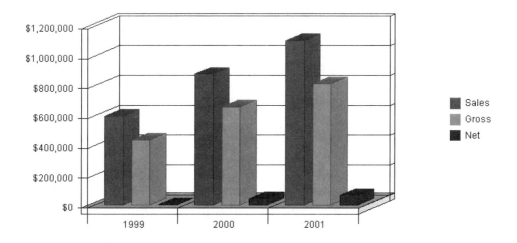

1.1 Objectives

1. Sales of over $1 million by 2001.

2. Gross margin higher than 80%.

3. Net income more than 10% of sales by the third year.

1.2 Mission

Acme Consulting offers high-tech manufacturers a reliable, high-quality alternative to in-house resources for business development, market development, and channel development on an international scale. A true alternative to in-house resources offers a very high level of practical experience, know-how, contacts, and confidentiality. Clients must know that working with Acme is a more professional, less risky way to develop new areas even than working completely in-house with their own people. Acme must also be able to maintain financial balance, charging a high value for its services, and delivering an even higher value to its clients. Initial focus will be development in the European and Latin American markets, or for European clients in the United States market.

1.3 Keys to Success

1. Excellence in fulfilling the promise—completely confidential, reliable, trustworthy expertise and information.

2. Developing visibility to generate new business leads.

3. Leveraging from a single pool of expertise into multiple revenue generation opportunities: retainer consulting, project consulting, market research, and market research published reports.

2.0 Company Summary

Acme Consulting is a new company providing high-level expertise in international high-tech business development, channel development, distribution strategies, and marketing of high-tech products. It will focus initially on providing two kinds of international triangles:

· Providing United States clients with development for European and Latin American markets.

· Providing European clients with development for the United States and Latin American markets.

As it grows it will take on people and consulting work in related markets, such as the rest of Latin America, the Far East, and similar markets. It will also look for additional leverage by taking brokerage positions and representation positions to create percentage holdings in product results.

2.1 Company Ownership

Acme Consulting will be created as a California C corporation based in Santa Clara County, owned by its principal investors and principal operators. As of this writing, it has not been chartered yet and is still considering alternatives of legal formation.

2.2 Start-up Summary

Total start-up expense (including legal costs, logo design, stationery and related expenses) come to $18,350. Start-up assets required include $3,000 in short-term assets (office furniture, etc.) and $50,000 in initial cash to handle the first few months of consulting operations as sales and accounts receivable play through the cash flow. The details are included in the following table:

Start-up Plan	
Start-up Expenses	
Legal	$1,000
Stationery etc.	$3,000
Brochures	$5,000
Consultants	$5,000
Insurance	$350
Expensed equipment	$3,000
Other	$1,000
Total Start-up Expense	$18,350
Start-up Assets Needed	
Cash Requirements	$25,000
Other Short-term Assets	$7,000
Total Short-term Assets	$32,000
Long-term Assets	$0
Total Assets	$32,000
Total Start-up Requirements:	$50,350
Left to finance:	$0
Start-up Funding Plan	
Investment	
Investor 1	$20,000
Investor 2	$20,000
Other	$10,000
Total investment	$50,000
Short-term Liabilities	
Unpaid Expenses	$350
Short-term Loans	$0
Interest-free Short-term Loans	$0
Subtotal Short-term Liabilities	$350
Long-term Liabilities	$0
Total Liabilities	$350
Loss at Start-up	($18,350)
Total Capital	$31,650
Total Capital and Liabilities	$32,000
Checkline	$0

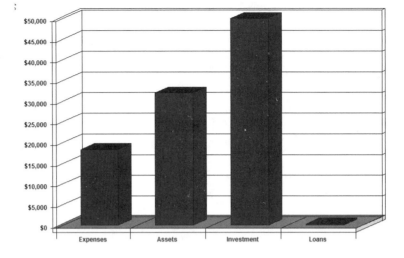

Start-up Financing

2.3 Company Services

Acme offers expertise in channel distribution/development, and market development, sold and packaged in various ways that allow clients to choose their preferred relationship: these include retainer consulting relationships, project-based consulting, relationship and alliance brokering, sales representation and market representation, project-based market research, published market research, and information forums.

2.4 Company Locations and Facilities

The initial office will be established in a quality office space in the Santa Clara County "Silicon Valley" area of California, the heart of the U.S. high tech industry.

3.0 Services

Acme offers the expertise a high-technology company needs to develop new product distribution and new market segments in new markets. This can be taken as high-level retainer consulting, market research reports, or project-based consulting.

3.1 Service Description

1. Retainer consulting: We represent a client company as an extension of its business development and market development functions. This begins with complete understanding of the client company's situation, objectives, and constraints. We then represent the client company quietly and confidentially, sifting through new market developments and new opportunities as is appropriate to the client, representing the client in initial talks with possible allies, vendors, and channels.

2. Project consulting: Proposed and billed on a per-project and per-milestone basis, project consulting offers a client company a way to harness our specific qualities and use our expertise to solve specific problems, develop and/or implement plans, and develop specific information.

3. Market research: Group studies available to selected clients at $5,000 per unit. A group study is a packaged and published complete study of a specific market, channel, or topic. Examples might be studies of developing consumer channels in Japan or Mexico, or implications of changing margins in software.

3.2 Competitive Comparison

The competition comes in several forms:

1. The most significant competition is no consulting at all, companies choosing to do business development, channel development and market research in-house. Their own managers do this on their own, as part of their regular business functions. Our key advantage in competition with in-house development is that managers are already overloaded with responsibilities, they don't have time for additional responsibilities in new market development or new channel development. Also, Acme can approach alliances, vendors, and channels on a confidential basis, gathering information and making initial contacts in ways that the corporate managers can't.

2. The high-level prestige management consulting: McKinsey, Bain, Arthur Anderson, Boston Consulting Group, etc. These are essentially generalists who take their name-brand management consulting into specialty areas. Their other very important weakness is the management structure that has the partners selling new jobs, and inexperienced associates delivering the work. We compete against them as experts in our specific fields, and with the guarantee that our clients will have the top-level people doing the actual work.

3. The third general kind of competitor is the international market research company: International Data Corporation (IDC), Dataquest, Stanford Research Institute, etc. These companies are formidable competitors for published market research and market forums, but cannot provide the kind of high-level consulting that Acme will provide.

4. The fourth kind of competition is the market-specific smaller house. For example: Nomura Research in Japan, Select S.A. de C.V. in Mexico (now affiliated with IDC).

5. Sales representation, brokering, and deal catalysts are an ad-hoc business form that will be defined in detail by the specific nature of each individual case.

3.3 Sales Literature

The business will begin with a general corporate brochure establishing the positioning. This brochure will be developed as part of the start-up expenses.

Literature and mailings for the initial market forums will be very important.

3.4 Fulfillment

1. The key fulfillment and delivery will be provided by the principals of the business. The real core value is professional expertise, provided by a combination of experience, hard work, and education (in that order).

2. We will turn to qualified professionals for freelance backup in market research and presentation and report development, which are areas that we can afford to subcontract without risking the core values provided to the clients.

3.5 Technology

Acme Consulting will maintain the latest Windows and Macintosh capabilities including:

1. Complete e-mail facilities on the Internet, Compuserve, America-Online, and Applelink, for working with clients directly through e-mail delivery of drafts and information.

2. Complete presentation facilities for preparation and delivery of multimedia presentations on Macintosh or Windows machines, in formats including on-disk presentation, live presentation, or video presentation.

3. Complete desktop publishing facilities for delivery of regular retainer reports, project output reports, marketing materials, and market research reports.

3.6 Future Services

In the future, Acme will broaden the coverage by expanding into coverage of additional markets (e.g., all of Latin America, Far East, Western Europe) and additional product areas (e.g., telecommunications and technology integration).

We are also studying the possibility of newsletter or electronic newsletter services, or perhaps special on-topic reports.

4.0 Market Analysis Summary

Acme will be focusing on high-technology manufacturers of computer hardware and software, services, and networking, who want to sell into markets in the United States, Europe, and Latin America. These are mostly larger companies, and occasionally medium-sized companies.

Our most important group of potential customers are executives in larger corporations. These are marketing managers, general managers, sales managers, sometimes charged with international focus and sometimes charged with market or even specific channel focus. They do not want to waste their time or risk their money looking for bargain information or questionable expertise. As they go into markets looking at new opportunities, they are very sensitive to risking their company's name and reputation.

4.1 Market Segmentation

Large manufacturer corporations: Our most important market segment is the large manufacturer of high-technology products, such as Apple, Hewlett-Packard, IBM, Microsoft, Siemens, or Olivetti. These companies will be calling on Acme for development functions that are better spun off than managed in-house, for market research, and for market forums.

Medium-sized growth companies: particularly in software, multimedia, and some related high-growth fields, Acme will offer an attractive development alternative to the company that is management constrained and unable to address opportunities in new markets and new market segments.

Market Analysis

Potential Customers	Growth	1999	2000	2001	2002	2003	CAGR
U.S. High Tech	10%	5,000	5,500	6,050	6,655	7,321	10.00%
European High Tech	15%	1,000	1,150	1,323	1,521	1,749	15.00%
Latin America	35%	250	338	456	616	832	35.07%
Other	2%	10,000	10,200	10,404	10,612	10,824	2.00%
Total	6.27%	16,250	17,188	18,233	19,404	20,726	6.27%

Potential Market by Segment

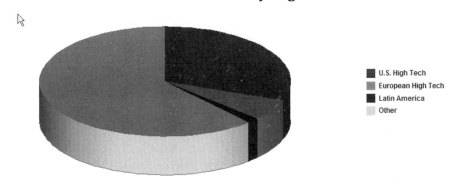

- U.S. High Tech
- European High Tech
- Latin America
- Other

4.2 Target Market Segment Strategy

As indicated by the previous table and illustration, we must focus on a few thousand well-chosen potential customers in the United States, Europe, and Latin America. These few thousand high-tech manufacturing companies are the key customers for Acme.

4.3 Service Business Analysis

The consulting "industry" is pulverized and disorganized, with thousands of smaller consulting organizations and individual consultants for every one of the few dozen well-known companies.

Consulting participants range from major international name-brand consultants to tens of thousands of individuals. One of Acme's challenges will be establishing itself as a real consulting company, positioned as a relatively risk-free corporate purchase.

4.3.1 Business Participants

At the highest level are the few well-established major names in management consulting. Most of these are organized as partnerships established in major markets around the world, linked together by interconnecting directors and sharing the name and corporate wisdom. Some evolved from accounting companies (e.g. Arthur Andersen, Touche Ross) and some from management consulting (McKinsey, Bain). These companies charge very high rates for consulting, and maintain relatively high overhead structures and fulfillment structures based on partners selling and junior associates fulfilling.

At the intermediate level are some function-specific or market-specific consultants, such as the market research firms (IDC, Dataquest) or channel development firms (ChannelCorp, Channel Strategies, ChannelMark).

Some kinds of consulting are little more than contract expertise provided by somebody who, while temporarily out of work, offers consulting services.

4.3.2 Distributing a Service

Consulting is sold and purchased mainly on a word-of-mouth basis, with relationships and previous experience being, by far, the most important factor.

The major name-brand houses have locations in major cities and major markets, and executive-level managers or partners develop new business through industry associations, business associations, chambers of commerce and industry, etc., and in some cases social associations such as country clubs.

The medium-level houses are generally area specific or function specific, and are not easily able to leverage their business through distribution.

4.3.3 Competition and Buying Patterns

The key element in purchase decisions made at the Acme client level is trust in the professional reputation and reliability of the consulting firm.

4.3.4 Main Competitors

1. The high-level prestige management consulting:

    Strengths: International locations managed by owner-partners with a high level of presentation and understanding of general business. Enviable reputations which make purchase of consulting an easy decision for a manager, despite the very high prices.

    Weaknesses: General business knowledge doesn't substitute for the specific market, channel, and distribution expertise of Acme, focusing on high-technology markets and products only. Also, fees are extremely expensive, and work is generally done by very junior-level consultants, even though sold by high-level partners.

2. The international market research company:

   Strengths: International offices, specific market knowledge, permanent staff developing market research information on permanent basis, good relationships with potential client companies.

   Weaknesses: Market numbers are not marketing, not channel development nor market development. Although these companies compete for some of the business Acme is after, they cannot really offer the same level of business understanding at a high level.

3. Market specific or function specific experts:

   Strengths: Expertise in market or functional areas. Acme should not try to compete with Nomura or Select in their markets with market research, or with ChannelCorp in channel management.

   Weaknesses: The inability to spread beyond a specific focus, or to rise above a specific focus, to provide actual management expertise, experience, and wisdom beyond the specifics.

4. The most significant competition is no consulting at all, companies choosing to do business development, channel development, and market research in-house.

   Strengths: No incremental cost except travel; also, the general work is done by the people who are entirely responsible, the planning is done by those who will implement it.

   Weaknesses: Most managers are terribly overburdened already, unable to find incremental resources in time and people to apply to incremental opportunities. Also, there is a lot of additional risk in market and channel development done in-house from the ground up. Finally, retainer-based antenna consultants can greatly enhance a company's reach and extend its position into conversations that might otherwise never have taken place.

5.0 Strategy and Implementation Summary

Acme will focus on three geographical markets, the United States, Europe, and Latin America, and in limited product segments: personal computers, software, networks, telecommunications, personal organizers, and technology integration products.

The target customer is usually a manager in a larger corporation, and occasionally an owner or president of a medium-sized corporation in a high-growth period.

5.1 Pricing Strategy

Acme Consulting will be priced at the upper edge of what the market will bear, competing with the name-brand consultants. The pricing fits with the general positioning of Acme as providing high-level expertise.

Consulting should be based on $5,000 per day for project consulting, $2,000 per day for market research, and $10,000 per month and up for retainer consulting. Market research reports should be priced at $5,000 per report, which will, of course, require that reports be very well planned, focused on very important topics, and very well presented.

5.2 Sales Forecast

The sales forecast monthly summary is included in the appendix. The annual sales projections are included here.

Sales Forecast

Sales	1999	2000	2001
Retainer Consulting	$200,000	$350,000	$425,000
Project Consulting	$270,000	$325,000	$350,000
Market Research	$122,000	$150,000	$200,000
Strategic Reports	$0	$50,000	$125,000
Other	$0	$0	$0
Total Sales	$592,000	$875,000	$1,100,000

Direct Cost of sales	1999	2000	2001
Retainer Consulting	$30,000	$38,000	$48,000
Project Consulting	$45,000	$56,000	$70,000
Market Research	$84,000	$105,000	$131,000
Strategic Reports	$0	$20,000	$40,000
Other	$0	$0	$0
Subtotal Cost of Sales	$159,000	$219,000	$289,000

5.3 Strategic Alliances

At this writing, strategic alliances with Smith and Jones are possibilities, given the content of existing discussions. Given the background of prospective partners, we might also be talking to European companies including Siemens, Olivetti, and others, and to United States companies related to Apple Computer. In Latin America we would be looking at the key local high-technology vendors, beginning with Printaform.

6.0 Management Summary

The initial management team depends on the founders themselves, with little backup. As we grow, we will take on additional consulting help, plus graphic/editorial, sales, and marketing.

6.1 Organizational Structure

Acme should be managed by working partners, in a structure taken mainly from Smith Partners. In the beginning we assume 3-5 partners:

·   Ralph Sampson.

·   At least one, probably two, partners from Smith and Jones.

·   One strong European partner, based in Paris.

      The organization has to be very flat in the beginning, with each of the founders responsible for his or her own work and management.

·   One other strong partner.

6.2 Management Team

The Acme business requires a very high level of international experience and expertise, which means that it will not be easily leveragable in the common consulting company mode in which partners run the business and make sales, while associates fulfill. Partners will necessarily be involved in the fulfillment of the core business proposition, providing the expertise to the clients. The initial personnel plan is still tentative. It should involve 3-5 partners, 1-3 consultants, one strong editorial/graphic person with good staff support, one strong marketing person, an office manager, and a secretary. Later, we add more partners, consultants, and sales staff. Founders' resumes are included as an attachment to this plan.

6.3 Personnel Plan

The detailed monthly personnel plan for the first year is included in the appendix. The annual personnel estimates are included here.

Personnel Plan

	1999	2000	2001
Partners	$144,000	$175,000	$200,000
Consultants	$0	$50,000	$63,000
Editorial/graphic	$18,000	$22,000	$26,000
VP Marketing	$20,000	$50,000	$55,000
Sales people	$0	$30,000	$33,000
Office Manager	$7,500	$30,000	$33,000
Secretarial	$5,250	$20,000	$22,000
Other	$0	$0	$0
Other	$0	$0	$0
Total Payroll	$194,750	$377,000	$432,000
Total Headcount	0	0	0
Payroll Burden	$27,265	$52,780	$60,480
Total Payroll Expenditures	$222,015	$429,780	$492,480

7.0 Financial Plan

7.1 Important Assumptions

The following table summarizes key financial assumptions, including 45-day average collection days, sales entirely on invoice basis, expenses mainly on net 30 basis, 35 days on average for payment of invoices, and present-day interest rates.

General Assumptions

	1999	2000	2001
Short-term Interest Rate %	8.00%	8.00%	8.00%
Long-term Interest Rate %	10.00%	10.00%	10.00%
Payment Days Estimator	35	35	35
Collection Days Estimator	45	45	45
Tax Rate %	25.00%	25.00%	25.00%
Expenses in Cash %	25.00%	25.00%	25.00%
Sales on Credit %	100.00%	100.00%	100.00%
Personnel Burden %	14.00%	14.00%	14.00%

7.2 Key Financial Indicators

The following benchmark chart indicates our key financial indicators for the first three years. We foresee major growth in sales and operating expenses, and a bump in our collection days as we spread the business during expansion.

Benchmark Comparison

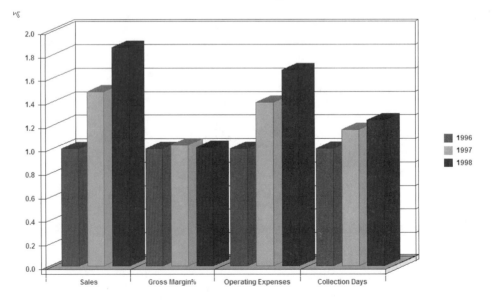

7.3 Break-even Analysis

This table and chart summarizes the break-even analysis, including monthly units and sales break-even points.

Break-even Analysis:
Monthly Units Break-even	12,500
Monthly Sales Break-even	$12,500

Assumptions:
Average Per-Unit Revenue	$1.00
Average Per-Unit Variable Cost	$0.20
Estimated Monthly Fixed Cost	$10,000

Break-even Analysis

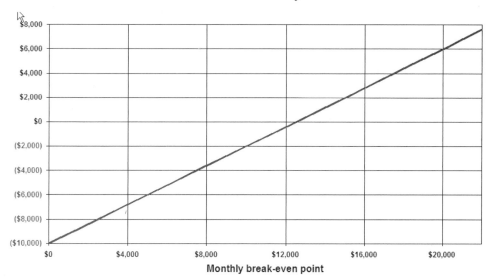

Monthly break-even point

7.4 Projected Profit and Loss

The detailed monthly pro forma income statement for the first year is included in the appendix. The annual estimates are included here.

Profit and Loss (Income Statement)

	1999	2000	2001
Sales	$592,000	$875,000	$1,100,000
Direct Cost of Sales	$159,000	$219,000	$289,000
Other	$0	$0	$0
Total Cost of Sales	$159,000	$219,000	$289,000
Gross Margin	$433,000	$656,000	$811,000
Gross Margin %	73.14%	74.97%	73.73%
Operating expenses:			
Advertising/Promotion	$36,000	$40,000	$44,000
Public Relations	$30,000	$30,000	$33,000
Travel	$90,000	$60,000	$110,000
Miscellaneous	$6,000	$7,000	$8,000
Travel	$0	$0	$0
Miscellaneous	$0	$0	$0
Payroll Expense	$194,750	$377,000	$432,000
Payroll Burden	$27,265	$52,780	$60,480
Depreciation	$0	$0	$0
Leased Equipment	$6,000	$7,000	$7,000
Utilities	$12,000	$12,000	$12,000
Insurance	$3,600	$2,000	$2,000
Rent	$18,000	$0	$0
Other	$0	$0	$0
Contract/Consultants	$0	$0	$0
Total Operating Expenses	$423,615	$587,780	$708,480
Profit Before Interest and Taxes	$9,385	$68,220	$102,520
Interest Expense Short-term	$3,600	$8,800	$12,800
Interest Expense Long-term	$5,000	$5,000	$5,000
Taxes Incurred	$196	$13,605	$21,180
Net Profit	$589	$40,815	$63,540
Net Profit/Sales	0.10%	4.66%	5.78%

7.5 Projected Cash Flow

Cash flow projections are critical to our success. The monthly cash flow is shown in the illustration, with one bar representing the cash flow per month and the other representing the monthly balance. The annual cash flow figures are included here. Detailed monthly numbers are included in the appendix.

Pro-Forma Cash Flow

	1999	2000	2001
Net Profit	$589	$40,815	$63,540
Plus:			
Depreciation	$0	$0	$0
Change in Accounts Payable	$25,896	$1,405	$10,967
Current Borrowing (repayment)	$60,000	$100,000	$0
Increase (decrease) Other Liabilities	$0	$0	$0
Long-term Borrowing (repayment)	$50,000	$0	$0
Capital Input	$0	$0	$0
Subtotal	$136,485	$142,220	$74,507
Less:			
Change in Accounts Receivable	$100,000	$47,804	$38,007
Change in Other ST Assets	$0	$0	$0
Capital Expenditure	$0	$0	$0
Dividends	$0	$0	$0
Subtotal	$100,000	$47,804	$38,007
Net Cash Flow	$36,485	$94,416	$36,500
Cash Balance	$61,485	$155,901	$192,401

Cash Analysis

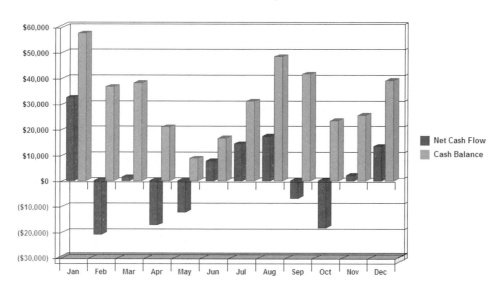

Page 15

7.6 Projected Balance Sheet

The balance sheet shows healthy growth of net worth, and strong financial position. The monthly estimates are included in the appendix.

Pro forma Balance Sheet

Assets

	Starting Balances	1999	2000	2001
Short-term Assets				
Cash	$25,000	$61,485	$155,901	$192,401
Accounts Receivable	$0	$100,000	$147,804	$185,811
Other Short-term Assets	$7,000	$7,000	$7,000	$7,000
Total Short-term Assets	$32,000	$168,485	$310,705	$385,212
Long-term Assets				
Capital Assets	$0	$0	$0	$0
Accumulated Depreciation	$0	$0	$0	$0
Total Long-term Assets	$0	$0	$0	$0
Total Assets	$32,000	$168,485	$310,705	$385,212

Liabilities and Capital

		1999	2000	2001
Accounts Payable	$5,000	$30,896	$32,301	$43,268
Short-term Notes	$0	$60,000	$160,000	$160,000
Other Short-term Liabilities	$0	$0	$0	$0
Subtotal Short-term Liabilities	$5,000	$90,896	$192,301	$203,268
Long-term Liabilities	$0	$50,000	$50,000	$50,000
Total Liabilities	$5,000	$140,896	$242,301	$253,268
Paid in Capital	$50,000	$50,000	$50,000	$50,000
Retained Earnings	($23,000)	($23,000)	($22,411)	$18,404
Earnings	$0	$589	$40,815	$63,540
Total Capital	$27,000	$27,589	$68,404	$131,944
Total Liabilities and Capital	$32,000	$168,485	$310,705	$385,212
Net Worth	$27,000	$27,589	$68,404	$131,944

SP1.18

7.7 Business Ratios

The following table shows the projected business ratios. We expect to maintain healthy ratios for profitability, risk, and return.

Ratio Analysis

Profitability Ratios:	**1999**	**2000**	**2001**
Gross Margin	73.14%	74.97%	73.73%
Net Profit Margin	0.10%	4.66%	5.78%
Return on Assets	0.35%	13.14%	16.49%
Return on Equity	2.13%	59.67%	48.16%

Activity Ratios	**1999**	**2000**	**2001**
AR Turnover	5.92	5.92	5.92
Collection Days	31	52	55
Inventory Turnover	0.00	0.00	0.00
Accts Payable Turnover	8.75	8.75	8.75
Total Asset Turnover	3.51	2.82	2.86

Debt Ratios	**1999**	**2000**	**2001**
Debt to Net Worth	5.11	3.54	1.92
Short-term Liab. to Liab.	0.65	0.79	0.80

Liquidity Ratios	**1999**	**2000**	**2001**
Current Ratio	1.85	1.62	1.90
Quick Ratio	1.85	1.62	1.90
Net Working Capital	$77,589	$118,404	$181,944
Interest Coverage	1.09	4.94	5.76

Additional Ratios	**1999**	**2000**	**2001**
Assets to Sales	0.28	0.36	0.35
Debt/Assets	84%	78%	66%
Current Debt/Total Assets	54%	62%	53%
Acid Test	0.75	0.85	0.98
Asset Turnover	3.51	2.82	2.86
Sales/Net Worth	21.46	12.79	8.34

This page intentionally blank.

Pro Forma Balance Sheet

Assets

	Starting Balances	Jan	Feb	Mar	Apr	May	Jun	Jul	Aug	Sep	Oct	Nov	Dec
Short-term Assets													
Cash	$25,000	$56,928	$36,767	$31,994	$37,163	$40,812	$35,086	$50,572	$71,398	$64,176	$43,072	$43,674	$61,485
Accounts Receivable	$0	$10,000	$14,795	$29,589	$44,000	$75,000	$104,000	$87,500	$60,000	$87,500	$120,000	$132,500	$100,000
Other ST Assets	$7,000	$7,000	$7,000	$7,000	$7,000	$7,000	$7,000	$7,000	$7,000	$7,000	$7,000	$7,000	$7,000
Total ST Assets	$32,000	$73,928	$58,561	$68,583	$88,163	$122,812	$146,086	$145,072	$138,398	$158,676	$170,072	$183,174	$168,485
Long-term Assets													
Capital Assets	$0	$0	$0	$0	$0	$0	$0	$0	$0	$0	$0	$0	$0
Accum. Depreciation	$0	$0	$0	$0	$0	$0	$0	$0	$0	$0	$0	$0	$0
Total LT Assets	$0	$0	$0	$0	$0	$0	$0	$0	$0	$0	$0	$0	$0
Total Assets	$32,000	$73,928	$58,561	$68,583	$88,163	$122,812	$146,086	$145,072	$138,398	$158,676	$170,072	$183,174	$168,485

Liabilities and Capital

	Starting Balances	Jan	Feb	Mar	Apr	May	Jun	Jul	Aug	Sep	Oct	Nov	Dec
Accounts Payable	$5,000	$14,475	$16,656	$17,951	$21,403	$26,149	$30,896	$24,855	$21,403	$33,053	$35,211	$36,074	$30,896
ST Notes	$0	$0	$0	$20,000	$40,000	$60,000	$60,000	$60,000	$60,000	$60,000	$60,000	$60,000	$60,000
Other ST Liabilities	$0	$0	$0	$0	$0	$0	$0	$0	$0	$0	$0	$0	$0
Subtotal ST Liabilities	$5,000	$14,475	$16,656	$37,951	$61,403	$86,149	$90,896	$84,855	$81,403	$93,053	$95,211	$96,074	$90,896
LT Liabilities	$0	$50,000	$50,000	$50,000	$50,000	$50,000	$50,000	$50,000	$50,000	$50,000	$50,000	$50,000	$50,000
Total Liabilities	$5,000	$64,475	$66,656	$87,951	$111,403	$136,149	$140,896	$134,855	$131,403	$143,053	$145,211	$146,074	$140,896
Paid in Capital	$50,000	$50,000	$50,000	$50,000	$50,000	$50,000	$50,000	$50,000	$50,000	$50,000	$50,000	$50,000	$50,000
Retained Earnings	($23,000)	($23,000)	($23,000)	($23,000)	($23,000)	($23,000)	($23,000)	($23,000)	($23,000)	($23,000)	($23,000)	($23,000)	($23,000)
Earnings	$0	($17,548)	($35,095)	($46,368)	($50,240)	($40,338)	($21,810)	($16,783)	($20,005)	($11,378)	($2,139)	$10,100	$589
Total Capital	$27,000	$9,453	($8,095)	($19,368)	($23,240)	($13,338)	$5,190	$10,218	$6,995	$15,623	$24,861	$37,100	$27,589
Total Liab. & Capital	$32,000	$73,928	$58,561	$68,583	$88,163	$122,812	$146,086	$145,072	$138,398	$158,676	$170,072	$183,174	$168,485
Net Worth	$27,000	$9,453	($8,095)	($19,368)	($23,240)	($13,338)	$5,190	$10,218	$6,995	$15,623	$24,861	$37,100	$27,589

Pro Forma Cash Flow

	Jan	Feb	Mar	Apr	May	Jun	Jul	Aug	Sep	Oct	Nov	Dec
Net Profit	($17,548)	($17,548)	($11,273)	($3,873)	$9,903	$18,528	$5,028	($3,223)	$8,628	$9,239	$12,239	($9,511)
Plus:												
Depreciation	$0	$0	$0	$0	$0	$0	$0	$0	$0	$0	$0	$0
Change in Accounts Payable	$9,475	$2,181	$1,295	$3,452	$4,747	$4,747	($6,041)	($3,452)	$11,651	$2,158	$863	($5,178)
Current Borrowing (repayment)	$0	$0	$20,000	$20,000	$20,000	$0	$0	$0	$0	$0	$0	$0
Increase (decrease) Other Liab.	$0	$0	$0	$0	$0	$0	$0	$0	$0	$0	$0	$0
LT Borrowing (repayment)	$50,000	$0	$0	$0	$0	$0	$0	$0	$0	$0	$0	$0
Capital Input	$0	$0	$0	$0	$0	$0	$0	$0	$0	$0	$0	$0
Subtotal	$41,928	($15,366)	$10,022	$19,580	$34,649	$23,274	($1,014)	($6,675)	$20,278	$11,396	$13,102	($14,689)
Less:												
Change in Accounts Receivable	$10,000	$4,795	$14,795	$14,411	$31,000	$29,000	($16,500)	($27,500)	$27,500	$32,500	$12,500	($32,500)
Change in Other ST Assets	$0	$0	$0	$0	$0	$0	$0	$0	$0	$0	$0	$0
Capital Expenditure	$0	$0	$0	$0	$0	$0	$0	$0	$0	$0	$0	$0
Dividends	$0	$0	$0	$0	$0	$0	$0	$0	$0	$0	$0	$0
Subtotal	$10,000	$4,795	$14,795	$14,411	$31,000	$29,000	($16,500)	($27,500)	$27,500	$32,500	$12,500	($32,500)
Net Cash Flow	$31,928	($20,161)	($4,773)	$5,169	$3,649	($5,726)	$15,486	$20,825	($7,222)	($21,104)	$602	$17,811
Cash Balance	$56,928	$36,767	$31,994	$37,163	$40,812	$35,086	$50,572	$71,398	$64,176	$43,072	$43,674	$61,485

General Assumptions

	Jan	Feb	Mar	Apr	May	Jun	Jul	Aug	Sep	Oct	Nov	Dec
Short-term Interest Rate %	8.00%	8.00%	8.00%	8.00%	8.00%	8.00%	8.00%	8.00%	8.00%	8.00%	8.00%	8.00%
Long-term Interest Rate %	10.00%	10.00%	10.00%	10.00%	10.00%	10.00%	10.00%	10.00%	10.00%	10.00%	10.00%	10.00%
Payment Days Estimator	35	35	35	35	35	35	35	35	35	35	35	35
Collection Days Estimator	45	45	45	45	45	45	45	45	45	45	45	45
Tax Rate %	25.00%	25.00%	25.00%	25.00%	25.00%	25.00%	25.00%	25.00%	25.00%	25.00%	25.00%	25.00%
Expenses in Cash %	25.00%	25.00%	25.00%	25.00%	25.00%	25.00%	25.00%	25.00%	25.00%	25.00%	25.00%	25.00%
Sales on Credit %	100.00%	100.00%	100.00%	100.00%	100.00%	100.00%	100.00%	100.00%	100.00%	100.00%	100.00%	100.00%
Personnel Burden %	14.00%	14.00%	14.00%	14.00%	14.00%	14.00%	14.00%	14.00%	14.00%	14.00%	14.00%	14.00%

Personnel Plan

	Jan	Feb	Mar	Apr	May	Jun	Jul	Aug	Sep	Oct	Nov	Dec
Partners	$12,000	$12,000	$12,000	$12,000	$12,000	$12,000	$12,000	$12,000	$12,000	$12,000	$12,000	$12,000
Consultants	$0	$0	$0	$0	$0	$0	$0	$0	$0	$0	$0	$0
Editorial/graphic	$0	$0	$0	$0	$0	$0	$0	$0	$0	$6,000	$6,000	$6,000
VP Marketing	$0	$0	$0	$0	$0	$0	$0	$0	$5,000	$5,000	$5,000	$5,000
Sales people	$0	$0	$0	$0	$0	$0	$0	$0	$0	$0	$0	$0
Office Manager	$0	$0	$0	$0	$0	$0	$0	$0	$0	$2,500	$2,500	$2,500
Secretarial	$0	$0	$0	$0	$0	$0	$0	$0	$0	$1,750	$1,750	$1,750
Other	$0	$0	$0	$0	$0	$0	$0	$0	$0	$0	$0	$0
Other	$0	$0	$0	$0	$0	$0	$0	$0	$0	$0	$0	$0
Total Payroll	$12,000	$12,000	$12,000	$12,000	$12,000	$12,000	$12,000	$12,000	$17,000	$27,250	$27,250	$27,250
Total Headcount	0	0	0	0	0	0	0	0	0	0	0	0
Payroll Burden	$1,680	$1,680	$1,680	$1,680	$1,680	$1,680	$1,680	$1,680	$2,380	$3,815	$3,815	$3,815
Total Payroll Expenditures	$13,680	$13,680	$13,680	$13,680	$13,680	$13,680	$13,680	$13,680	$19,380	$31,065	$31,065	$31,065

Profit and Loss (Income Statement)

	Jan	Feb	Mar	Apr	May	Jun	Jul	Aug	Sep	Oct	Nov	Dec
Sales	$10,000	$10,000	$20,000	$34,000	$58,000	$75,000	$50,000	$35,000	$70,000	$85,000	$90,000	$55,000
Direct Cost of Sales	$2,500	$2,500	$4,000	$8,000	$13,500	$19,000	$12,000	$8,000	$21,500	$24,000	$25,000	$19,000
Other	$0	$0	$0	$0	$0	$0	$0	$0	$0	$0	$0	$0
Total Cost of Sales	$2,500	$2,500	$4,000	$8,000	$13,500	$19,000	$12,000	$8,000	$21,500	$24,000	$25,000	$19,000
Gross Margin	$7,500	$7,500	$16,000	$26,000	$44,500	$56,000	$38,000	$27,000	$48,500	$61,000	$65,000	$36,000
Gross Margin %	75.00%	75.00%	80.00%	76.47%	76.72%	74.67%	76.00%	77.14%	69.29%	71.76%	72.22%	65.45%
Operating expenses:												
Advertising/Promotion	$3,000	$3,000	$3,000	$3,000	$3,000	$3,000	$3,000	$3,000	$3,000	$3,000	$3,000	$3,000
Public Relations	$2,500	$2,500	$2,500	$2,500	$2,500	$2,500	$2,500	$2,500	$2,500	$2,500	$2,500	$2,500
Travel	$7,500	$7,500	$7,500	$7,500	$7,500	$7,500	$7,500	$7,500	$7,500	$7,500	$7,500	$7,500
Miscellaneous	$500	$500	$500	$500	$500	$500	$500	$500	$500	$500	$500	$500
Travel	$0	$0	$0	$0	$0	$0	$0	$0	$0	$0	$0	$0
Miscellaneous	$0	$0	$0	$0	$0	$0	$0	$0	$0	$0	$0	$0
Payroll Expense	$12,000	$12,000	$12,000	$12,000	$12,000	$12,000	$12,000	$12,000	$17,000	$27,250	$27,250	$27,250
Payroll Burden	$1,680	$1,680	$1,680	$1,680	$1,680	$1,680	$1,680	$1,680	$2,380	$3,815	$3,815	$3,815
Depreciation	$0	$0	$0	$0	$0	$0	$0	$0	$0	$0	$0	$0
Leased Equipment	$500	$500	$500	$500	$500	$500	$500	$500	$500	$500	$500	$500
Utilities	$1,000	$1,000	$1,000	$1,000	$1,000	$1,000	$1,000	$1,000	$1,000	$1,000	$1,000	$1,000
Insurance	$300	$300	$300	$300	$300	$300	$300	$300	$300	$300	$300	$300
Rent	$1,500	$1,500	$1,500	$1,500	$1,500	$1,500	$1,500	$1,500	$1,500	$1,500	$1,500	$1,500
Other	$0	$0	$0	$0	$0	$0	$0	$0	$0	$0	$0	$0
Contract/Consultants	$0	$0	$0	$0	$0	$0	$0	$0	$0	$0	$0	$0
Total Operating Expenses	$30,480	$30,480	$30,480	$30,480	$30,480	$30,480	$30,480	$30,480	$36,180	$47,865	$47,865	$47,865
Profit Before Int. & Taxes	($22,980)	($22,980)	($14,480)	($4,480)	$14,020	$25,520	$7,520	($3,480)	$12,320	$13,135	$17,135	($11,865)
Interest Expense ST	$0	$0	$133	$267	$400	$400	$400	$400	$400	$400	$400	$400
Interest Expense LT	$417	$417	$417	$417	$417	$417	$417	$417	$417	$417	$417	$417
Taxes Incurred	($5,849)	($5,849)	($3,758)	($1,291)	$3,301	$6,176	$1,676	($1,074)	$2,876	$3,080	$4,080	($3,170)
Net Profit	($17,548)	($17,548)	($11,273)	($3,873)	$9,903	$18,528	$5,028	($3,223)	$8,628	$9,239	$12,239	($9,511)
Net Profit/Sales	-175.48%	-175.48%	-56.36%	-11.39%	17.07%	24.70%	10.06%	-9.21%	12.33%	10.87%	13.60%	-17.29%

Sales Forecast

Sales	Jan	Feb	Mar	Apr	May	Jun	Jul	Aug	Sep	Oct	Nov	Dec
Retainer Consulting	$10,000	$10,000	$10,000	$10,000	$20,000	$20,000	$20,000	$20,000	$20,000	$20,000	$20,000	$20,000
Project Consulting	$0	$0	$10,000	$20,000	$30,000	$40,000	$20,000	$10,000	$30,000	$45,000	$50,000	$15,000
Market Research	$0	$0	$0	$4,000	$8,000	$15,000	$10,000	$5,000	$20,000	$20,000	$20,000	$20,000
Strategic Reports	$0	$0	$0	$0	$0	$0	$0	$0	$0	$0	$0	$0
Other	$0	$0	$0	$0	$0	$0	$0	$0	$0	$0	$0	$0
Total Sales	$10,000	$10,000	$20,000	$34,000	$58,000	$75,000	$50,000	$35,000	$70,000	$85,000	$90,000	$55,000

Direct Cost of sales

	Jan	Feb	Mar	Apr	May	Jun	Jul	Aug	Sep	Oct	Nov	Dec
Retainer Consulting	$2,500	$2,500	$2,500	$2,500	$2,500	$2,500	$2,500	$2,500	$2,500	$2,500	$2,500	$2,500
Project Consulting	$0	$0	$1,500	$3,500	$5,000	$6,500	$3,500	$1,500	$5,000	$7,500	$8,500	$2,500
Market Research	$0	$0	$0	$2,000	$6,000	$10,000	$6,000	$4,000	$14,000	$14,000	$14,000	$14,000
Strategic Reports	$0	$0	$0	$0	$0	$0	$0	$0	$0	$0	$0	$0
Other	$0	$0	$0	$0	$0	$0	$0	$0	$0	$0	$0	$0
Subtotal Cost of Sales	$2,500	$2,500	$4,000	$8,000	$13,500	$19,000	$12,000	$8,000	$21,500	$24,000	$25,000	$19,000

SAMPLE PLAN: AMT, Inc.

This sample business plan has been made available to users of Business Plan Pro®, business planning software published by Palo Alto Software. Names, locations and numbers may have been changed, and substantial portions of the original plan text may have been omitted to preserve confidentiality and protect proprietary information.

You are welcome to use this plan as a starting point to create your own, but you do not have permission to reproduce, publish, distribute or even copy this plan as it exists here.

Requests for reprints, academic use, and other dissemination of this sample plan should be emailed to the marketing department of Palo Alto Software at marketing@paloalto.com. For product information visit our Website: www.paloalto.com or call: 1-800-229-7526.

American Management Technologies (AMT), Inc.
Table of Contents

1.0 Executive Summary

By focusing on its strengths, its key customers, and the underlying values they need, American Management Technology, Inc. (AMT, Inc.) will increase sales to approximately $9 million in three years, while also improving the gross margin on sales and cash management and working capital.

This business plan leads the way. It renews our vision and strategic focus: adding value to our target market segments, the small business and high-end home office users, in our local market. It also provides the step-by-step plan for improving our sales, gross margin, and profitability.

This plan includes this summary, and chapters on the company, products and services, market focus, action plans and forecasts, management team, and financial plan.

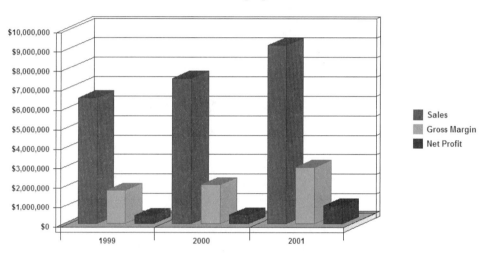

Business Plan Highlights

1.1 Objectives

1. Sales increasing to approximately $9 million by the third year.

2. Bring gross margin back up to above 30%, and maintain that level.

3. Sell $2 million of service, support, and training by 2001.

4. Improve inventory turnover to 6 turns next year, 7 in 2000, and 8 in 2001.

1.2 Mission

AMT is built on the assumption that the management of information technology for business is like legal advice, accounting, graphic arts, and other bodies of knowledge, in that it is not inherently a do-it-yourself prospect. Smart business people who aren't computer hobbyists need to find quality vendors of reliable hardware, software, service, and support. They need to use these quality vendors as they use their other professional service suppliers, as trusted allies. AMT is such a vendor. It serves its clients as a trusted ally, providing them with the loyalty of a business partner and the economics of an outside vendor. We make sure that our clients have what they need to run their businesses as well as possible, with maximum efficiency and reliability. Many of our information applications are mission critical, so we give our clients the assurance that we will be there when they need us.

1.3 Keys to Success

1. Differentiate from box-pushing, price-oriented businesses by offering and delivering service and support — and charging for it.

2. Increase gross margin to more than 25%.

3. Increase our non-hardware sales to 20% of the total sales by the third year.

2.0 Company Summary

AMT is a computer reseller based in the Uptown area. It was founded as a consulting-oriented VAR, became a reseller to fill the market need for personal computers, and is emphasizing service and support to differentiate itself from more price oriented national chains.

2.1 Company Ownership

AMT is a privately-held C corporation owned in majority by its founder and president, Ralph Jones. There are six part owners, including four investors and two past employees. The largest of these (in percent of ownership) are Frank Dudley, our attorney, and Paul Karots, our public relations consultant. Neither owns more than 15%, but both are active participants in management decisions.

2.2 Company History

AMT has been caught in the vise grip of margin squeezes that have affected computer resellers worldwide. Although the chart titled Past Financial Performance shows that we have had healthy growth in sales, it also shows declining gross margin and declining profits. The more detailed numbers in the following table include other indicators of some concern:

The gross margin % has been declining steadily, as we see in the chart. Inventory turnover is getting steadily worse. All of these concerns are part of the general trend affecting computer resellers. The margin squeeze is happening throughout the computer industry worldwide.

Past Performance

	1996	1997	1998
Sales	$3,773,889	$4,661,902	$5,301,059
Gross Margin	$1,189,495	$1,269,261	$1,127,568
Gross % (calculated)	31.52%	27.23%	21.27%
Operating Expenses	$752,083	$902,500	$1,052,917
Collection period (days)	48	52	65
Inventory turnover	7	6	5

Balance Sheet

Short-term Assets

	1998
Cash	$55,432
Accounts receivable	$395,107
Inventory	$251,012
Other Short-term Assets	$25,000
Total Short-term Assets	$726,551
Long-term Assets	
Capital Assets	$350,000
Accumulated Depreciation	$50,000
Total Long-term Assets	$300,000
Total Assets	$1,026,551

Capital and Liabilities

	1998
Accounts Payable	$223,897
Short-term Notes	$90,000
Other ST Liabilities	$15,000
Subtotal Short-term Liabilities	$328,897
Long-term Liabilities	$284,862
Total Liabilities	$613,759
Paid in Capital	$500,000
Retained Earnings	($161,860)
Earnings	$74,652
Total Capital	$412,792
Total Capital and Liabilities	$1,026,551

Other Inputs	1998
Payment days	30
Sales on credit	$3,445,688
Receivables turnover	8.72

SP2.5

Past Financial Performance

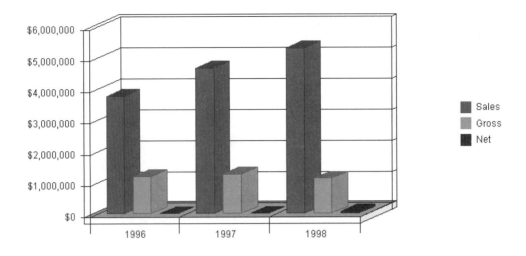

2.3 Company Locations and Facilities

We have one location—a 7,000 square foot store in a suburban shopping center located conveniently close to the downtown area. It includes a training area, service department, offices, and showroom area.

3.0 Products and Services

AMT provides both computer products and services to make them useful to small business. We are especially focused on providing network systems and services to small and medium business. The systems include both PC-based LAN systems and minicomputer server-based systems. Our services include design and installation of network systems, training, and support.

3.1 Product and Service Description

In personal computers, we support three main lines:

1. The Super Home is our smallest and least expensive line, initially positioned by its manufacturer as a home computer. We use it mainly as a cheap workstation for small business installations. Its specifications include ...[additional specifics omitted].

2. The Power User is our main upscale line. It is our most important system for high-end home and small business main workstations, because of .... Its key strengths are .... Its specifications include ....[additional specifics omitted].

3. The Business Special is an intermediate system, used to fill the gap in the positioning. Its specifications include ... [additional specifics omitted].

In peripherals, accessories and other hardware, we carry a complete line of necessary items from cables to forms to mousepads ... [additional specifics omitted].

In service and support, we offer a range of walk-in or depot service, maintenance contracts and on-site guarantees. We have not had much success selling service contracts. Our networking capabilities ...[additional specifics omitted].

In software, we sell a complete line of ... [additional specifics omitted].

In training, we offer ... [additional specifics omitted].

3.2 Competitive Comparison

The only way we can hope to differentiate well is to define the vision of the company to be an information technology ally to our clients. We will not be able to compete in any effective way with the chains using boxes or products as appliances. We need to offer a real alliance.

The benefits we sell include many intangibles: confidence, reliability, knowing that somebody will be there to answer questions and help at the important times.

These are complex products, products that require serious knowledge and experience to use, and our competitors sell only the products themselves.

Unfortunately, we cannot sell the products at a higher price just because we offer services; the market has shown that it will not support that concept. We have to also sell the service and charge for it separately.

3.3 Sales Literature

Copies of our brochure and advertisements are attached as appendices. Of course, one of our first tasks will be to change the message of our literature to make sure we are selling the company, rather than the product.

3.4 Sourcing

Our costs are part of the margin squeeze. As competition on price increases, the squeeze between manufacturers' price into channels and end-users' ultimate buying price continues.

With the hardware lines, our margins are declining steadily. We generally buy at ... Our margins are thus being squeezed from the 25% of five years ago to more like 13-15% at present. In the mainline peripherals a similar trend shows, with prices for printers and monitors declining steadily. We are also starting to see that same trend with software ....

In order to hold costs down as much as possible, we concentrate our purchasing with Hauser, which offers 30-day net terms and overnight shipping from the warehouse in Dayton. We need to concentrate on making sure our volume gives us negotiating strength.

In accessories and add-ons we can still get decent margins, 25% to 40%.

For software, margins are ...

3.5 Technology

We have for years supported both Windows and Macintosh technology for CPUs, although we've switched vendors many times for the Windows (and previously DOS) lines. We are also supporting Novell, Banyon, and Microsoft networking, Xbase database software, and Claris application products.

3.6 Service and Support

Our strategy hinges on providing excellent service and support. This is critical. We need to differentiate on service and support, and to therefore deliver as well.

1. Training: details would be essential in a real business plan, but not in this sample plan.

2. Upgrade offers: details would be essential in a real business plan, but not in this sample plan.

3. Our own internal training: details would be essential in a real business plan, but not in this sample plan.

4. Installation services: details would be essential in a real business plan, but not in this sample plan.

5. Custom software services: details would be essential in a real business plan, but not in this sample plan.

6. Network configuration services: details would be essential in a real business plan, but not in this sample plan.

3.7 Future Products and Services

We must remain on top of the new technologies, because this is our bread and butter. For networking, we need to provide better knowledge of cross platform technologies. Also, we are under pressure to improve our understanding of direct-connect Internet and related communications. Finally, although we have a good command of desktop publishing, we are concerned about getting better at the integration of technologies that creates fax, copier, printer, and voice mail as part of the computer system.

4.0 Market Analysis Summary

AMT focuses on local markets, small business and home office, with special focus on the high-end home office and the 5-20 unit small business office.

4.1 Market Segmentation

The segmentation allows some room for estimates and nonspecific definitions. We focus on a small-medium level of small business, and it is hard to find information to make an exact classification. Our target companies are large enough to need the high-quality information technology management we offer, but too small to have a separate computer management staff such as an MIS department. We say that our target market has 10-50 employees, and needs 5-20 workstations tied together in a local area network; the definition is flexible.

Defining the high-end home office is even more difficult. We generally know the characteristics of our target market, but we can't find easy classifications that fit into available demographics. The high-end home office business is a business, not a hobby. It generates enough money to merit the owner's paying real attention to the quality of information technology management, meaning that there is both budget and concerns that warrant working with our level of quality service and support. We can assume that we aren't talking about home offices used only part-time by people who work elsewhere during the day, and that our target market home office wants to have powerful technology and a lot of links between computing, telecommunications, and video.

Market Analysis

Potential Customers	Growth	1999	2000	2001	2002	2003	CAGR
Consumer	2%	12,000	12,240	12,485	12,735	12,990	2.00%
Small Business	5%	15,000	15,750	16,538	17,365	18,233	5.00%
Large Business	8%	33,000	35,640	38,491	41,570	44,896	8.00%
Government	-2%	36,000	35,280	34,574	33,883	33,205	-2.00%
Other	0%	19,000	19,000	19,000	19,000	19,000	0.00%
Total	2.78%	115,000	117,910	121,088	124,553	128,324	2.78%

Potential Market by Segment

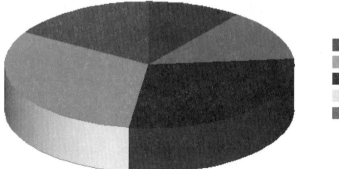

Consumer
Small Business
Large Business
Government
Other

4.2 Target Market Segment Strategy

We are part of the computer reselling business, which includes several kinds of businesses:

1. Computer dealers: storefront computer resellers, usually less than 5,000 square feet, often focused on a few main brands of hardware, usually offering only a minimum of software, and variable amounts of service and support. These are usually old-fashioned (1980s-style) computer stores and they usually offer relatively few reasons for buyers to shop with them. Their service and support is not usually very good and their prices are usually higher than the larger stores.

2. Chain stores and computer superstores: these include major chains such as CompUSA, Computer City, Future Shop, etc. They are almost always more than 10,000 square feet of space, usually offer decent walk-in service, and are often warehouse-like locations where people go to find products in boxes with very aggressive pricing, and little support.

3. Mail order: the market is served increasingly by mail order businesses that offer aggressive pricing of boxed product. For the purely price-driven buyer, who buys boxes and expects no service, these are very good options.

4. Others: there are many other channels through which people buy their computers, usually variations of the main three types above.

4.2.1 Market Needs

Since our target market is the service seeker, the most important market needs are support, service, training, and installation, in that order. One of the key points of our strategy is the focus on target segments that know and understand these needs and are willing to pay to have them filled.

All personal computer users need support and service. The self reliant ones, however, supply those needs themselves. In home offices, these are the knowledgeable computer users who like to do it themselves. Among the businesses, these are businesses that have people on staff.

4.2.2 Market Trends

The most obvious and important trend in the market is declining prices. This has been true for years, but the trend seems to be accelerating. We see the major brand-name manufacturers putting systems together with amazing specs—more power, more speed, more memory, more disk storage—at amazing prices. The major chain shops are selling brand-name powerful computers for less than $1,000.

This may be related to a second trend, which is the computer as throw-away appliance. By the time a system needs upgrading, it is cheaper to buy completely new. The increasing power and storage of a sub-$1000 system means buyers are asking for less service.

A third trend is ever greater connectivity. Everybody wants onto the Internet, and every small office wants a LAN. A lot of small offices want their LAN connected to the Internet.

4.2.3 Market Growth

As prices fall, unit sales increase. The published market research on sales of personal computers is astounding, as the United States market alone is absorbing more than 30 million units per year, and sales are growing at more than 20 percent per year. We could quote Dataquest, Infocorp, IDC, or others; it doesn't matter, they all agree on high growth of CPU sales.

Where growth is not as obvious is the retail market. A report in CRW says Dell is now selling $5 million monthly over the Web, and we assume Gateway and Micron are both close to that. Direct mail has given way to the Web, but catalogs are still powerful, and the non-retail sale is more accepted every day. The last study we saw published has retail sales growing at 5% per year, while Web sales and direct sales are growing at 25% or 30%.

4.3 Industry Analysis

We are part of the computer reselling business, which includes several kinds of businesses:

1. Computer dealers: storefront computer resellers, usually less than 5,000 square feet, often focused on a few main brands of hardware, usually offering only a minimum of software, and variable amounts of service and support. These are usually old-fashioned (1980s-style) computer stores and they usually offer relatively few reasons for buyers to shop with them. Their service and support is not usually very good and their prices are usually higher than the larger stores.

2. Chain stores and computer superstores: these include major chains such as CompUSA, Computer City, Future Shop, etc. They are almost always more than 10,000 square feet of space, usually offer decent walk-in service, and are often warehouse-like locations where people go to find products in boxes with very aggressive pricing, and little support.

3. Mail order: the market is served increasingly by mail order businesses that offer aggressive pricing of boxed product. For the purely price-driven buyer, who buys boxes and expects no service, these are very good options.

4. Others: there are many other channels through which people buy their computers, usually variations of the main three types above.

4.3.1 Industry Participants

1. The national chains are a growing presence. CompUSA, Computer City, Incredible Universe, Babbages, Egghead, and others. They benefit from national advertising, economies of scale, volume buying, and a general trend toward name-brand loyalty for buying in the channels as well as for products.

2. Local computer stores are threatened. These tend to be small businesses, owned by people who started them because they liked computers. They are undercapitalized and under-managed. Margins are squeezed as they compete against the chains, in a competition based on price more than on service and support.

4.3.2 Distribution Patterns

Small Business target buyers are accustomed to buying from vendors who visit their offices. They expect the copy machine vendors, office products vendors, and office furniture vendors, as well as the local graphic artists, freelance writers, or whomever, to visit their office to make their sales.

There is usually a lot of leakage in ad-hoc purchasing through local chain stores and mail order. Often the administrators try to discourage this, but are only partially successful.

Unfortunately our Home Office target buyers may not expect to buy from us. Many of them turn immediately to the superstores (office equipment, office supplies, and electronics) and mail order to look for the best price, without realizing that there is a better option for them at only a little bit more.

4.3.3 Competition and Buying Patterns

The Small Business buyers understand the concept of service and support, and are much more likely to pay for it when the offering is clearly stated.

There is no doubt that we compete much more against all the box pushers than against other service providers. We need to effectively compete against the idea that businesses should buy computers as plug-in appliances that don't need ongoing service, support, and training.

Our focus group sessions indicated that our target Home Offices think about price but would buy based on quality service if the offering were properly presented. They think about price because that's all they ever see. We have very good indications that many would rather pay 10-20% more for a relationship with a long-term vendor providing backup and quality service and support; they end up in the box-pusher channels because they aren't aware of the alternatives.

Availability is also very important. The Home Office buyers tend to want immediate, local solutions to problems.

4.3.4 Main Competitors

Chain stores:

We have Store 1 and Store 2 already within the valley, and Store 3 is expected by the end of next year. If our strategy works, we will have differentiated ourselves sufficiently to not have to compete against these stores.

Strengths: national image, high volume, aggressive pricing, economies of scale.

Weaknesses: lack of product, service and support knowledge, lack of personal attention.

Other local computer stores:

Store 4 and Store 5 are both in the downtown area. They are both competing against the chains in an attempt to match prices. When asked, the owners will complain that margins are squeezed by the chains and customers buy on price only. They say they tried offering services and that buyers didn't care, instead preferring lower prices. We think the problem is also that they didn't really offer good service, and also that they didn't differentiate from the chains.

5.0 Strategy and Implementation Summary

The home offices in Tintown are an important growing market segment. Nationally, there are approximately 30 million home offices, and the number is growing at 10% per year. Our estimate in this plan for the home offices in our market service area is based on an analysis published four months ago in the local newspaper.

Home offices include several types. The most important, for our plan's focus, are the home offices that are the only offices of real businesses, from which people make their primary living. These are likely to be professional services such as graphic artists, writers, and consultants, some accountants and the occasional lawyer, doctor, or dentist. There are also part-time home offices with people who are employed during the day but work at home at night, people who work at home to provide themselves with a part-time income, or people who maintain home offices relating to their hobbies; we will not be focusing on this segment.

Small business within our market includes virtually any business with a retail, office, professional, or industrial location outside of someone's home, and fewer than 30 employees. We estimate 45,000 such businesses in our market area.

The 30-employee cutoff is arbitrary. We find that the larger companies turn to other vendors, but we can sell to departments of larger companies, and we shouldn't be giving up leads when we get them.

5.1 Strategy Pyramids

For placing emphasis on service and support, our main tactics are networking expertise, excellent training, and developing our own proprietary software/network administrative system. Our specific programs for networking include mailers and internal training. Specific programs for training include direct mail promotion, and train-the-trainers programs. For developing our own proprietary systems, our programs are company direct mail marketing, and working with VARs.

Our second strategy is emphasizing relationships. The tactics are marketing the company (instead of the products), more regular contacts with the customer, and increasing sales per customer. Programs for marketing the company include new sales literature, revised ad strategy, and direct mail. Programs for more regular contacts include callbacks after installation, direct mail, and sales management. Programs for increasing sales per customer include upgrade mailings and sales training.

5.2 Value Proposition

Our value proposition has to be different from the standard box-oriented retail chain. We offer our target customer, who is service seeking and not self reliant, a vendor who acts as a strategic ally, at a premium price that reflects the value of reassurance that systems will work.

5.3 Competitive Edge

Our competitive edge is our positioning as a strategic ally with our clients, who are clients more than customers. By building a business based on long-standing relationships with satisfied clients, we simultaneously build defenses against competition. The longer the relationship stands, the more we help our clients understand what we offer them and why they need it.

5.4 Marketing Strategy

The marketing strategy is the core of the main strategy:

1. Emphasize service and support.

2. Build a relationship business.

3. Focus on small business and high-end home office as key target markets.

5.4.1 Positioning Statements

For businesspeople who want to be sure their computer systems are always working reliably, AMT is a vendor and trusted strategic ally who makes sure their systems work, their people are trained, and their down time is minimal. Unlike the chain retail stores, it knows the customer and goes to his or her site when needed, and offers proactive support, service, training, and installation.

5.4.2 Pricing Strategy

We must charge appropriately for the high-end, high-quality service and support we offer. Our revenue structure has to match our cost structure, so the salaries we pay to assure good service and support must be balanced by the revenue we charge.

We cannot build the service and support revenue into the price of products. The market can't bear the higher prices and the buyer feels ill-used when they see the same product priced lower at the chains. Despite the logic behind this, the market doesn't support this concept.

Therefore, we must make sure that we deliver and charge for service and support. Training, service, installation, networking support—all of this must be readily available and priced to sell and deliver revenue.

5.4.3 Promotion Strategy

We depend on newspaper advertising as our main way to reach new buyers. As we change strategies, however, we need to change the way we promote ourselves:

1. Advertising

   We'll be developing our core positioning message: "24 Hour On-Site Service - 365 Days a Year With No Extra Charges" to differentiate our service from the competition. We will be using local newspaper advertising, radio, and cable TV to launch the initial campaign.

2. Sales Brochure

   Our collaterals have to sell the store, and visiting the store, not the specific book or discount pricing.

3. Direct Mail

   We must radically improve our direct mail efforts, reaching our established customers with training, support services, upgrades, and seminars.

4. Local Media

It's time to work more closely with the local media. We could offer the local radio a regular talk show on technology for small business, as one example.

5.4.4 Distribution Strategy

Our most important marketing program is [specifics omitted]. [Name] will be responsible, with budget of $XX,XXX and milestone date of [date]. This program is intended to [objectives omitted]. Achievement should be measured by [specific concrete measurement].

Another key marketing program is [specifics omitted]. [Name] will be responsible, with budget of $XX,XXX and milestone date of [date]. This program is intended to [objectives omitted]. Achievement should be measured by [specific concrete measurement].

5.5 Sales Strategy

1. We need to sell the company, not the product. We sell AMT, not Apple, IBM, Hewlett-Packard, or Compaq, or any of our software brand names.

2. We have to sell our service and support. The hardware is like the razor, and the support, service, software services, training, and seminars are the razor blades. We need to serve our customers with what they really need.

3. The Yearly Total Sales chart summarizes our ambitious sales forecast. We expect sales to increase from $5.3 million last year to more than $7 million next year and $9 million in the last year of this plan.

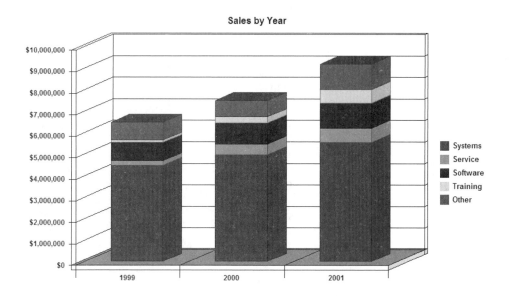

5.5.1 Sales Forecast

The important elements of the sales forecast are shown in the Total Sales by Month in Year 1 table. The non-hardware sales increase to about $2 million total in the third year.

Sales Forecast

Unit Sales	1999	2000	2001
Systems	2,255	2,500	2,800
Service	3,128	6,000	7,500
Software	3,980	5,000	6,500
Training	2,230	4,000	8,000
Other	2,122	2,500	3,000
Total Unit Sales	13,715	20,000	27,800

Unit Prices	1999	2000	2001
Systems	$1,980.80	$1,984.50	$1,980.80
Service	$68.47	$84	$87
Software	$212.86	$195	$180
Training	$46.58	$72	$79
Other	$394.21	$300	$394

Sales	1999	2000	2001
Systems	$4,466,708	$4,961,240	$5,546,245
Service	$214,159	$504,000	$652,500
Software	$847,183	$975,000	$1,170,000
Training	$103,865	$288,000	$632,000
Other	$836,520	$750,000	$1,182,639
Total Sales	$6,468,434	$7,478,240	$9,183,384

Direct Unit Costs	1999	2000	2001
Systems	$1,700.00	$1,686.82	$1,683.68
Service	$58.08	$33.60	$34.80
Software	$120.00	$117.00	$108.00
Training	$11.10	$21.60	$23.70
Other	$90.00	$90.00	$118.26

Direct Cost of Sales	1999	2000	2001
Systems	$3,833,500	$4,217,054	$4,714,308
Service	$181,680	$201,600	$261,000
Software	$477,600	$585,000	$702,000
Training	$24,753	$86,400	$189,600
Other	$190,980	$225,000	$354,792
Subtotal Direct Cost of Sales	$4,708,513	$5,315,054	$6,221,700

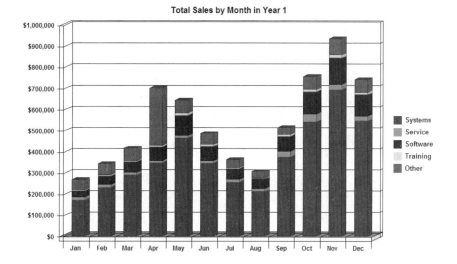

Total Sales by Month in Year 1

5.5.2 Sales Programs

1. Direct mail: Use great detail to describe your company's programs here.

2. Seminars: Use great detail to describe your company's programs here.

5.6 Strategic Alliances

Our important milestones are shown on the following table. Row by row, they track the need to follow up on strategy with specific activities. Most of the activities on the list can be easily tied to our strategic goals of selling more service and enhancing the relationship with the customer.

Business Plan Milestones

Milestone	Manager	Planned Date	Department	Budget	Actual Date	Actual Budget	Date Variance	Budget Variance
Corporate identity	TJ	12/17/98	Marketing	$10,000	1/15/99	$12,004	(29)	($2,004)
Seminar implementation	IR	1/10/99	Sales	$1,000	12/27/98	$5,000	14	($4,000)
Business plan review	RJ	1/10/99	GM	$0	1/23/99	$500	(13)	($500)
Upgrade mailer	IR	1/16/99	Sales	$5,000	2/12/99	$12,500	(27)	($7,500)
New corporate brochure	TJ	1/16/99	Marketing	$5,000	1/15/99	$5,000	1	$0
Delivery vans	SD	1/25/99	Service	$12,500	2/26/99	$3,500	(32)	$9,000
Direct mail	IR	2/16/99	Marketing	$3,500	2/25/99	$2,500	(9)	$1,000
Advertising	RJ	2/16/99	GM	$115,000	3/6/99	$100,000	(19)	$15,000
X4 prototype	SG	2/25/99	Product	$2,500	2/25/99	$181,500	0	($179,000)
Service revamp	SD	2/25/99	Product	$2,500	2/25/99	$2,500	0	$0
6 Presentations	IR	2/25/99	Sales	$0	1/10/99	$0	46	$0
X4 Testing	SG	3/6/99	Product	$1,000	1/16/99	$0	50	$1,000
3 Accounts	SD	3/17/99	Sales	$0	3/17/99	$0	0	$0
L30 prototype	PR	3/26/99	Product	$2,500	4/11/99	$0	(16)	$2,500
Tech99 Expo	TB	4/12/99	Marketing	$15,000	1/25/99	$0	78	$15,000
VP S&M hired	JK	6/11/99	Sales	$1,000	7/25/99	$181,500	(44)	($180,500)
Mailing system	SD	7/25/99	Service	$5,000	7/14/99	$7,654	11	($2,654)
Totals				$181,500		$514,158	11	($332,658)

6.0 Management Summary

Our management philosophy is based on responsibility and mutual respect. People who work at AMT want to work at AMT because we have an environment that encourages creativity and achievement.

6.1 Organizational Structure

1.   The team includes 22 employees, under a president and four managers.

2.   Our main management divisions are sales, marketing, service, and administration. Service handles service, support, training, and development.

6.2 Management Team

Ralph Jones, President: 46 years old, founded AMT in 1984 to focus on reselling high-powered personal computers to small business. Degree in computer science, 15 years with Large Computer Company, Inc. in positions ending with project manager. Ralph has been attending courses at the local Small Business Development Center for more than six years now, steadily adding business skills and business training to his technical background.

Sabrina Benson, VP Marketing: 36 years old, joined us last year following a very successful career with Continental Computers. Her hiring was the culmination of a long recruiting search. With Continental she managed the VAR marketing division. She is committed to re-engineering AMT to be a service and support business that sells computers, not vice-versa. MBA, undergraduate degree in history.

Gary Andrews, VP Service and Support: 48 years old, has been with AMT for seven years, and prior to that spent 18 years with Large Computers, Inc. in programming and service-related positions, . MS in computer science and BS in electrical engineering.

Laura Dannis, VP Sales: 32 years old, joined AMT part-time in 1991 and went full-time in 1992. A former teacher, she has very high people skills. BA in elementary education. She has also taken several sales management courses at the local SBDC.

John Peters, Director of Administration: 43 years old, started with AMT as a part-time bookkeeper in 1987, and has become the full-time administrative and financial backbone of the company.

6.3 Management Team Gaps

At present we believe we have a good team for covering the main points of the business plan. The addition of Sabrina Benson was important as a way to cement our fundamental repositioning and re-engineering.

At present, we are weakest in the area of technical capabilities to manage the database marketing programs and upgraded service and support, particularly with cross-platform networks. We also need to find a training manager.

6.4 Personnel Plan

The Personnel Plan reflects the need to bolster our capabilities to match our positioning. Our total headcount should increase to 22 this first year, and to 30 by the third year.

Personnel Plan

Production	1999	2000	2001
Manager	$36,000	$40,000	$40,000
Assistant	$12,000	$13,000	$14,000
Technical	$12,500	$35,000	$35,000
Technical	$12,500	$35,000	$35,000
Technical	$24,000	$27,500	$27,500
Fulfillment	$24,000	$30,000	$60,000
Fulfillment	$18,000	$22,000	$50,000
Other	$0	$0	$0
Subtotal	$139,000	$202,500	$261,500
Sales and Marketing Personnel			
Manager	$72,000	$76,000	$80,000
Technical sales	$60,000	$63,000	$85,000
Technical sales	$45,500	$46,000	$46,000
Salesperson	$40,500	$55,000	$64,000
Salesperson	$40,500	$50,000	$55,000
Salesperson	$33,500	$34,000	$45,000
Salesperson	$31,000	$38,000	$45,000
Salesperson	$21,000	$30,000	$33,000
Salesperson	$0	$30,000	$33,000
Other	$0	$0	$0
Subtotal	$344,000	$422,000	$486,000
General and Administrative Personnel			
President	$66,000	$69,000	$95,000
Finance	$28,000	$29,000	$30,000
Admin Assistant	$24,000	$26,000	$28,000
Bookkeeping	$18,000	$25,000	$30,000
Clerical	$12,000	$15,000	$18,000
Clerical	$7,000	$15,000	$18,000
Clerical	$0	$0	$15,000
Other	$0	$0	$0
Subtotal	$155,000	$179,000	$234,000
Other Personnel			
Programming	$36,000	$40,000	$44,000
Other technical	$0	$30,000	$33,000
Other	$0	$0	$0
Subtotal	$36,000	$70,000	$77,000

Total Payroll	$674,000	$873,500	$1,058,500
Payroll Burden	$107,840	$139,760	$169,360
Total Payroll Expenditures	$781,840	$1,013,260	$1,227,860

6.5 Other Management Considerations

Our attorney, Frank Dudley, is also a cofounder. He invested significantly in the company over a period of time during the 1980's. He remains a good friend of Ralph and has been a steady source of excellent legal and business advice.

Paul Karots, public relations consultant, is also a cofounder and co-owner. Like Dudley, he invested in the early stages and remains a trusted confidant and vendor of public relations and advertising services.

7.0 Financial Plan

The most important element in the financial plan is the critical need for improving several of the key factors that impact cash flow:

1. We must at any cost stop the slide in inventory turnover and develop better inventory management to bring the turnover back up to 8 turns by the third year. This should also be a function of the shift in focus towards service revenues to add to the hardware revenues.

2. We must also bring the gross margin back up to 25%. This too is related to improving the mix between hardware and service revenues, because the service revenues offer much better margins.

3. We plan to borrow another $150,000 long-term this year. The amount seems in line with the balance sheet capabilities.

7.1 Important Assumptions

The financial plan depends on important assumptions, most of which are shown in Table 7.1. The key underlying assumptions are:

1. We assume a slow-growth economy, without major recession.

2. We assume of course that there are no unforeseen changes in technology to make products immediately obsolete.

On our General Assumptions table, the most ambitious and also the most questionable assumption is our projected improvement in inventory turnover. This is critical to healthy cash flow, but will also be difficult.

General Assumptions

	1999	**2000**	**2001**
Short-term Interest Rate %	8.00%	8.00%	8.00%
Long-term Interest Rate %	8.50%	8.50%	8.50%
Payment Days Estimator	45	45	45
Collection Days Estimator	45	45	45
Inventory Turnover Estimator	7.00	7.00	7.00
Tax Rate %	20.00%	20.00%	20.00%
Expenses in Cash %	14.00%	14.00%	14.00%
Sales on Credit %	70.00%	70.00%	70.00%
Personnel Burden %	16.00%	16.00%	16.00%

7.2 Key Financial Indicators

The Benchmark Comparison chart highlights our ambitious plans to correct declining gross margin and inventory turnover. The chart illustrates why we think the ambitious sales increases we plan are reasonable. We have had similar increases in the recent past.

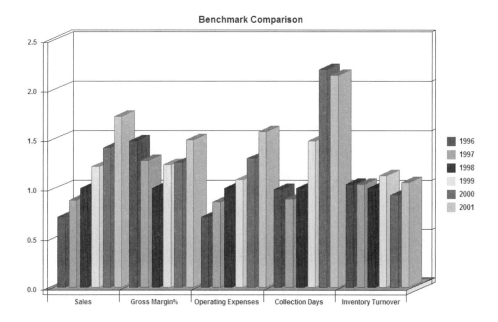

7.3 Break-even Analysis

For our break-even analysis, we assume running costs of approximately $96,000 per month, which includes our full payroll, rent, and utilities, and an estimation of other running costs. Payroll alone, at our present run rate, is only about $55,000.

Margins are harder to assume. Our overall average of $343/248 is based on past sales. We hope to attain a margin that high in the future.

The chart shows that we need to sell about $350,000 per month to break even, according to these assumptions. This is about half of our planned 1999 sales level, and significantly below our last year's sales level, so we believe we can maintain it.

Break-even Analysis:

Monthly Units Break-even	824
Monthly Sales Break-even	$352,336

Assumptions:

Average Per-Unit Revenue	$427.69
Average Per-Unit Variable Cost	$311.41
Estimated Monthly Fixed Cost	$95,792

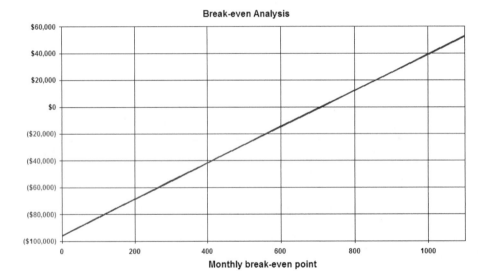

Break-even Analysis

Monthly break-even point

SP2.22

7.4 Projected Profit and Loss

The most important assumption in the Projected Profit and Loss statement is the gross margin, which is supposed to increase. This is up from barely 21% in the last year. The increase in gross margin is based on changing our sales mix, and it is critical.

Month-by-month assumptions for profit and loss are included in the appendices.

Profit and Loss (Income Statement)

	1999	2000	2001
Sales	$6,468,434	$7,478,240	$9,183,384
Direct Cost of Sales	$4,708,513	$5,315,054	$6,221,700
Production payroll	$139,000	$202,500	$261,500
Other	$6,000	$6,600	$7,260
Total Cost of Sales	$4,853,513	$5,524,154	$6,490,460
Gross Margin	$1,614,921	$1,954,086	$2,692,924
Gross Margin %	24.97%	26.13%	29.32%
Operating expenses:			
Sales and Marketing Expenses			
Sales and Marketing Payroll	$344,000	$422,000	$486,000
Ads	$125,000	$140,000	$175,000
Catalog	$25,000	$19,039	$19,991
Mailing	$113,300	$120,000	$150,000
Promo	$16,000	$20,000	$25,000
Shows	$20,200	$25,000	$30,000
Literature	$7,000	$10,000	$12,500
PR	$1,000	$1,250	$1,500
Seminar	$31,000	$45,000	$60,000
Service	$10,250	$12,000	$15,000
Training	$5,400	$7,000	$15,000
Total Sales and Marketing Expenses	$698,150	$821,289	$989,991
Sales and Marketing %	10.79%	10.98%	10.78%
General and Administrative Expenses			
General and Administrative Payroll	$155,000	$179,000	$234,000
Payroll Burden	$107,840	$139,760	$169,360
Depreciation	$12,681	$13,315	$13,981
Leased Equipment	$30,000	$31,500	$33,075
Utilities	$9,000	$9,450	$9,923
Insurance	$6,000	$6,300	$6,615
Rent	$84,000	$88,200	$92,610
Other	$0	$0	$0
Other	$6,331	$6,648	$6,980

Total General and Administrative Expenses	$410,852	$474,173	$566,544
General and Administrative %	6.35%	6.34%	6.17%
Other Expenses			
Other Payroll	$36,000	$70,000	$77,000
Contract/Consultants	$1,500	$5,000	$30,000
Other			
Total Other Expenses	$37,500	$75,000	$107,000
Other %	0.58%	1.00%	1.17%
Total Operating Expenses	$1,149,502	$1,370,462	$1,663,535
Profit Before Interest and Taxes	$465,419	$583,624	$1,029,389
Interest Expense Short-term	$7,867	$8,000	$8,000
Interest Expense Long-term	$29,628	$26,833	$21,162
Taxes Incurred	$85,585	$109,758	$200,045
Net Profit	$342,339	$439,033	$800,182
Net Profit/Sales	5.29%	5.87%	8.71%

7.5 Projected Cash Flow

The cash flow depends on assumptions for inventory turnover, payment days, and accounts receivable management. Our projected 45-day collection days is critical, and it is also reasonable. We need $150,000 in new financing in March to get through a cash flow dip as we build up for midyear sales.

Pro-Forma Cash Flow

	1999	2000	2001
Net Profit	$342,339	$439,033	$800,182
Plus:			
Depreciation	$12,681	$13,315	$13,981
Change in Accounts Payable	$537,079	$96,220	$152,274
Current Borrowing (repayment)	$10,000	$0	$0
Increase (decrease) Other Liabilities	$0	$0	$0
Long-term Borrowing (repayment)	$63,292	($64,953)	($68,484)
Capital Input	$325,000	$0	$0
Subtotal	$1,290,391	$483,615	$897,953
Less:	1999	2000	2001
Change in Accounts Receivable	$449,771	$131,896	$222,718
Change in Inventory	$746,874	$137,884	$198,673
Change in Other ST Assets	$0	$0	$0
Capital Expenditure	$90,000	$200,000	$400,000
Dividends	$0	$0	$0
Subtotal	$1,286,645	$469,780	$821,391
Net Cash Flow	$3,746	$13,835	$76,562
Cash Balance	$59,178	$73,013	$149,575

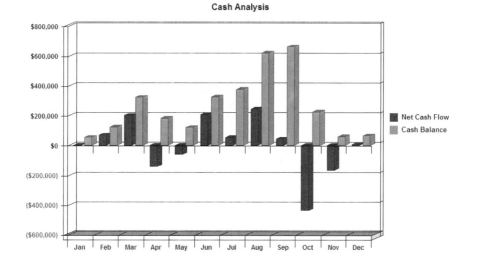

Cash Analysis

7.6 Projected Balance Sheet

The Projected Balance Sheet is quite solid. We do not project any real trouble meeting our debt obligations—as long as we can achieve our specific objectives.

Pro forma Balance Sheet
Assets

	Starting Balances	1999	2000	2001
Short-term Assets				
Cash	$55,432	$59,178	$73,013	$149,575
Accounts Receivable	$395,107	$844,878	$976,775	$1,199,493
Inventory	$251,012	$997,886	$1,135,770	$1,334,443
Other Short-term Assets	$25,000	$25,000	$25,000	$25,000
Total Short-term Assets	$726,551	$1,926,942	$2,210,558	$2,708,511
Long-term Assets				
Capital Assets	$350,000	$440,000	$640,000	$1,040,000
Accumulated Depreciation	$50,000	$62,681	$75,996	$89,977
Total Long-term Assets	$300,000	$377,319	$564,004	$950,023
Total Assets	$1,026,551	$2,304,261	$2,774,562	$3,658,534

Liabilities and Capital

		1999	2000	2001
Accounts Payable	$223,897	$760,976	$857,196	$1,009,471
Short-term Notes	$90,000	$100,000	$100,000	$100,000
Other Short-term Liabilities	$15,000	$15,000	$15,000	$15,000
Subtotal Short-term Liabilities	$328,897	$875,976	$972,196	$1,124,471
Long-term Liabilities	$284,862	$348,154	$283,201	$214,717
Total Liabilities	$613,759	$1,224,130	$1,255,397	$1,339,188
Paid in Capital	$500,000	$825,000	$825,000	$825,000
Retained Earnings	($161,860)	($87,208)	$255,131	$694,165
Earnings	$74,652	$342,339	$439,033	$800,182
Total Capital	$412,792	$1,080,131	$1,519,165	$2,319,347
Total Liabilities and Capital	$1,026,551	$2,304,261	$2,774,562	$3,658,534
Net Worth	$412,792	$1,080,131	$1,519,165	$2,319,347

7.7 Business Ratios

The table follows with our main business ratios. We do intend to improve gross margin, collection days, and inventory turnover.

Ratio Analysis

Profitability Ratios:	1999	2000	2001
Gross Margin	24.97%	26.13%	29.32%
Net Profit Margin	5.29%	5.84%	8.68%
Return on Assets	14.86%	15.74%	21.83%
Return on Equity	31.69%	28.78%	34.46%
Activity Ratios	1999	2000	2001
AR Turnover	5.36	5.36	5.36
Collection Days	50	64	62
Inventory Turnover	7.77	5.18	5.25
Accts Payable Turnover	5.90	5.90	5.90
Total Asset Turnover	2.81	2.70	2.51
Debt Ratios	1999	2000	2001
Debt to Net Worth	1.13	0.83	0.58
Short-term Liab. to Liab.	0.72	0.77	0.84
Liquidity Ratios	1999	2000	2001
Current Ratio	2.20	2.27	2.40
Quick Ratio	1.06	1.10	1.22
Net Working Capital	$1,050,966	$1,235,842	$1,578,874
Interest Coverage	12.41	16.66	35.19
Additional Ratios	1999	2000	2001
Assets to Sales	0.36	0.37	0.40
Debt/Assets	53%	45%	37%
Current Debt/Total Assets	38%	35%	31%
Acid Test	0.10	0.10	0.15
Asset Turnover	2.81	2.70	2.51
Sales/Net Worth	5.99	4.93	3.97

This page intentionally blank.

AMT, Inc. - Appendix Tables

Pro Forma Balance Sheet

Assets

	Starting Balances	Jan	Feb	Mar	Apr	May	Jun	Jul	Aug	Sep	Oct	Nov	Dec
Short-term Assets													
Cash	$55,432	$108,508	$141,078	$153,148	$5,027	$32,208	$73,174	$58,626	$23,036	$11,478	$21,518	$7,873	$59,178
Accounts Receivable	$395,107	$277,923	$354,332	$430,575	$636,674	$696,256	$565,392	$423,890	$341,268	$466,541	$707,840	$918,115	$844,878
Inventory	$251,012	$333,445	$444,104	$544,477	$699,578	$879,836	$648,051	$459,866	$401,460	$666,411	$994,975	$1,250,220	$997,886
Other ST Assets	$25,000	$25,000	$25,000	$25,000	$25,000	$175,000	$175,000	$475,000	$475,000	$325,000	$25,000	$25,000	$25,000
Total ST Assets	$726,551	$744,876	$964,514	$1,153,200	$1,366,278	$1,783,300	$1,461,618	$1,417,381	$1,240,763	$1,469,430	$1,749,332	$2,201,208	$1,926,942
Long-term Assets													
Capital Assets	$350,000	$375,000	$375,000	$390,000	$390,000	$440,000	$440,000	$440,000	$440,000	$440,000	$440,000	$440,000	$440,000
Accum. Depreciation	$50,000	$51,000	$52,010	$53,030	$54,060	$55,100	$56,150	$57,211	$58,283	$59,366	$60,460	$61,565	$62,681
Total LT Assets	$300,000	$324,000	$322,990	$336,970	$335,940	$384,900	$383,850	$382,789	$381,717	$380,634	$379,540	$378,435	$377,319
Total Assets	$1,026,551	$1,068,876	$1,287,504	$1,490,170	$1,702,218	$2,168,200	$1,845,468	$1,800,170	$1,622,480	$1,850,064	$2,128,872	$2,579,643	$2,304,261

Liabilities and Capital

	Jan	Feb	Mar	Apr	May	Jun	Jul	Aug	Sep	Oct	Nov	Dec
Accounts Payable	$223,897	$268,569	$369,549	$428,414	$560,724	$702,163	$514,886	$378,036	$324,275	$555,293	$795,989	$984,178	$760,976
Short-term Notes	$90,000	$90,000	$190,000	$220,000	$140,000	$140,000	$0	$100,000	$0	$0	$0	$200,000	$100,000
Other ST Liabilities	$15,000	$15,000	$15,000	$15,000	$15,000	$15,000	$15,000	$15,000	$15,000	$15,000	$15,000	$15,000	$15,000
Subtotal ST Liabilities	$328,897	$373,569	$574,549	$663,414	$715,724	$857,163	$529,886	$493,036	$339,275	$570,293	$810,989	$1,199,178	$875,976
Long-term Liabilities	$284,862	$281,920	$278,958	$375,974	$372,970	$369,944	$366,897	$363,828	$360,737	$357,624	$354,490	$351,333	$348,154
Total Liabilities	$613,759	$655,489	$853,506	$1,039,388	$1,088,694	$1,227,107	$896,783	$856,863	$700,012	$927,917	$1,165,479	$1,550,511	$1,224,130
Paid in Capital	$500,000	$500,000	$525,000	$525,000	$525,000	$825,000	$825,000	$825,000	$825,000	$825,000	$825,000	$825,000	$825,000
Retained Earnings	($161,860)	($87,208)	($87,208)	($87,208)	($87,208)	($87,208)	($87,208)	($87,208)	($87,208)	($87,208)	($87,208)	($87,208)	($87,208)
Earnings	$74,652	$595	($3,795)	$12,990	$175,732	$203,300	$210,893	$205,515	$184,676	$184,355	$225,601	$291,340	$342,339
Total Capital	$412,792	$413,387	$433,997	$450,782	$613,524	$941,092	$948,685	$943,307	$922,468	$922,147	$963,393	$1,029,132	$1,080,131
Total Liab. & Capital	$1,026,551	$1,068,876	$1,287,504	$1,490,170	$1,702,218	$2,168,200	$1,845,468	$1,800,170	$1,622,480	$1,850,064	$2,128,872	$2,579,643	$2,304,261
Net Worth	$412,792	$413,387	$433,997	$450,782	$613,524	$941,092	$948,685	$943,307	$922,468	$922,147	$963,393	$1,029,132	$1,080,131

Pro Forma Cash Flow

	Jan	Feb	Mar	Apr	May	Jun	Jul	Aug	Sep	Oct	Nov	Dec
Net Profit	$595	($4,390)	$16,784	$162,743	$27,568	$7,593	($5,378)	($20,839)	($321)	$41,246	$65,739	$50,999
Plus:												
Depreciation	$1,000	$1,010	$1,020	$1,030	$1,040	$1,050	$1,061	$1,072	$1,083	$1,094	$1,105	$1,116
Change in Accounts Payable	$44,672	$100,980	$58,866	$132,310	$141,439	($187,277)	($136,850)	($53,761)	$231,018	$240,697	$188,189	($223,202)
Current Borrowing (repayment)	$0	$100,000	$30,000	($80,000)	$0	($140,000)	$100,000	($100,000)	$0	$0	$200,000	($100,000)
Increase (decrease) Other Liabilities												
Long-term Borrowing (repayment)	($2,942)	($2,962)	$97,017	($3,005)	($3,026)	($3,047)	($3,069)	($3,091)	($3,113)	($3,135)	($3,157)	($3,179)
Capital Input	$0	$25,000	$0	$0	$300,000	$0	$0	$0	$0	$0	$0	$0
Subtotal	$43,325	$219,638	$203,686	$213,078	$467,021	($321,682)	($44,236)	($176,618)	$228,667	$279,902	$451,876	($274,266)
Less:												
Change in Accounts Receivable	($117,184)	$76,409	$76,243	$206,099	$59,582	($130,864)	($141,502)	($82,622)	$125,273	$241,299	$210,276	($73,237)
Change in Inventory	$82,433	$110,659	$100,373	$155,101	$180,258	($231,784)	($188,186)	($58,406)	$264,951	$328,563	$255,245	($252,334)
Change in Other ST Assets	$0	$0	$0	$0	$150,000	$0	$300,000	$0	($150,000)	($300,000)	$0	$0
Capital Expenditure	$25,000	$0	$15,000	$0	$50,000	$0	$0	$0	$0	$0	$0	$0
Dividends	$0	$0	$0	$0	$0	$0	$0	$0	$0	$0	$0	$0
Subtotal	($9,751)	$187,068	$191,616	$361,200	$439,840	($362,648)	($29,688)	($141,028)	$240,224	$269,862	$465,521	($325,571)
Net Cash Flow	$53,076	$32,570	$12,071	($148,122)	$27,181	$40,967	($14,549)	($35,590)	($11,557)	$10,040	($13,645)	$51,305
Cash Balance	$108,508	$141,078	$153,148	$5,027	$32,208	$73,174	$58,626	$23,036	$11,478	$21,518	$7,873	$59,178

General Assumptions

	Jan	Feb	Mar	Apr	May	Jun	Jul	Aug	Sep	Oct	Nov	Dec
Short-term Interest Rate %	8.00%	8.00%	8.00%	8.00%	8.00%	8.00%	8.00%	8.00%	8.00%	8.00%	8.00%	8.00%
Long-term Interest Rate %	8.50%	8.50%	8.50%	8.50%	8.50%	8.50%	8.50%	8.50%	8.50%	8.50%	8.50%	8.50%
Payment Days Estimator	45	45	45	45	45	45	45	45	45	45	45	45
Collection Days Estimator	45	45	45	45	45	45	45	45	45	45	45	45
Inventory Turnover Estimator	7.00	7.00	7.00	7.00	7.00	7.00	7.00	7.00	7.00	7.00	7.00	7.00
Tax Rate %	20.00%	20.00%	20.00%	20.00%	20.00%	20.00%	20.00%	20.00%	20.00%	20.00%	20.00%	20.00%
Expenses in Cash %	14.00%	14.00%	14.00%	14.00%	14.00%	14.00%	14.00%	14.00%	14.00%	14.00%	14.00%	14.00%
Sales on Credit %	70.00%	70.00%	70.00%	70.00%	70.00%	70.00%	70.00%	70.00%	70.00%	70.00%	70.00%	70.00%
Personnel Burden %	16.00%	16.00%	16.00%	16.00%	16.00%	16.00%	16.00%	16.00%	16.00%	16.00%	16.00%	16.00%

Personnel Plan

Production

	Jan	Feb	Mar	Apr	May	Jun	Jul	Aug	Sep	Oct	Nov	Dec
Manager	$1,000	$1,000	$1,000	$1,000	$1,000	$1,000	$1,000	$1,000	$1,000	$1,000	$1,000	$1,000
Assistant	$3,000	$3,000	$3,000	$3,000	$3,000	$3,000	$3,000	$3,000	$3,000	$3,000	$3,000	$3,000
Technical	$0	$0	$0	$0	$0	$0	$0	$2,500	$2,500	$2,500	$2,500	$2,500
Technical	$0	$0	$0	$0	$0	$0	$0	$2,500	$2,500	$2,500	$2,500	$2,500
Fulfillment	$2,000	$2,000	$2,000	$2,000	$2,000	$2,000	$2,000	$2,000	$2,000	$2,000	$2,000	$2,000
Fulfillment	$2,000	$2,000	$2,000	$2,000	$2,000	$2,000	$2,000	$2,000	$2,000	$2,000	$2,000	$2,000
Fulfillment	$1,500	$1,500	$1,500	$1,500	$1,500	$1,500	$1,500	$1,500	$1,500	$1,500	$1,500	$1,500
Other	$0	$0	$0	$0	$0	$0	$0	$0	$0	$0	$0	$0
Subtotal	$9,500	$9,500	$9,500	$9,500	$9,500	$9,500	$9,500	$14,500	$14,500	$14,500	$14,500	$14,500

Sales and Marketing

	Jan	Feb	Mar	Apr	May	Jun	Jul	Aug	Sep	Oct	Nov	Dec
Manager	$6,000	$6,000	$6,000	$6,000	$6,000	$6,000	$6,000	$6,000	$6,000	$6,000	$6,000	$6,000
Technical sales	$5,000	$5,000	$5,000	$5,000	$5,000	$5,000	$5,000	$5,000	$5,000	$5,000	$5,000	$5,000
Technical sales	$3,500	$3,500	$3,500	$3,500	$3,500	$4,000	$4,000	$4,000	$4,000	$4,000	$4,000	$4,000
Salesperson	$2,500	$2,500	$2,500	$2,500	$2,500	$4,000	$4,000	$4,000	$4,000	$4,000	$4,000	$4,000
Salesperson	$2,500	$2,500	$2,500	$2,500	$2,500	$4,000	$4,000	$4,000	$4,000	$4,000	$4,000	$4,000
Salesperson	$2,500	$2,500	$2,500	$2,500	$2,500	$3,000	$3,000	$3,000	$3,000	$3,000	$3,000	$3,000
Salesperson	$2,000	$2,000	$2,000	$2,000	$2,000	$3,000	$3,000	$3,000	$3,000	$3,000	$3,000	$3,000
Salesperson	$0	$0	$0	$0	$0	$3,000	$3,000	$3,000	$3,000	$3,000	$3,000	$3,000
Salesperson	$0	$0	$0	$0	$0	$0	$0	$0	$0	$0	$0	$0
Other	$0	$0	$0	$0	$0	$0	$0	$0	$0	$0	$0	$0
Subtotal	$24,000	$24,000	$24,000	$24,000	$24,000	$32,000	$32,000	$32,000	$32,000	$32,000	$32,000	$32,000

General and Administrative

	Jan	Feb	Mar	Apr	May	Jun	Jul	Aug	Sep	Oct	Nov	Dec
President	$5,500	$5,500	$5,500	$5,500	$5,500	$5,500	$5,500	$5,500	$5,500	$5,500	$5,500	$5,500
Finance	$0	$0	$0	$0	$0	$4,000	$4,000	$4,000	$4,000	$4,000	$4,000	$4,000
Admin Assistant	$2,000	$2,000	$2,000	$2,000	$2,000	$2,000	$2,000	$2,000	$2,000	$2,000	$2,000	$2,000
Bookkeeping	$1,500	$1,500	$1,500	$1,500	$1,500	$1,500	$1,500	$1,500	$1,500	$1,500	$1,500	$1,500
Clerical	$1,000	$1,000	$1,000	$1,000	$1,000	$1,000	$1,000	$1,000	$1,000	$1,000	$1,000	$1,000
Clerical	$0	$0	$0	$0	$0	$1,000	$1,000	$1,000	$1,000	$1,000	$1,000	$1,000
Clerical	$0	$0	$0	$0	$0	$0	$0	$0	$0	$0	$0	$0
Other	$0	$0	$0	$0	$0	$0	$0	$0	$0	$0	$0	$0
Subtotal	$10,000	$10,000	$10,000	$10,000	$10,000	$15,000	$15,000	$15,000	$15,000	$15,000	$15,000	$15,000

Other Personnel

	Jan	Feb	Mar	Apr	May	Jun	Jul	Aug	Sep	Oct	Nov	Dec
Programming	$3,000	$3,000	$3,000	$3,000	$3,000	$3,000	$3,000	$3,000	$3,000	$3,000	$3,000	$3,000
Other technical	$0	$0	$0	$0	$0	$0	$0	$0	$0	$0	$0	$0
$0												
Other	$0	$0	$0	$0	$0	$0	$0	$0	$0	$0	$0	$0
Subtotal	$3,000	$3,000	$3,000	$3,000	$3,000	$3,000	$3,000	$3,000	$3,000	$3,000	$3,000	$3,000

	Jan	Feb	Mar	Apr	May	Jun	Jul	Aug	Sep	Oct	Nov	Dec
Total Headcount	0	0	0	0	0	0	0	0	0	0	0	0
Total Payroll	$46,500	$46,500	$46,500	$46,500	$46,500	$59,500	$59,500	$64,500	$64,500	$64,500	$64,500	$64,500
Payroll Burden	$7,440	$7,440	$7,440	$7,440	$7,440	$9,520	$9,520	$10,320	$10,320	$10,320	$10,320	$10,320
Total Payroll Expenditures	$53,940	$53,940	$53,940	$53,940	$53,940	$69,020	$69,020	$74,820	$74,820	$74,820	$74,820	$74,820

Profit and Loss (Income Statement)

	Jan	Feb	Mar	Apr	May	Jun	Jul	Aug	Sep	Oct	Nov	Dec
Sales	$268,365	$342,146	$415,767	$701,651	$643,826	$485,790	$362,662	$306,194	$513,389	$754,505	$934,341	$739,799
Direct Cost of Sales	$184,510	$249,061	$307,612	$398,087	$503,238	$368,030	$258,255	$219,185	$373,740	$565,402	$714,295	$567,100
Production payroll	$9,500	$9,500	$9,500	$9,500	$9,500	$9,500	$9,500	$14,500	$14,500	$14,500	$14,500	$14,500
Other	$500	$500	$500	$500	$500	$500	$500	$500	$500	$500	$500	$500
Total Cost of Sales	$194,510	$259,061	$317,612	$408,087	$513,238	$378,030	$268,255	$234,185	$388,740	$580,402	$729,295	$582,100
Gross Margin	$73,856	$83,086	$98,155	$293,564	$130,589	$107,760	$94,407	$72,009	$124,649	$174,103	$205,046	$157,699
Gross Margin %	27.52%	24.28%	23.61%	41.84%	20.28%	22.18%	26.03%	23.52%	24.28%	23.08%	21.95%	21.32%

Operating expenses:

Sales & Marketing Expenses

	Jan	Feb	Mar	Apr	May	Jun	Jul	Aug	Sep	Oct	Nov	Dec
Sales & Marketing Payroll	$24,000	$24,000	$24,000	$24,000	$24,000	$32,000	$32,000	$32,000	$32,000	$32,000	$32,000	$32,000
Ads	$5,000	$5,000	$7,000	$10,000	$15,000	$10,000	$4,000	$4,000	$20,000	$15,000	$20,000	$10,000
Catalog	$2,000	$3,000	$2,000	$2,000	$2,000	$2,000	$2,000	$2,000	$2,000	$2,000	$2,000	$2,000
Mailing	$3,000	$11,800	$5,500	$10,500	$10,500	$5,500	$10,500	$10,500	$10,500	$22,000	$8,000	$5,000
Promo	$0	$0	$0	$0	$0	$0	$0	$0	$1,000	$0	$15,000	$0
Shows	$0	$0	$0	$0	$0	$0	$3,200	$0	$10,000	$7,000	$0	$0
Literature	$0	$7,000	$0	$0	$0	$0	$0	$0	$0	$0	$0	$0
PR	$0	$0	$0	$1,000	$0	$0	$0	$0	$0	$0	$0	$0
Seminar	$1,000	$0	$0	$5,000	$5,000	$5,000	$5,000	$5,000	$5,000	$0	$0	$0
Service	$2,000	$1,000	$1,000	$500	$2,500	$500	$500	$500	$500	$500	$500	$250
Training	$450	$450	$450	$450	$450	$450	$450	$450	$450	$450	$450	$450
Total Sales & Mktg. Exp.	$37,450	$52,250	$39,950	$53,450	$59,450	$55,450	$57,650	$54,450	$81,450	$78,950	$77,950	$49,700
Sales and Marketing %	13.95%	15.27%	9.61%	7.62%	9.23%	11.41%	15.90%	17.78%	15.87%	10.46%	8.34%	6.72%

General & Administrative Expenses

	Jan	Feb	Mar	Apr	May	Jun	Jul	Aug	Sep	Oct	Nov	Dec
General & Admin. Payroll	$10,000	$10,000	$10,000	$10,000	$10,000	$15,000	$15,000	$15,000	$15,000	$15,000	$15,000	$15,000
Payroll Burden	$7,440	$7,440	$7,440	$7,440	$7,440	$9,520	$9,520	$10,320	$10,320	$10,320	$10,320	$10,320
Depreciation	$1,000	$1,010	$1,020	$1,030	$1,040	$1,050	$1,061	$1,072	$1,083	$1,094	$1,105	$1,116
Leased Equipment	$2,500	$2,500	$2,500	$2,500	$2,500	$2,500	$2,500	$2,500	$2,500	$2,500	$2,500	$2,500

Profit & Loss (cont'd.)

	Jan	Feb	Mar	Apr	May	Jun	Jul	Aug	Sep	Oct	Nov	Dec
Utilities	$750	$750	$750	$750	$750	$750	$750	$750	$750	$750	$750	$750
Insurance	$500	$500	$500	$500	$500	$500	$500	$500	$500	$500	$500	$500
Rent	$7,000	$7,000	$7,000	$7,000	$7,000	$7,000	$7,000	$7,000	$7,000	$7,000	$7,000	$7,000
Other	$0	$0	$0	$0	$0	$0	$0	$0	$0	$0	$0	$0
Other	$500	$505	$510	$515	$520	$525	$530	$535	$540	$545	$550	$556
Total Gen. & Admin. Exp.	$29,690	$29,705	$29,720	$29,735	$29,750	$36,845	$36,861	$37,677	$37,693	$37,709	$37,725	$37,742
General & Admin. %	11.06%	8.68%	7.15%	4.24%	4.62%	7.58%	10.16%	12.30%	7.34%	5.00%	4.04%	5.10%
Other Expenses												
Other Payroll	$3,000	$3,000	$3,000	$3,000	$3,000	$3,000	$3,000	$3,000	$3,000	$3,000	$3,000	$3,000
Contract/Consultants	$125	$125	$125	$125	$125	$125	$125	$125	$125	$125	$125	$125
Other	9/6/00	9/6/00	9/6/00	9/6/00	9/6/00	9/6/00	9/6/00	9/6/00	9/6/00	9/6/00	9/6/00	9/6/00
Total Other Expenses	$3,375	$3,375	$3,375	$3,375	$3,375	$3,375	$3,375	$3,375	$3,375	$3,375	$3,375	$3,375
Other %	1.26%	0.99%	0.81%	0.48%	0.52%	0.69%	0.93%	1.10%	0.66%	0.45%	0.36%	0.46%
Total Operating Exp.	$70,515	$85,330	$73,045	$86,560	$92,575	$95,670	$97,886	$95,502	$122,518	$120,034	$119,050	$90,817
Profit Before Int. & Taxes	$3,341	($2,244)	$25,110	$207,004	$38,014	$12,090	($3,479)	($23,493)	$2,131	$54,069	$85,996	$66,882
Interest Expense ST	$600	$1,267	$1,467	$933	$933	$0	$667	$0	$0	$0	$1,333	$667
Interest Expense LT	$1,997	$1,976	$2,663	$2,642	$2,620	$2,599	$2,577	$2,555	$2,533	$2,511	$2,489	$2,466
Taxes Incurred	$149	($1,097)	$4,196	$40,686	$6,892	$1,898	($1,345)	($5,210)	($80)	$10,312	$16,435	$12,750
Net Profit	$595	($4,390)	$16,784	$162,743	$27,568	$7,593	($5,378)	($20,839)	($321)	$41,246	$65,739	$50,999
Net Profit/Sales	0.22%	-1.28%	4.04%	23.19%	4.28%	1.56%	-1.48%	-6.81%	-0.06%	5.47%	7.04%	6.89%

Sales Forecast

Unit Sales

	Jan	Feb	Mar	Apr	May	Jun	Jul	Aug	Sep	Oct	Nov	Dec
Systems	85	115	145	190	245	175	120	100	180	275	350	275
Service	200	200	200	200	244	256	269	282	296	311	327	343
Software	150	200	250	330	430	310	210	180	320	490	620	490
Training	145	155	165	170	225	200	150	150	200	220	250	200
Other	160	176	192	240	200	175	125	100	104	200	250	200
Total Unit Sales	740	846	952	1,130	1,344	1,116	874	812	1,100	1,496	1,797	1,508

Unit Prices

	Jan	Feb	Mar	Apr	May	Jun	Jul	Aug	Sep	Oct	Nov	Dec
Systems	$2,000.00	$2,000.00	$2,000.00	$1,828.95	$1,890.63	$1,966.17	$2,131.58	$2,115.38	$2,083.33	$1,966.40	$1,980.29	$1,984.50
Service	$75	$69	$58	$46	$50	$47	$50	$50	$91	$124	$75	$67
Software	$200	$200	$200	$200	$223	$217	$242	$253	$220	$211	$204	$207
Training	$37	$35	$39	$41	$56	$50	$33	$33	$50	$55	$60	$50
Other	$300	$300	$300	$300	$300	$300	$300	$300	$300	$300	$300	$300

Sales

	Jan	Feb	Mar	Apr	May	Jun	Jul	Aug	Sep	Oct	Nov	Dec
Systems	$170,000	$230,000	$290,000	$347,500	$463,203	$344,079	$255,789	$211,538	$375,000	$540,761	$693,100	$545,736
Service	$15,000	$13,846	$11,667	$9,231	$12,200	$11,947	$13,450	$14,100	$26,909	$38,418	$24,525	$22,867
Software	$30,000	$40,000	$50,000	$66,000	$95,923	$67,264	$50,923	$45,556	$70,280	$103,326	$126,715	$101,196
Training	$5,365	$5,500	$6,500	$7,000	$12,500	$10,000	$5,000	$5,000	$10,000	$12,000	$15,000	$10,000
Other	$48,000	$52,800	$57,600	$271,920	$60,000	$52,500	$37,500	$30,000	$31,200	$60,000	$75,000	$60,000
Total Sales	$268,365	$342,146	$415,767	$701,651	$643,826	$485,790	$362,662	$306,194	$513,389	$754,505	$934,341	$739,799

Direct Unit Costs

		Jan	Feb	Mar	Apr	May	Jun	Jul	Aug	Sep	Oct	Nov	Dec
Systems	85.00%	$1,700.00	$1,700.00	$1,700.00	$1,700.00	$1,700.00	$1,700.00	$1,700.00	$1,700.00	$1,700.00	$1,700.00	$1,700.00	$1,700.00
Service	40.00%	$30.00	$60.00	$60.00	$60.00	$60.00	$60.00	$60.00	$60.00	$60.00	$60.00	$60.00	$60.00
Software	60.00%	$120.00	$120.00	$120.00	$120.00	$120.00	$120.00	$120.00	$120.00	$120.00	$120.00	$120.00	$120.00
Training	30.00%	$11.10	$11.10	$11.10	$11.10	$11.10	$11.10	$11.10	$11.10	$11.10	$11.10	$11.10	$11.10
Other	30.00%	$90.00	$90.00	$90.00	$90.00	$90.00	$90.00	$90.00	$90.00	$90.00	$90.00	$90.00	$90.00

Direct Cost of Sales

	Jan	Feb	Mar	Apr	May	Jun	Jul	Aug	Sep	Oct	Nov	Dec
Systems	$144,500	$195,500	$246,500	$323,000	$416,500	$297,500	$204,000	$170,000	$306,000	$467,500	$595,000	$467,500
Service	$6,000	$12,000	$12,000	$12,000	$14,640	$15,360	$16,140	$16,920	$17,760	$18,660	$19,620	$20,580
Software	$18,000	$24,000	$30,000	$39,600	$51,600	$37,200	$25,200	$21,600	$38,400	$58,800	$74,400	$58,800
Training	$1,610	$1,721	$1,832	$1,887	$2,498	$2,220	$1,665	$1,665	$2,220	$2,442	$2,775	$2,220
Other	$14,400	$15,840	$17,280	$21,600	$18,000	$15,750	$11,250	$9,000	$9,360	$18,000	$22,500	$18,000
Subtotal Direct Cost of Sales	$184,510	$249,061	$307,612	$398,087	$503,238	$368,030	$258,255	$219,185	$373,740	$565,402	$714,295	$567,100

This page intentionally blank.

HURDLE: WORKBOOK

Use it with Business Plan Software

This workbook is best used along with either Business Plan Pro® or Business Plan Pro® Premier planning software published by Palo Alto Software, Inc.

Use it to Develop A Plan

Take notes for your plan and write draft topics, gather information, and organize your thoughts. Then later you can incorporate this initial work into your plan on the computer. You can also share the main ideas with others, to stir the thinking process.

Use it with Clients, Colleagues, or Students

Use this workbook with clients, colleagues, or students. They can use the workbook to prepare drafts of topics, take notes, and gather information. You can use the workbook to absorb their inputs, then create a plan.

Use it with Tables

The workbook anticipates the information you'll want to add to your business plan tables. Use it to start the process.

For product information, contact Palo Alto Software, Inc. at:

U.S. Sales:	(800) 229-7526
Phone:	(541) 683-6162
Fax:	(541) 683-6250
Email:	sales@paloalto.com
Websites:	www.paloalto.com

PERMISSION TO COPY WORKBOOK PAGES GRANTED ONLY FOR USE WITH BUSINESS PLAN PRO® SOFTWARE.
FOR MORE INFORMATION CALL (800) 229-7526.

WB.1

1.0 Executive Summary

Although this topic appears first in the plan, you normally write it last. Wait until you're almost done so you can include the main highlights. You should cover the most important facts, such as sales growth, profitability, strategic focus, and those facts may change during the planning process.

The contents of the summary depend on the goals of your plan. For example, if you are selling a business idea to investors, then you should include highlights that will invite and encourage potential investors to read on. That might be growth rates, competitive edge, an exciting new technology, etc.

....

....

....

....

....

....

....

....

....

....

....

....

1.1 Objectives

Objectives are business goals. Set your market share objectives, sales objectives, and profit objectives. Companies need to set objectives and plan to achieve them.

Make sure your objectives are concrete and measurable. Be specific, such as achieving a given level of sales or profits, a percentage of gross margin, a growth rate, or a market share. Don't use generalities like "being the best" or "growing rapidly."

....

....

....

....

....

....

....

....

....

....

....

1.2 Mission Statement

Use the mission statement to define your business concept. A company mission statement should define underlying goals (such as making a profit) and objectives in broad strategic terms, including what market is served and what benefits are offered.

....

....

....

....

....

....

....

....

....

....

....

....

1.3 Keys to Success

The idea of keys to success is based on the need for focus. You can't focus efforts on a few priorities unless you limit the number of priorities. In practice, lists of more than three or four priorities are usually less effective. The more priorities (beyond three or four), the less chance of implementation.

Virtually every business has different keys to success. These are a few factors that make the difference between success and failure. This depends on who you are and what services you offer.

....

....

....

....

....

....

....

....

....

....

....

....

PERMISSION TO COPY WORKBOOK PAGES GRANTED ONLY FOR USE WITH BUSINESS PLAN PRO® SOFTWARE.
FOR MORE INFORMATION CALL (800) 229-7526.

WB.5

2.0 Company Description

Take a paragraph or two to introduce your business. Explain where it will be established, what type of legal entity you expect to form, who will own it, and how ownership will be divided.

....

....

....

....

....

....

....

....

....

....

....

....

2.1 Company Ownership

In this topic, describe the ownership and legal establishment of the company. This is mainly specifying whether your company is a corporation, partnership, sole proprietorship, or some other kind of legal entity, such as a limited liability partnership. You should also explain who owns the company, and, if there is more than one owner, in what proportion.

....

....

....

....

....

....

....

....

....

....

....

PERMISSION TO COPY WORKBOOK PAGES GRANTED ONLY FOR USE WITH BUSINESS PLAN PRO® SOFTWARE.
FOR MORE INFORMATION CALL (800) 229-7526.

WB.7

2.2 Start-up Plan

This topic appears when you're a start-up and your plan is for a new company with no history.

This topic explains the details of your expenses and assets listed in your start-up table that will be linked to this topic.

The cash you want to have in the bank at start-up is different from the money raised to start the business. The total money raised must match what was spent as expenses and assets. The cash at start-up is one of the assets. If you increase the amount of money raised, then you have to increase the start-up assets, usually by increasing the starting cash.

You have to fund start-up expenses as well as starting assets.

As with every business balance, assets must be equal to capital plus liabilities. Therefore, add up the investment you expect plus all the initial liabilities. Subtract that sum from total assets. The difference is called loss at start-up.

You can tell that you have not accounted for all your incoming financing by looking at the "loss at start-up" value. That should be the same number as total start-up expenses (except negative). If it is more negative than start-up expenses are positive, then you have brought in funds that haven't been accounted for. You can fix that by adding more money into your starting cash to account for the additional financing.

Start-up Plan	
Start-up Expenses	
Legal	
Stationery, etc.	
Brochures	
Consultants	
Insurance	
Rent	
Research and Development	
Expensed Equipment	
Other	
Total Start-up Expense	
Start-up Assets Needed	
Cash Requirements	
Start-up Inventory	
Other Short-term Assets	
Total Short-term Assets	
Long-term Assets	
Total Assets	
Total Start-up Requirements	
Left to Finance:	
Start-up Funding Plan	
Investment	
Investor 1	
Investor 2	
Other	
Total Investment	
Short-term Liabilities	
Unpaid Expenses	
Short-term Loans	
Interest-free Short-term Loans	
Subtotal Short-term Liabilities	
Long-term Liabilities	
Total Liabilities	
Loss at Start-up	
Total Capital	
Total Capital and Liabilities	
Checkline	

2.2 Company History

This topic appears when your business plan is for an existing or ongoing company, instead of a start-up company.

Use this topic to cover past performance. The topic is normally linked to the past performance table, which presents financial highlights for the last three years and starting balances for the next three. Explain why your sales and profits have changed. If you've had important events, like particularly bad years or good years, or new services, new locations, new partners, etc., then include that background here.

Past Performance	Y1	Y2	Y3
Sales			
Gross Margin			
Gross % (calculated)			
Operating Expenses			
Collection period (days)			
Inventory turnover			
Balance Sheet			
Short-term Assets	Y1	Y2	Y3
Cash			
Accounts receivable			
Inventory			
Other Short-term Assets			
Total Short-term Assets			
Long-term Assets			
Capital Assets			
Accumulated Depreciation			
Total Long-term Assets			
Total Assets			
Capital and Liabilities			
	Y1	Y2	Y3
Accounts Payable			
Short-term Notes			
Other ST Liabilities			
Subtotal Short-term Liabilities			
Long-term Liabilities			
Total Liabilities			
Paid in Capital			
Retained Earnings			
Earnings			
Total Capital			
Total Capital and Liabilities			
Other Inputs			
Payment days			
Sales on credit			
Receivables turnover			

2.3 Company Locations and Facilities

Briefly describe offices and locations of your company, the nature and function of each, square footage, lease arrangements, etc. For example, if you are a service business, you probably don't have major manufacturing plants, but you might have Internet services, office facilities, and telephone systems that are relevant to providing service. It is conceivable that your Internet connection, as one hypothetical case, might be critical to your business.

3.0 Product (or Service) Description

NOTE: References to products are interchangeable with services.

List and describe the products your company will sell. For each of them, cover the main points, including what it is, what customer need does it address, at what relative price point, and how is it different from other products or services that address the same need. If you think it's important, describe the technology involved, the manufacturing cost, distribution, packaging, pricing, what sorts of customers make purchases, and why. What are the important features and benefits?

....

....

....

....

....

....

....

....

....

....

....

PERMISSION TO COPY WORKBOOK PAGES GRANTED ONLY FOR USE WITH BUSINESS PLAN PRO® SOFTWARE.
FOR MORE INFORMATION CALL (800) 229-7526.

WB.11

3.1 Product (or Service) Description

NOTE: References to products are interchangeable with services.

The previous topic was the summary, so this one provides more detail. List and describe the products your company manufactures. For each product, cover the main points, including what the product is, technology, manufacturing cost, distribution, packaging, pricing, what sorts of customers make purchases and why. What customer need does each product fill? What are the important features and benefits?

....

....

....

....

....

....

....

....

....

....

....

....

3.2 Competitive Comparison

NOTE: References to products are interchangeable with services.

Use this topic for a general comparison of your product offering as one of several choices a potential buyer can make. There is a separate topic in the market analysis chapter for detailed comparison of strengths and weaknesses of your specific competitors.

....

....

....

....

....

....

....

....

....

....

....

....

3.3 Sales Literature

List any existing sales literature you will include with your finished plan.

....

....

....

....

....

....

....

....

....

....

....

3.4 Sourcing

How do you get the products you sell and at what cost? Use this topic to explain in as much detail as you think practical, depending on the specifics of your plan. Additional details depend on the nature of your business and the purpose of your plan. If you are a manufacturer or a retailer, you should describe your sources of materials.

PERMISSION TO COPY WORKBOOK PAGES GRANTED ONLY FOR USE WITH BUSINESS PLAN PRO® SOFTWARE.
FOR MORE INFORMATION CALL (800) 229-7526.

WB.15

3.5 Technology

Describe the current, and new, technologies which impact your ability to produce these goods or services.

....

....

....

....

....

....

....

....

....

....

....

....

3.6 Future Products (or Services)

What future products or services are on your drawing board? Is there a relationship between market segments, market demand, market needs, and product development?

....

....

....

....

....

....

....

....

....

....

....

4.0 Market Analysis Summary

This first paragraph is a simple summary. Assume this paragraph might be included in a loan application or summary memo, so you need it to summarize the rest of the chapter. What information would be most important if you had only one brief topic to include about your market?

Without going into great detail, you should generally describe the different groups of target customers included in your market analysis, and refer briefly to why you are selecting these as targets. You may also want to summarize market growth, citing highlights of growth projections.

....

....

....

....

....

....

....

....

....

....

....

....

4.1 Market Segmentation

Explain the potential customers analysis table, which is normally linked to it. Your analysis is based on a list of potential customer groups, each of which is a market segment. Explain how your segments are defined. The market segmentation concept is crucial to market assessment and market strategy. Divide the market into workable market segments—by age, income, product type, geography, buying patterns, customer needs, or other classification.

Market Analysis Potential Customers	# of Customers	Growth rate (%)

....

....

....

....

....

....

....

....

....

4.2 Target Market Segment Strategy

In this topic you should introduce the strategy behind your market segmentation and your choice of target markets. Explain why your business is focusing on these specific target market groups. What makes these groups more interesting than the other groups that you've ruled out? Why are the characteristics you specify important?

....

....

....

....

....

....

....

....

....

....

....

....

4.2.1 Market Needs

This topic is a good reminder that all marketing should be based on underlying needs. For each market segment included in your strategy, explain the market needs that lead to this group's wanting to buy your product or service.

....

....

....

....

....

....

....

....

....

....

....

....

4.2.2 Market Trends

To describe market trends, think strategically. What factors seem to be changing the market or changing the business? What developing trends can make a difference? Market trends could be changes in demographics, changes in customer needs, new sense of style or fashion, or something else. It depends on what business you are in.

4.2.3 Market Growth

Use this topic to explain and discuss market growth. Ideally you cite experts, a market expert, market research firm, trade association, or credible journalist, projecting market growth. This is particularly important when your plan is related to finding investors or supporting a loan application because market growth enhances the implied value of your business.

....

....

....

....

....

....

....

....

....

....

....

4.3 Industry Analysis

This topic summarizes the sub-topics that follow, explaining the type of business. The sub-topics look at the size and concentration of businesses in this group, the way services are bought and sold, and specific competitors. Depending on what you need for your specific plan, you could leave a brief summary in this topic and let the main information come in the following ones, or you could decide that all you need is a paragraph or two here, then delete the sub-topics. Remember that form follows function, so if describing your industry doesn't change any of your business decisions, and you are not using the plan to describe your business to an outsider, then you may not need to include this description at all.

A complete business plan discusses industry economics, participants, distribution patterns, factors in the competition, and whatever else describes the nature of this business to outsiders. For research, there are websites for analysis, financial statistics, demographics, trade associations, and just about everything you'll need for a complete business plan.

NOTE: Please refer to Chapter 8, The Business You're In, *for suggested resources.*

....

....

....

....

....

....

....

....

....

....

....

4.3.1 Industry Participants

Explain the nature of the industry. There is a huge difference, for example, between an industry like long-distance trunk services, in which there are only a few huge companies in any one country, and one like dry cleaning, in which there are tens of thousands of smaller participants. This topic is supposed to present a summary of this factor.

....

....

....

....

....

....

....

....

....

....

....

4.3.2 Distribution Patterns

Explain how distribution works in this industry. Does it have regional distributors, as is the case for computer products, magazines, or auto parts? Does it depend on direct sales to large industrial customers? Do manufacturers support their own direct sales forces?

....

....

....

....

....

....

....

....

....

....

....

....

4.3.3 Competition and Buying Patterns

Explain the general nature of competition in this business and how the customers seem to choose one provider over another. In the computer business, for example, competition might depend on reputation and trends in one part of the market and on channels of distribution and advertising in another. In many business-to-business industries, the nature of competition depends on direct selling because channels are impractical. Price is vital in products competing with each other on retail shelves, but delivery and reliability might be more important for materials used by manufacturers in volume, for which a shortage can affect an entire production line.

....

....

....

....

....

....

....

....

....

....

....

4.3.4 Main Competitors

You've referred to competition already in previous topics, in terms of general factors and the nature of competition. Use this topic to list your specific competitors and the strengths and weaknesses of each.

....

....

....

....

....

....

....

....

....

....

....

....

5.0 Strategy and Implementation Summary

Summarize the sales and marketing strategy. Details will come in the following topics, so keep this summary short, covering just the main points.

....

....

....

....

....

....

....

....

....

....

....

....

5.1 Strategy Pyramids

This topic is intended to help you think about strategy, not to make a business plan more difficult. If this framework for analysis doesn't work for you, don't worry about it.

Imagine a pyramid made of three levels. The top of the pyramid is a single box, which contains a strategy. Strategy is an area of resource focus. In the middle level, you have three or so boxes which contain tactics. In the third level, you have four to six boxes that stand for programs.

A strategy is a main focus, which might be on a specific target market. Tactics are there to implement strategies. Programs are specific business activities, each of which has concrete dates and responsibilities, and probably a budget. Your definitions don't have to be exact.

NOTE: Please refer to Chapter 17, Strategy is Focus, *in the main section of the Hurdle book for a more specific example.*

....

....

....

....

....

....

....

....

....

....

....

....

5.2 Value Proposition

Value-based marketing is another conceptual framework. Like the pyramid in the previous topic, it doesn't have to be in your business plan at all, but we add it here because some people find that the framework helps them develop strategy. Obviously, this has to be a quick treatment. There are textbooks written about value-based marketing, and the business literature on this topic is rich and varied.

NOTE: Please refer to Chapter 17, Strategy is Focus, *in the main section of the Hurdle book for a more specific example.*

....

....

....

....

....

....

....

....

....

....

....

....

PERMISSION TO COPY WORKBOOK PAGES GRANTED ONLY FOR USE WITH BUSINESS PLAN PRO® SOFTWARE.
FOR MORE INFORMATION CALL (800) 229-7526.

WB.31

5.3 Competitive Edge

So, what is your competitive edge? How is your company different from all others? In what way does it stand out? Is there a sustainable value there, something that you can maintain and develop over time? For example, a graphic design firm might have its head start in Internet Web page design or its Common Gateway Interface (CGI) programming staff as a competitive edge that puts it ahead of most competitors. An accounting practice might have its well-known senior partner whose books are used as textbooks. A restaurant might have its excellent location or its well-known master chef. The competitive edge might be different for any given company, even between one company and another in the same industry.

NOTE: Please refer to Chapter 17, Strategy is Focus, in the main section of the Hurdle book for a more specific example.

....

....

....

....

....

....

....

....

....

....

....

....

5.4 Marketing Strategy

This topic introduces marketing strategy. Sales strategy comes later. Your marketing strategy normally involves target market focus, emphasis on certain services or media, or ways to position your company and your products or service uniquely.

Your marketing strategy depends a great deal on which market segments you've chosen as target market groups. You covered this in the previous chapter, the market analysis, but it is also critical to market strategy. Also, if you've been through the previous topics, including the strategy pyramid, the value proposition, and competitive edge, then you probably have marketing strategy on the way. Obviously, you want to make sure to preserve the same basic focus and themes.

....

....

....

....

....

....

....

....

....

....

....

....

PERMISSION TO COPY WORKBOOK PAGES GRANTED ONLY FOR USE WITH BUSINESS PLAN PRO® SOFTWARE. FOR MORE INFORMATION CALL (800) 229-7526.

WB.33

5.4.1 Positioning Statement

Use this topic for your marketing positioning statements. The positioning statements should include a strategic focus on the most important target market, that market's most important market need, how your product meets that need, who is the main competition, and how your product is better than the competition.

Consider this simple template:

For [target market description] who [target market need], [this product] [how it meets the need]. Unlike [key competition], it [most important distinguishing feature].

....

....

....

....

....

....

....

....

....

....

....

....

....

5.4.2 Pricing Strategy

Provide detail on product pricing and relate your pricing to strategy. Your value proposition, for example, will normally include implications about relative pricing. Therefore, you should check whether your detailed product-by-product pricing matches the implied pricing in the value proposition. Pricing is also supposed to be intimately related to the positioning statement in the previous topic, since pricing is probably the most important factor in product positioning.

PERMISSION TO COPY WORKBOOK PAGES GRANTED ONLY FOR USE WITH BUSINESS PLAN PRO® SOFTWARE.
FOR MORE INFORMATION CALL (800) 229-7526.

WB.35

5.4.3 Promotion Strategy

Think of promotion in a broader sense than simply sales promotion. How will you spread the word about your business to your future customers? Think of it in the broader context, including the whole range of advertising, public relations, events, direct mail, seminars, and sales literature.

Think strategically. What, in general, is your strategy about communicating with people? Do you go for expensive ads in mass media, or targeted marketing in specialized publications, or even more targeted with direct mail? Do you have a way to leverage the news media or reviewers? Do you advertise more effectively through public relations events, trade shows, newspaper, or radio? What about telemarketing, the World Wide Web, or even multilevel marketing?

5.4.4 Distribution Strategy

What is your strategy for distributing your products? Remember, strategy is focus, so think about emphasizing your strengths and protecting your weaknesses. You should also refer to your discussion of distribution patterns in the previous chapter to consider how your strategy fits in with the rest of your industry.

Are you focusing on a specific channel, area of distribution, or means of distribution? Is there some special advantage you have that you want to emphasize to differentiate from your competition? Is there anything unique in your distribution plans that your competitors can't imitate? In what way does your plan for distribution emphasize your strengths and move away from your weaknesses?

....

....

....

....

....

....

....

....

....

....

....

PERMISSION TO COPY WORKBOOK PAGES GRANTED ONLY FOR USE WITH BUSINESS PLAN PRO® SOFTWARE.
FOR MORE INFORMATION CALL (800) 229-7526.

WB.37

5.4.5 Marketing Programs

Details and specifics are critical to implementation. Use this topic to list the specific information related to marketing programs in your Milestones table (attached to Workbook topic 5.7) with the specific persons responsible, deadlines, and budgets.

Each marketing program in your Milestones table should appear in this topic, along with relevant details. You may go over them again in the text related to that table, but for this topic you want to cement your marketing strategy with programs that make it real. How is this strategy to be implemented? Do you have concrete and specific plans? How will implementation be measured?

....

....

....

....

....

....

....

....

....

....

....

....

5.5 Sales Strategy

Describe sales strategy as it differs from marketing strategy. Sales should close the deals that marketing opens. Sales strategies deal with how and when to close sales prospects, how to compensate salespeople, how to optimize order processing and database management, how to maneuver price, delivery, and conditions. This topic is the summary, to be followed by a detailed sales forecast and a discussion of specific sales programs.

....

....

....

....

....

....

....

....

....

....

....

PERMISSION TO COPY WORKBOOK PAGES GRANTED ONLY FOR USE WITH BUSINESS PLAN PRO® SOFTWARE.
FOR MORE INFORMATION CALL (800) 229-7526.

WB.39

5.5.1 Sales Forecast

Break down your sales—by product or by service. The best forecasts will list one full year by month, plus two additional years by year.

You also need to project costs of sales, just as you project sales. Usually you'll use the same sales break down for costs as for sales.

Sales Forecast	M1	M2	M3	M4	M5	M6	M7	M8	M9	M10	M11	M12	Y1
Sales													
Total													
Cost of Sales													
Total													

5.5.2 Sales Programs

Details and specifics are important to implementation. Use this topic to list the specific information related to sales programs in your Milestones table, with the persons responsible, deadlines, and budgets.

....

....

....

....

....

....

....

....

....

....

....

....

PERMISSION TO COPY WORKBOOK PAGES GRANTED ONLY FOR USE WITH BUSINESS PLAN PRO® SOFTWARE.
FOR MORE INFORMATION CALL (800) 229-7526.

WB.41

5.6 Strategic Alliances

Explain your strategic alliances, such as co-marketing, co-development, commissions and cooperative arrangements. Is your fate tied to that of any other company? Can you link your promotions or distribution strategies to another company or companies? Does this affect your marketing strategy, competitive edge, or positioning?

....

....

....

....

....

....

....

....

....

....

....

....

5.7 Milestones

The milestones are critical. This is where a business plan becomes a real plan, with measurable activities instead of just a document. Include as many specific programs as possible. For each program, give it a name, a person responsible, a milestone date, and a budget.

Milestone	Manager	Planned Date	Department	Budget

6.0 Management Summary

As with the other first topics in chapters, this summary may be used to stand for the rest of the chapter as part of a Summary Memo. If you only have one or two paragraphs to include about your personnel and management team, this is it.

....

....

....

....

....

....

....

....

....

....

....

6.1 Organizational Structure

The organizational structure of a company is what you frequently see as an organizational chart (also known as an "org chart"). If you have access to a graphic of an organizational chart (from a drawing program or one of the specialized organizational charting software packages available), then you can include the drawing into your business plan at this point. If not, you may want to include a chart as an illustration in the appendix. You can also just use text to describe the organizational structure in words, without a chart.

PERMISSION TO COPY WORKBOOK PAGES GRANTED ONLY FOR USE WITH BUSINESS PLAN PRO® SOFTWARE. FOR MORE INFORMATION CALL (800) 229-7526.

WB.45

6.2 Management Team

List the most important members of the management team. Include summaries of their backgrounds and experience, using them like brief resumes. Describe their functions with the company.

....

....

....

....

....

....

....

....

....

....

....

6.3 Management Team Gaps

Specify where the team is weak because of gaps in coverage of key management functions. How will these weaknesses be corrected? How will the more important gaps be filled?

....

....

....

....

....

....

....

....

....

....

....

PERMISSION TO COPY WORKBOOK PAGES GRANTED ONLY FOR USE WITH BUSINESS PLAN PRO® SOFTWARE.
FOR MORE INFORMATION CALL (800) 229-7526.

WB.47

6.4 Personnel Plan

Use the Personnel table to project employees, salaries, and departments. A standard plan would list one full year by month, plus two additional years by year. Use the text topic to explain the plan, assumptions, personnel needs, costs, and benefits.

Personnel Plan	M1	M2	M3	M4	M5	M6	M7	M8	M9	M10	M11	M12	Y1
Subtotal													
Tax, insurance, etc.													
Total													

7.0 Financial Plan

This is another summary topic, which is followed by detailed topics covering your General Assumptions, Break-even Analysis, Profit and Loss, Cash Flow, Balance Sheet, and Ratios.

....

....

....

....

....

....

....

....

....

....

....

....

7.1 Important Assumptions

Discuss your important assumptions about your business. Explain how key assumptions have affected your financial projections. There might be additional assumptions, such as assuming general economic conditions, or that your competition isn't going to release a new product during the next 12 months.

....

....

....

....

....

....

....

....

....

....

....

....

7.2 Key Financial Indicators

This topic compares five key indicators in regard to how much they change over time. The indicators include sales, gross margin, operating expenses, inventory turnover, and collection days. We chose these five indicators because they all have an impact on the health of a business. We focus not on gross amounts as much as changes.

The indicator value is a good way to compare different concepts. Sales and operating expenses are measured in gross amounts, gross margin is in percentage terms, collection days are in days (how many days do you wait to get the money), and inventory turnover is in turns per year (cost of goods sold divided by average inventory). With sales, gross margin, and inventory turnover, the higher the better. With operating expenses and collection days, the lower the better.

....

....

....

....

....

....

....

....

....

....

....

7.3 Break-even Analysis

Collect the data to do a break-even analysis. Determine (or guess) your average monthly fixed costs and revenues. For a product business, record your average unit price and average unit cost. What do you have to sell each month in order for your income to exceed your fixed and product costs?

Use the text area to explain your assumptions, and the significance of the analysis.

NOTE: *Please refer to* Chapter 16, Finish the Financials, *in the main section of the Hurdle book for more specific information on Break-even Analysis.*

Assumptions	
Average Unit Sale	
Average Per-unit Cost	
Monthly Fixed Cost	
Calculating Fixed Cost	
Rent	
Utilities	
Insurance	
Salaries, Benefits, etc.	
Other	
Other	
Other	

....

....

....

....

....

....

....

....

....

....

....

....

7.4 Projected Profit and Loss

Take a deep breath. You've already collected some of the information you need here, so now you can begin to put it together. Again, the goal is to create a plan showing one full year by month, plus two additional years by year. You roughed out your fixed costs; now you'll list the details. You have already forecasted your sales and product costs. You have your payroll costs. Remember, you will most likely revise these numbers as you complete this plan.

Profit and Loss	M1	M2	M3	M4	M5	M6	M7	M8	M9	M10	M11	M12	Y1
Sales													
Cost of sales													
Gross Margin													
Less Operating Expenses:													
Salaries and benefits													
Rent & utilities													
Advertising & promotion													
Subtotal													
Gross Profit													
Interest expense													
Taxes													
Net Profit													

7.5 Projected Cash Flow

Fill in the Cash Flow table. A standard plan would list one full year by month, plus two additional years by year. In most business plans, the cash flow is negative for some months, so the net cash flow row can show negative values. The cash balance, however, must not go below zero ever, because that would be equivalent to a negative balance in the checking accounts, which means bounced checks and bad problems. Normally you will have to borrow money off of a credit line to support your weak months and pay it off during your strong months. You might also be looking for new investment to improve your cash flow, or taking out a long-term loan or selling assets.

Cash Received	M1	M2	M3	M4	M5	M6	M7	M8	M9	M10	M11	M12	Y1
Cash Sales													
From Receivables													
From Sale of Inventory													
From Sale of Other Current Assets													
From Sale of Capital Assets													
From New Capital													
New Short-term Loans													
New Long-term Loans													
New Other Liabilities (taxes, etc.)													
Subtotal													

Cash Expenditures	M1	M2	M3	M4	M5	M6	M7	M8	M9	M10	M11	M12	Y1
Pay Accounts Payable													
Payroll and Payroll Burden													
Cash Payments													
Inventory Paid in Cash													
Principle Payments Short-term Debt													
Principle Payments Other Liabilities													
Principle Payments Long-term Debt													
Purchase of Short-term Assets													
Purchase of Capital Assets													
Payments of Dividends or Draw													
Subtotal													
Net Cash Flow													
Cash Balance													

7.6 Projected Balance Sheet

Here is a sample Balance Sheet table. This example has been greatly simplified for input purposes. To see an example of a completed Balance Sheet table, please refer to *Chapter 16: Finish the Financials*, Figure 16-1, in the main portion of this book.

Balance Sheet		Y1	Y2	Y3
Assets				
	Bank balance			
	Accounts Receivable			
	Inventory			
Total				
Capital and Liabilities				
Liabilities				
	Accounts Payable			
	Short-term debt			
Total Liabilities				
Capital				
	Paid-in			
	Earnings			
Total				

7.7 Business Ratios

Here is a sample of a Business Ratios table.

Profitability Ratios:	Y1	Y2	Y3
Gross Margin			
Net Profit Margin			
Return on Assets			
Return on Equity			
Activity Ratios:			
AR Turnover			
Collection Days			
Inventory Turnover			
Accts Payable Turnover			
Total Asset Turnover			
Debt Ratios:			
Debt to Net Worth			
Short-term Liab. To Liab.			
Liquidity Ratios:			
Current Ratio			
Quick Ratio			
Net Working Capital			
Interest Coverage			
Additional Ratios:			
Assets to Sales			
Debt/Assets			
Current Debt/Total Assets			
Acid Test			
Asset Turnover			
Sales/Net Worth			
Dividend Payout			

Appendix A:

GLOSSARY

A

Accounts payable   Bills to be paid as part of the normal course of business.

Accounts receivable   Debts owed to your company, usually from sales on credit.

Accumulated depreciation Total accumulated depreciation reduces the formal accounting value (called book value) of assets. Each month's accumulated balance is the same as last month's balance plus this month's depreciation.

Acid test   Short-term assets minus accounts receivable and inventory, divided by short-term liabilities. This is a test of a company's ability to meet its immediate cash requirements.

Assets   Property that a business owns, including cash and receivables, inventory, etc. Assets are any possessions that have value in an exchange. The more formal definition is the entire property of a person, association, corporation, or estate applicable or subject to the payment of debts. What most people understand as business assets are cash and investments, accounts receivable, inventory, office equipment, plant and equipment, etc. Assets can be long-term or short-term, and the distinction between these two categories might be whether they last three years, five years, 10 years, or whatever; normally the accountants decide for each company and what's important is consistency. The government also has a say in defining assets, because it has to do with tax treatment; when you buy a piece of equipment, if you call that purchase an expense then you can deduct it from taxable income. If you call it an asset you can't deduct it, but you can list it on your financial statement among the assets. The tax code controls how businesses decide to categorize spending into assets or expenses.

Asset turnover   Sales divided by total assets. Important for comparison over time and to other companies of the same industry.

B

Break-even point   The unit sales volumes or actual sales amounts that a company needs to equal its running expense rate and not lose or make money in a given month. The formula for break-even point in units is:

                          =Regular running costs/(Unit Price-Unit Variable Cost)

                          The formula for break-even point in sales amount is:

                          =Regular running costs/(1-(Unit Variable Cost/Unit Price))

A.1

Burden rate | Refers to personnel burden, the sum of employer costs over and above salaries (including employer taxes, benefits, etc.).

C

Capital assets | Long-term assets, also known as Plant and Equipment.

Capital expenditure | Spending on capital assets (also called plant and equipment, or fixed assets).

Capital input | New money being invested in the business. New capital will increase your cash, and will also increase the total amount of paid-in capital.

Cash | The bank balance, or checking account balance, or real cash in bills and coins.

Collection days | See Collection period, below.

Collection period (days) | The average number of days that pass between delivering an invoice and receiving the money. The formula is:

=(Accounts_receivable_balance*360)/(Sales_on_credit*12)

Commissions | Gross margin multiplied by the commissions percentage.

Commissions percent | An assumed percentage used to calculate commissions expense as the product of this percentage multiplied by gross margin.

Cost of sales | The costs associated with producing the sales. In a standard manufacturing or distribution company, this is about the same as the cost of the goods sold. In a services company, this is more likely to be personnel costs for people delivering the service, or subcontracting costs.

Current assets | The same as short-term assets.

Current debt | Short-term debt, short-term liabilities.

Current liabilities | Short-term debt, short-term liabilities.

D

Debt and equity | The sum of liabilities and capital. This should always be equal to total assets.

Depreciation | An accounting and tax concept used to estimate the loss of value of assets over time. For example, cars depreciate with use.

Directory | A computer term related to the operating system on IBM and compatible computers. Disk storage space is divided into directories.

Dividends | Money distributed to the owners of a business as profits.

E

Earnings — Also called income or profits, earnings are the famous "bottom line": sales less costs of sales and expenses.

EBIT — Earnings before interest and taxes.

Equity — Business ownership; capital. Equity can be calculated as the difference between assets and liabilities.

Expense — Webster's calls it "a spending or consuming; disbursement, expenditure." What's important about expenses for the purpose of business accounting is that expenses are deductible against taxable income. Common expenses are rent, salaries, advertising, travel, etc. Questions arise because some businesses have trouble distinguishing between expenses and purchase of assets, especially with development expenses. When your business purchases office equipment, if you call that an expense then you can deduct that amount from taxable income, so it reduces taxes.

F

Fiscal year — Standard accounting practice allows the accounting year to begin in any month. Fiscal years are numbered according to the year in which they end. For example, a fiscal year ending in February of 1992 is Fiscal 1992, even though most of the year takes place in 1991.

Fixed costs — Running costs that take time to wind down: usually rent, overhead, some salaries. Technically, fixed costs are those that the business would continue to pay even if it went bankrupt. In practice, fixed costs are usually considered the running costs.

G

Gross margin — Sales minus cost of sales.

Gross margin percent — Gross margin divided by sales, displayed as a percentage. Acceptable levels depend on the nature of the business.

I

Interest expense — Interest is paid on debts, and interest expense is deducted from profits as expenses. Interest expense is either long-term or short-term interest.

Inventory — Goods in stock, either finished goods or materials to be used to manufacture goods.

Inventory turnover — Total cost of sales divided by inventory. Usually calculated using the average inventory over an accounting period, not an ending-inventory value.

Inventory turns   Inventory turnover (above).

L

Labor

The labor costs associated with making goods to be sold. This labor is part of the cost of sales, part of the manufacturing and assembly. The row heading refers to fulfillment costs as well, for service companies.

Liabilities

Debts; money that must be paid. Usually debt on terms of less than five years is called short-term liabilities, and debt for longer than five years in long-term liabilities.

Long-term assets

Assets like plant and equipment that are depreciated over terms of more than five years, and are likely to last that long, too.

Long-term interest rate

The interest rate charged on long-term debt.

Long-term liabilities

This is the same as long-term loans. Most companies call a debt long-term when it is on terms of five years or more.

M

Materials

Included in the cost of sales. These are materials involved in the assembly or manufacture of goods for sale.

N

Net cash flow

This is the projected change in cash position, an increase or decrease in cash balance.

Net profit

The operating income less taxes and interest. The same as earnings, or net income.

Net worth

This is the same as assets minus liabilities, and the same as total equity.

O

Other short-term assets

These might be securities, business equipment, etc.

Other ST liabilities

These are short-term debts that don't cause interest expenses. For example, they might be loans from founders or accrued taxes (taxes owed, already incurred, but not yet paid).

P

Paid-in capital	Real money paid into the company as investments. This is not to be confused with par value of stock, or market value of stock. This is actual money paid into the company as equity investments by owners.
Payment days	The average number of days that pass between receiving an invoice and paying it. It is not a simple estimate; it is calculated with a financial formula: =(Accounts_payable_balance*360)/(Total entries to accounts payable*12)
Payroll burden	Payroll burden includes payroll taxes and benefits. It is calculated using a percentage assumption that is applied to payroll. For example, if payroll is $1,000 and the burden rate is 10 percent, the burden is an extra $100. Acceptable payroll burden rates vary by market, by industry, and by company.
Personnel burden	Payroll burden. See above description.
Plant and equipment	This is the same as long-term, fixed, or capital assets.
Product development	Expenses incurred in development of new products (salaries, laboratory equipment, test equipment, prototypes, research and development, etc.).
Profit before int and taxes	This is also called EBIT, for Earnings Before Interest and Taxes. It is gross margin minus operating expenses.

R

Receivables turnover	Sales on credit for an accounting period divided by the average accounts receivables balance.
Retained earnings	Earnings (or losses) that have been reinvested into the company, not paid out as dividends to the owners. When retained earnings are negative, the company has accumulated losses.
Return on assets	Net profits divided by total assets. A measure of profitability.
Return on investment	Net profits divided by net worth or total equity; yet another measure of profitability. Also called ROI.
Return on sales	Net profits divided by sales; another measure of profitability.
ROI	Return on investment; net profits divided by net worth or total equity, another measure of profitability.

S

Sales break-even	The sales volume at which costs are exactly equal to sales. The exact formula is: =Fixed_costs/(1-(Unit_Variable_Cost/Unit_Price))
Sales on credit	Sales made on account; shipments against invoices to be paid later.

Short term	Normally used to distinguish between short-term and long-term, when referring to assets or liabilities. Definitions vary because different companies and accountants handle this in different ways. Accounts payable is always a short-term liability, and cash, accounts receivable and inventory are always short-term assets. Most companies call any debt of less than five-year terms short-term debt. Assets that depreciate over more than five years (e.g., plant and equipment) are usually long-term assets.
Short term assets	Cash, securities, bank accounts, accounts receivable, inventory, business equipment, assets that last less than five years or are depreciated over terms of less than five years.
Short term notes	These are the same as short-term loans. These are debts with terms of five years or less.
Starting date	The starting date for the entire business plan.

T

Tax rate percent	An assumed percentage applied against pre-tax income to determine taxes.
Taxes incurred	Taxes owed but not yet paid.

U

Unit variable cost	The specific labor and materials associated with a single unit of goods sold. Does not include general overhead.
Units break-even	The unit sales volume at which the fixed and variable costs are exactly equal to sales. The formula is:

$$UBE = Fixed\_costs/(Unit\_Price - Unit\_Variable\_Cost)$$

Appendix B:

INDEX

This page intentionally blank.

Palo Alto Software publishes a full range of planning software for entrepreneurs and business owners. Visit our website at www.paloalto.com.

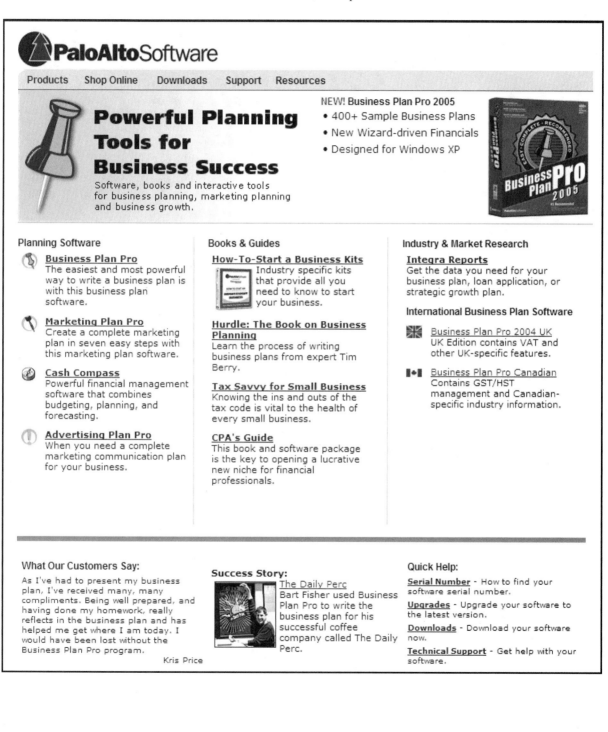